Coaching Creativity

Creativity and coaching are two of the buzzwords of the twenty-first century and yet little is known about how to coach creativity. In business, education, health and many other fields there is an increasing acknowledgement of the importance of innovation and recognition of what is lost when creativity is lacking.

In *Coaching Creativity*, Jen Gash explores the history, science and practice of 'creativity' by artists, makers and creators, translating this into practical advice for coaches. The book investigates the concept of creativity and examines the theories surrounding it from psychological, neurological and biological perspectives. It then takes a more practical look at the 'doing' of creativity and explores the use of creativity in therapeutic settings. A model of coaching creativity is presented which acknowledges its diverse and individual nature. The book also includes tools, case studies and ideas for coaching creativity including contributions from a wide range of coaches.

Coaching Creativity will be inspiring reading for coaches of all backgrounds, including business and organisational coaches, those in training, and others in the helping professions looking to enhance their practice. It is essential reading for all coaches who aim to support clients' creative goals and use creativity in their own practice. It fills important gaps in current coach education and practice.

Jen Gash is a coach, entrepreneur and occupational therapist in private practice. Her personal experience as an artist and writer led her to explore the creative process and prompted her research into the complex world of creativity. Jen's inspiring career has seen her work across the public and private sectors. She is based in South Gloucestershire, UK and works internationally across a variety of multi-media platforms.

'For coaching wishing to work creatively, this is the book for you! Jen Gash offers coaches a new and exciting way to think about their work, freeing them from technocratic and skills-based coaching approaches. This book is rich and has real depth. It will change the way you coach!' – **Professor Simon Western, adjunct professor, University College Dublin**

'Jen Gash is well equipped to explore and elucidate this subject as she is an artist and a coach. In this well researched and thoroughly referenced book she explores the history and development of our understanding of creativity. A series of real life case studies demonstrate how coaches might helpfully use creative processes in their work with clients. A useful text for coaches wanting to explore and expand their creativity and use it in their work.' – **Jenny Bird, MCC, co-author of** *The Art of Coaching* **(Routledge, 2016)**

'Jen Gash's book is a clever and comprehensive take on coaching and creativity, weaving together science and the arts. Its scope extends from the philosophical roots of creativity to coaching future innovation. It's a fascinating read with lots of inspiration for applying the knowledge, I'm already using the ideas in my coaching practice and business.' – **Miriam Akhtar, MAPP, positive psychologist, UK**

'Many books on creativity promise to inspire us with the joy of the new while in reality bogging us down in programmatic constraints. Many books on coaching offer to transport us to fresh paradigms but somehow amid a rash of tools and techniques leave us firmly in the box we were trying to get out of in the first place. Jen Gash's offering on the other hand pulls off the unusual feat of being intellectually provocative while at the same time inviting us to experiment with fresh coaching directions rather than simply leaving us captive within the confines of functional thinking. I applaud the readability and sheer zest that runs through this book – thank you Jen.' – **Dr Daniel Doherty, FHEA FCIPD FRSA M.ED PhD, senior lecturer in Leadership Work and Organisation, Middlesex Business School**

'Jen Gash combines learning and laughter to write in a distinctive voice about creativity, psychology, neuroscience and coaching. Her thorough exploration, suggested model and practical examples will enhance coaches' understanding and their ability to work with both paradox and flow.' – **Sarah Gornall, coach supervisor & executive coach**

Coaching Creativity

Transforming your practice

Jen Gash

LONDON AND NEW YORK

First published 2017
by Routledge
2 Park Square, Milton Park, Abingdon, Oxon OX14 4RN

and by Routledge
711 Third Avenue, New York, NY 10017

Routledge is an imprint of the Taylor & Francis Group, an informa business

© 2017 Jen Gash

The right of Jen Gash to be identified as author of this work has been asserted by her in accordance with sections 77 and 78 of the Copyright, Designs and Patents Act 1988.

All rights reserved. No part of this book may be reprinted or reproduced or utilised in any form or by any electronic, mechanical, or other means, now known or hereafter invented, including photocopying and recording, or in any information storage or retrieval system, without permission in writing from the publishers.

Trademark notice: Product or corporate names may be trademarks or registered trademarks, and are used only for identification and explanation without intent to infringe.

British Library Cataloguing in Publication Data
A catalogue record for this book is available from the British Library

Library of Congress Cataloging in Publication Data
Names: Gash, Jen, author.
Title: Coaching creativity : transforming your practice / Jen Gash.
Description: Abingdon, Oxon ; New York, NY : Routledge, 2017. |
 Includes bibliographical references and index.
Identifiers: LCCN 2016009873| ISBN 9781138960794 (hardback) |
 ISBN 9781138960800 (pbk.)
Subjects: LCSH: Creative ability. | Creative ability in business. |
 Personal coaching.
Classification: LCC BF408 .G336 2017 | DDC 153.3/5—dc23
LC record available at https://lccn.loc.gov/2016009873

ISBN: 978-1-138-96079-4 (hbk)
ISBN: 978-1-138-96080-0 (pbk)
ISBN: 978-1-315-66018-9 (ebk)

Typeset in Times New Roman
by Swales & Willis Ltd, Exeter, Devon, UK

To Maggie Jeffery, my soulmate, colleague, mum and best friend.

Contents

List of figures x
List of contributors xi
Foreword xiii
Preface xvi
Acknowledgements xviii

PART I
This crazy thing called creativity — 1

1 Buzzwords and sexy shortcuts — 3
2 Time and place – how we got to here — 9

PART II
Creative human — 19

3 Creativity and the psyche — 21
4 Creativity, neurology and the physical body — 37
5 Creativity and human 'doing'? — 50

PART III
Creativity as a means and also as an end — 65

6 Creative therapy — 67
7 This crazy thing called coaching — 75
8 Coaching as 'creative' process — 77
9 Creative 'doing' as part of coaching — 83

viii Contents

| 10 | Coaching as activating, integrating and supporting creativity | 86 |
| 11 | Proposing a model for coaching creativity | 88 |

PART IV
Coaching the creative process — 97

12	The vessel wall – containing the process	99
13	Enabling expansion – stretching, filling and activating the space	105
14	Enabling contraction and integration	111
15	The point of creative action	114
16	Reducing 'blocks' and restrictions	124

PART V
An invitation to coach in a different way — 141

17 Writing – journaling, poetry and story — 143
   Journaling 143
   Poetry 146
   Story 152

18 Visual processes — 155
   Working with metaphor using a visual process 155
   Drawing my rather full plate 156
   Drawing my business garden 157
   Drawing organisational values 159
   Drawing goals 160
   How does your river flow? 161
   A vision in collage 164

19 Humour and provocation — 167
   Humour 167
   Provocation 168

20 Evocative environments, evocative objects — 170
   Evocative environments 170
   Evocative objects 173

21 Imagining, being and becoming — 176
   Windows to other selves 176
   Visualisation – sculpting new pathways 179
   Being the metaphor 180

22 The 'we' of creativity 182
   *Improvisation in leadership coaching: knowing what to do
      when we don't know what to do 182*
   Coaching in the 'key' of life 188
   Coaching using party games 191

Index 194

Figures

11.1	Expansion and contraction of the blood vessel creates flow	90
11.2	The creative process described by artists and creatives	91
11.3	How coaching supports and enables the creative process	93
11.4	Common creative challenges faced in coaching	95
13.1	Enabling healthy expansion: stretching, filling and activating the space	106
17.1	Ishikawa: engineering a poem	150
18.1	Life river cross section	161

Contributors

David Adams, FCA, accountant, poet and coach. Based in central London where the bulk of his practice is located together with the USA, where he delivers workshops for Unlocking Creativity™ two or three times each year, as well as in the UK generally. His UK practice consists of a mixture of peer group facilitation and coaching for business owners and managers together with executive coaching for corporate leaders. In addition, he holds a number of non-executive directorships.

Sue Blow, MA, MBA, PGCertEd, has worked in management development and learning for more than twenty years. Her key areas of expertise are in coaching, facilitation and process consultancy, but she also has significant experience in researching, designing and delivering training programmes.

Dr Sam Chittenden, Director, Different Development Ltd. Sam uses creative approaches to leadership and organisational development. She is also an actor/director, and runs The Mastery of Self Expression workshops in Brighton, UK.

Kathy Denton, MSc Occupational Psychology, Chartered Psychologist (Occupational), Accredited EMCC Senior Practitioner and Director of Kathy Denton Ltd. Kathy is an experienced business coach using creative methods to optimise individual and team potential.

Dr Daniel Doherty is a senior lecturer at Middlesex University, London, UK, in the Department of Leadership. He is part of the coaching education there, as well as being founder and chair of the Critical Coaching Research Group. In addition to this academic focus he is a Master Practitioner in coaching, which he has practised at executive level for thirty years. Outside of work he likes to write freely and to sing in many choirs.

Peter Mayes is a highly experienced executive coach, business mentor, consultant and trainer with a track record in the corporate work spanning twenty-five years. An Accredited Executive Coach (Association for Coaching) and credentialed coach (ACC, ICF). Working throughout the UK, Europe and the Middle East within the manufacturing and service industries with multinationals at strategic and operational levels. As a qualified ILM level 7 in coaching and mentoring, Master NLP Practitioner with an MSc in Strategic Human Resource Development, he brings extensive skills and insight to the partnership of working with executives and teams.

Peter Moolan Feroze is a creativity specialist working with schools and business organisations and is a post graduate of the Royal Academy of Arts. He is an external consultant to the London Business School and an Associate of Steele Consulting. He uses drawing, painting and philosophy to release the whole person at work.

Kate Taylor Hewett is a coach, social entrepreneur and meditation teacher based in South West England. Her 'whole person' coaching approach draws on mind–body approaches, the Analytic-Network Coaching framework and a wide range of eclectic life experiences ranging from an international corporate career to Indian spiritual exploration.

Foreword

One historical link made in this book is through the concepts of 'mythos' and 'logos'. This is intriguing and resonates with other thinking. For example, in the modern world the psychologist Bruner believed that we have two ways of organising ourselves – the scientific and the narrative. Back to Ancient Greece, Aristotle had his take on these ideas with his concepts of 'phronesis' and 'techne'.

Techne is akin to the modern world's understanding of scientific thinking and behaviour. Techne leads to the mastery of something.

Phronesis is linked to the idea of noticing or attentiveness to a specific situation. It involves flexibility of thought, sensitivity of context, an orientation to the subject and critical interpretation.

Techne is about pre-planned learning whereas phronesis is exercised in the course of what might be called 'hot action', it happens in the moment as an act of creativity. Rather like when a coach is working.

However, the approach taken by most of the professional bodies is techne at the expense of phronesis. This is a problem because the coaching professionalisation agenda has become dominated by techne through standards, competence frameworks and alleged quality assurance. Bruner's notion of 'scientific' organisation is dominating here and alternatives are squeezed out, marginalised or simply ignored.

There is a huge paradox in the coaching literature where, almost to a writer, there are big claims for coaching in terms of its ability to develop individualism, creative and innovative thought, change and the tolerance of complexity – to mention a few commonly cited benefits. The simple truth is that a techne-informed approach just doesn't cut it and can't alone deliver on these claims.

For example, one problem with techne is the concept of 'skill level ranking', that is, novice coach, master coach, supervisor coach. Whilst there is a conventional logic to the skills-ranking approach, it is, however, an *exclusive* and not an *inclusive* approach to coaching. This will mean that some potentially good coaches will drop out or be damaged by this approach. If one subscribes to the scientific logic way of organising this will not be viewed as a problem. In a Darwinian survival of the fittest world this would be an acceptable loss in the interests of standards.

A further paradox is unveiled in the coaching literature, which, again almost to an author, favours a person centred humanistic approach (see Cox et al, 2014,

Garvey et al 2014, du Toit 2014, Rogers 2012, Connor and Pokora 2012, Western 2012, Garvey 2011, Parsloe and Leedham 2009, Whitmore 2009, Rosinski 2004). This philosophy is an inclusive one and clearly at odds with the 'ranking' philosophy employed by professional bodies.

Another problem of the techne approach is that the education system for coaches is instructor led. This may seem an odd criticism. However, it assumes that the instructor has the knowledge and the experience and the learner learns it! The learner is taught and the instructor teaches to the standards set by the assessment or accreditation process. So far so good but, again, this is at odds with the professed philosophy of coaching that is dominated by the discourse of the 'learner's agenda' (see Cox et al 2014, Garvey et al 2014, du Toit 2014, Rogers 2012, Connor and Pokora 2012, Western 2012, Garvey 2011, Parsloe and Leedham 2009, Whitmore 2009, Rosinski 2004). However, the techne discourse positions the coach as an expert and so instructor led is clearly acceptable in a world dominated by the techne discourse.

As this book clearly professes, humans are complex and coaching is complex. Coaching is varied in its application and is employed in a range of contexts. Its potential for doing *good* and making a positive difference to people is huge. Techne makes it easier to judge if outcomes or objectives are met. Techne treats learning as a linear activity (Garvey et al 2014) where the learner moves in a straight line rather like moving along a road or up a staircase. This approach is attractive for if we know the destination then the most helpful thing we can do is accelerate the journey and get to a pre-specified destination as quickly as possible.

Some human progress happens in this way but this is only a fraction of human capability and it does not develop the essential quality of 'phronesis' so needed by a coach and coachee. Techne is necessary but phronesis is essential.

This book explores what it is to be human and what it is to coach a fellow human. It sets out to explore our whole capabilities through the lens of creativity. It is about noticing and relationships. It is like fresh air blowing through the rather tired and lifeless managerialism of the coaching professional bodies. They have become 'exclusive'. This book reignites the 'inclusive' debate by elegantly arguing for a more democratised and egalitarian view of creativity located within the coaching process. It is, at times, challenging and playful and this is a challenge for all of us as we face the new challenges in the world – to be seriously playful and playfully serious; to perhaps focus more or our phronesis or narrative selves in order to unlock our full capabilities. This book also reminds us that paradoxes create creative opportunities so, rather than taking up positions – techne vs phronesis; science vs narrative; mythos vs logos – we are invited to go with the flow of these tension for out of these comes something new. It's a great invitation. Are we bold enough to embrace it?

Bob Garvey
Professor of Business Education
York St John Business School,
York, UK
r.garvey@yorksj.ac.uk

References

Connor, M. and Pokora, J. (2012) *Coaching and Mentoring at Work: Developing Effective Practice*. Maidenhead: McGraw-Hill.

Cox, E. Bachkirova, T. and Clutterbuck, D. (eds) (2014) *The Complete Handbook of Coaching* (2nd edn). London: Sage.

du Toit, A. (2014) *Making Sense of Coaching*. London: Sage.

Garvey, B. (2011) *A Very Short, Slightly Interesting and Reasonably Cheap Book on Coaching and Mentoring*. London: Sage.

Garvey, B., Stokes, P. and Megginson, D. (2014) *Coaching and Mentoring Theory and Practice* (2nd edn). London: Sage.

Parsloe, E. and Leedham, M. (2009) *Coaching and Mentoring: Practical Conversations to Improve Learning*. London: Kogan Page.

Rogers, J. (2012) *Coaching Skills: A Handbook* (3rd edn). Maidenhead: Open University Press.

Rosinski, P. (2004) *Coaching Across Cultures*. London: Nicholas Brealey.

Schön, D. A. (1987) *Educating the Reflective Practitioner: Towards a New Design for Teaching and Learning in the Profession*. San Francisco, CA: Jossey-Bass.

Swailes, S. and Roodhouse, S. (2003) Structural barriers to the take-up of higher level NVQs, *Journal of Vocational Education and Training*, 55(1), 85–110.

Western, S. (2012) *Coaching and Mentoring: A Critical Text*. London: Sage

Whitmore, J (2009) *Coaching for Performance: Growing Human Potential and Purpose* (4th edn). London: Nicholas Brealey.

Preface

I am a coach, an Occupational Therapist but first and foremost, a painter. Painting allows me to experiment with ideas through playing with paint. I usually start several new canvases at once and don't really worry about what I produce or where it might end up. Writing a book, however, is very different. If you keep turning up with different ideas, more material and new juicy references to mention, you could go round in circles for years. If I hadn't learned to understand how creativity works for me and against me, I doubt this book would have ever happened.

I imagine I am a coach's nightmare client. I never bring the same topic or idea more than once, but I repeatedly bring the same old beliefs and stuck patterns over and over again. I don't do plans and certainly don't do accountability, meaning that my coaches don't see me for months then get a frantic email for help. I am highly sensitive, as many creative people are, and find it difficult to operate in a world where feedback is considered important and readily given.

My coaches spend a lot of time helping me process and reframe what I always perceive as criticism. I talk metaphorically and visually all the time; I know I am a nightmare to keep up with, let alone understand. My favourite coaching action step of all time was when I said I would 'go and do a jigsaw', to try to help me focus and piece my fragile 'self' back together again.

I know many coaches who could have written this book, but once I had got over the fact that it was me doing so, I settled into the lovely fight that ensued. The fight between my expansive creative mind, my oscillating self-belief, my busy home life, the need to earn money and needing to find time to paint, without which, nothing seems to work. However, I felt addressing creativity as a coaching profession, was essential at this moment in time.

The importance of creativity to our world cannot be understated. We are living in times of great change where creative resilient responses will be profoundly necessary to facilitate these changes. Re-hashing old methods and re-inventing the same old wheel won't cut the mustard in terms of the challenges we will face over the coming decade. True transformation through true creativity is needed and heaps of courage to go with it.

At work, companies are told to 'innovate or die' but how creativity manifests (or doesn't) at work is complex to say the least – what organisations want from creativity is even more complex.

The search for a meaningful life has become more and more evident in recent years. Human beings' need for creativity and connection to a craft or activity is being acknowledged once more and re-examined in light of increasing levels of depression, stress and ill health.

For these reasons, I believe that the coaching profession needs to understand much more about creativity and how we support creative people through the systems we work with.

The reasons for writing this book are multiple:

- Creativity is poorly understood but desperately needed in the world today.
- Creativity is an innate human capacity and promotes mental and physical wellbeing.
- Bringing a creative idea into form often requires very different qualities and skills than those needed to come up with the idea in the first place.
- Creativity is at the heart of the coaching process – something not often explored.
- Creative people, goals and projects present many unique challenges for coaches.
- Coaches regularly confirm that gaining a deeper understanding of creativity has been important and hugely relevant to their work.

This book follows a fairly traditional format, taking the reader through an exploration of creativity and its history, culture, research, science and theory. This is followed by a discussion about creativity and how it shows up in coaching. A model of creativity and coaching is presented, which guides the practice and principles explored. Finally, some practical coaching tools and processes for the reader to play with and use in their practice.

Some key themes will be woven throughout:

- How to take the best from research about creativity, the practice of artists and makers and use it to inform our coaching practice.
- What to consider when coaching highly creative people
- How to use more creative methods in coaching.

In Part I you will hear Jen the researcher and scientist and later on you start to hear Jen the creative and pragmatist. These changing voices worried me at times, but slowly I came to realise that this is what I was aiming to do all along; build a grounded, solid, theoretical base to start with so I could then let go, dance and have fun, confident that the floor would not give way.

Welcome to my dance floor!

Bristol, September 2016

Acknowledgements

So many people need to be acknowledged for their role in making this book become reality. I have had support and endless conversations with many colleagues over the last few years and have gained tremendous support and encouragement throughout. The coaches at Bristol and Bath Coaching Group and the Critical Coaching Research Group, also based in Bristol, have helped me test out ideas and explore coaching in all sorts of ways. Dan Doherty requires a special thank you, for helping me develop a more critical overview of my work and for keeping me going. Thank you also to James O'Connell at Odd Shoe Designs who designed the diagrams.

My love for occupational therapy, coaching and creativity grew exponentially when I 'met' Jill Badonsky, OT, poet and creator of Kaizen Muse™ Creativity Coaching – without Jill, there would be no book. Coaching questions throughout the book highlighted by (JB) are attributed to Jill. Stewart Geddes RWA, my painting mentor, also needs a special mention as does Jo Birch, my coach and coaching supervisor. She has also seen me through this process, which extends way beyond the creation of this book.

Clearly my long-suffering family all need acknowledging – my husband Jeff, my children Jillie and Janey and not forgetting Bob. However, my mum, Maggie Jeffery is the person who has stood by me and scraped me off the floor many times in recent months. Not only has she helped with the editing and referencing, but every day for the last few months she made me a packed lunch, ensuring I ate something other than biscuits.

Part I

This crazy thing called creativity

The planet does not need more successful people. The planet desperately needs more peacemakers, healers, restorers, storytellers and lovers of all kinds.
Dalai Lama

Chapter 1

Buzzwords and sexy shortcuts

'Coaching' – such a fashionable word, so twenty-first century

In the last twenty years or so, the 'coaching' world has expanded. Hundreds of coaching schools and programmes have sprung up all around the world and there has been a proliferation of coaches; life coaches, business coaches, wellbeing coaches, executive coaches and so on. The term 'coach' is, however, unprotected, meaning that anyone can call themselves a coach.

Slowly, in the same way that other new professions have evolved, the coaching profession has itself grown up. Whilst some may see it as becoming too institutionalised, systems of training and accreditation have developed, alongside clear standards of practice and an ethical framework.

However, this thing we call 'coaching' isn't confined to those accredited coaches operating within a professional body such as the ICF (International Coach Federation) or the EMCC (European Mentoring and Coaching Council). People who use a 'coach approach' to their work are also carrying out great work. These include therapists, mentors, teachers and educationalists, as well as facilitators of all sorts.

Throughout this book, the term coach will be used in such a way to be inclusive to everyone using coaching in their work and perhaps other areas of life too.

'Creativity' – such a sexy word isn't it?

The word 'creativity', like 'coaching' is also a great buzzword and used these days almost as much as lovely words such as 'empowerment', 'potential' and 'authenticity'. These words are beautiful language shortcuts—ways of helping us to communicate large complex topics succinctly—but as we discuss 'creativity' further, a vast array of differing meaning, definition, opinion and understanding will be unearthed.

Creativity, and what it means to people, is as broad as you can imagine. Complexity deepens further if we start to look at the ways in which creativity is discussed in different settings.

In organisations the word innovation is often used interchangeably with creativity and is usually the preferred term. Perhaps creativity is seen as too fluffy and not business like. It's difficult to evaluate and is often relegated to 'team bonding days', where the use of coloured post-it notes is encouraged, to tick the box labelled 'do something creative'. However, innovation just cannot take place without creativity.

Thirty years ago, if someone said they worked in a creative business, you could reasonably assume that person was an artist, musician or writer. However, these days the term is also used to describe people and businesses in print media, television, software, app development and other online media. I often wonder if messy, mucky and quirky activities have been completely hijacked by technology firms who seem to want to claim 'creativity' as their own concept, as if it's something new!

When talking about creativity in education, it used to mean ensuring a goodly amount of painting, drawing, collage and model making. Now it often means teaching kids thinking skills, rather than allowing them to experiment, take risks, get messy and make mistakes!

At home and in our leisure time, creativity can have all sorts of meanings. With increasing amounts of free time (yes I know it doesn't feel like it), recent years have seen a growing interest in crafts, such as card making, creative baking, knitting and sewing, jewellery making and all sorts of other activities.

So creativity and what it means to us as individuals, groups and organisations is hugely complex. In the last fifty years, creativity as a concept has started to be explored, researched and categorised, but before we start looking at some of those theories and definitions, please take some time to explore what *you* think, understand and believe about this thing called creativity.

As coaches we know how important self-awareness is and that how we think and feel about certain topics and issues affects our stance as a coach (however much we would like to think it doesn't). Surfacing and acknowledging these personal beliefs and values around creativity is crucial, so please take some time to reflect on these questions:

> What does 'creativity' mean to you?
>
> Where does 'creativity' come from?
>
> Do you believe you are 'creative'? What do you feel has helped shape that belief?
>
> When someone says they are a 'creative' person, what do you immediately think?
>
> What assumptions do you make if people say they would like to be more 'creative'?

If you spent time considering those questions, I imagine the concept of creativity started to unravel. Perhaps it became complex and included types of 'thinking', 'doing' and 'being'. Many deeply held images and beliefs about creativity probably started to arise.

As the journey through this book progresses, we will explore various aspects of creativity, but it's always helpful to start somewhere, perhaps with a definition or two. One of the best discussions regarding a definition of creativity can be found in James Kaufman's *101 Creativity*. It's a brilliant resource and very readable.

> *Creativity research is much more than a basic definition and the concept of divergent thinking. When I talk about creativity, am I talking about a beautiful piece of art or an ingenious computer program? How about the sensation of the 'a-ha' process when I suddenly understand what I need to do next? Maybe, instead, I'm talking about how a creative person behaves. Or maybe it's the synergy that happens when many different people share and exchange ideas together. Throwing all of these things together and labelling them as 'creativity' is not much different than using the word 'love' to mean your feelings for your mom, your best friend, your significant other, and spicy calamari. It may be technically correct, but it's not terribly useful.*
>
> (Kaufman 2009, p. 21)

A shorter definition could go something like this:

> creativity = bringing something new into being

It is generally agreed by many researchers, that creativity manifests in the following three arenas:

- Hands-On Creativity (art, crafts and bodily/physical creativity).
- Mathematical/Scientific Creativity.
- Creativity in Empathy/Communication (creativity in the areas of interpersonal relationships, communication, solving personal problems and writing).

(Kaufman and Baer 2004)

Before we hold on too tightly to this definition of 'creativity' and those three arenas, we should consider creativity's history. Until the 1950s the term creativity didn't exist. The desire to study this thing we now call creativity meant that psychologists effectively had to invent it. This happened mostly through the work of American psychologists Guilford, Osborn and Torrance in the 1950s and 1960s, who we will meet later.

Today, many would argue that creativity is a highly problematic concept. As Readman notes:

6 This crazy thing called creativity

> *What is really intriguing about creativity as a concept ... is that it is able to attach itself to different interests with a high degree of promiscuity; it is simultaneously bereft of and rich in meaning, and has a polymorphous quality which makes it impossible to pin down ... Yet, despite its instability there are many documents and practices which claim to have secured the term for the purposes of, promoting, implementing, or assessing it.*
>
> (Readman 2010, p. 14)

Yes, as we will see, there are many, many ways the phrase creativity is used nowadays. There are multiple meanings and, as we will see, creativity certainly is a concept with a deeply cultural and sociological history. However, a debate as to the genealogy of the word creativity is not terribly helpful here.

Like me, I imagine you seek to make sense of this thing called creativity, rather than get more confused. In an attempt to do so, the four 'Ps' of creativity were proposed by Rhodes in 1961: process, product, person/personality and place/press. In 2010 Kaufman added two more: persuasion and potential.

Process: theories that focus on the creative process and 'aim to understand the nature of the mental mechanisms that occur, when a creative person is engaged in creative thinking or creative activity' (Kaufman 2010). This creative process is also central to the coaching process, as we will later see.

Product: theories of creativity that focus on what has been produced – the 'products', such as works of art, invention, publications and musical compositions.

Person/Personality: what is it that makes a person creative or think that they are not creative? Or what constitutes a creative personality? Creativity research shows, however, that 'personality' is just one influence on creative behaviour, rather than a complete explanation (Feist and Barron 2003 in Kaufman and Sternberg 2010).

Place/Press: this considers how the place or the environment 'presses' on the individual and affects the creative behaviour/process. Are there opportunities for creativity to flourish in the work environment? How does the home environment promote, enable or restrict creative behaviour? How do social and cultural issues press on individuals in terms of their creativity or desired creative outcome?

Persuasion: here creative individuals initiate or influence the direction taken by a group/movement/domain – 'my idea will change the world: it will revolutionise ... '. We see creative forces in action especially in newspapers, on television, in social media and during elections or political campaigns. Political 'spin doctors' must be amongst the most persuasive and highly creative individuals known.

Potential: here, as yet unfulfilled, ideas and possibilities are acknowledged. This is the starting point from which support may be required to move towards optimum performance and fulfilment. Some would argue that creative potential has also become a device for wealth creation and capitalism.

As you start to ponder these, I imagine you can see how coaching has a potential role and relationship with them all:

- By its very nature, coaching is a highly creative *process* – but it is also often sought to facilitate creative thinking in individuals and teams.
- People often come to coaching wishing to *produce* a creative work: write a book, start a business, start a creative hobby, or finish a project.
- Coaching increases *personal* awareness and can help us understand the relationship our *personality* has with our creativity.
- Through coaching clients become aware of the impact of their social and physical environment on their desired outcomes (*place/press*).
- Often coaching clients might want to influence or *persuade* a situation or work environment, or start a new 'cause'.
- And, of course, belief in personal *potential*, which is close to our hearts in the coaching domain.

It is helpful to really reflect upon these differing aspects of creativity, as we tend to lump things together when we talk about creativity and coaching.

I talk to hundreds of coaches each year and in those discussions many are talking about creative thinking (*process*). Others talk about creativity and mean using creative activities as part of their coaching (*products* used in the *process*). Some might talk about innovation at work but actually mean that more creativity, thinking and ideas (*process*) are desired or some help is needed to put an idea into action (continual cycle of *process* and *product* occurring in a *place*).

From a client perspective, individuals may seek coaching to become more creative and through discussion it becomes clear that they want to *produce* things, for example, create a watercolour painting or a write a book. Some clients want to be more creative at work but sometimes we meet a client who has the opposite issue – too many ideas, too much creativity – and that presents a very different challenge at work.

Naturally, as coaches we know the importance of unpicking terms and language with our clients, but as a profession we need more clarity ourselves rather than blandly using the word creativity to cover so many aspects of our involvement.

It may well feel like we revisit these two questions many times during our journey through this book:

What is creativity?

What is coaching?

And of course as coaches, you will all know how we often need to revisit the same questions repeatedly!

The complexity inherent in our understanding of the word creativity has developed through our social and cultural history and our relationship with this thing called 'creating'. We must first, therefore, take a look back, before we can go forward.

Learning Points

- Coaching is a new profession.
- Coaching skills are used by a variety of people, in many settings.
- Creativity is a complex term, varying widely in its meaning and usage.
- Creativity as a term did not exist until the 1950s.
- Simply put, creativity means 'bringing something new into being'.
- There are three main arenas where creativity is seen: hands on creativity (art, craft, dance etc.); mathematical/scientific creativity; creativity in empathy and communication.
- Coaching has a relationship with and a potential role in many aspects of creativity.

References

Feist, G. J. (1998) A meta-analysis of personality in scientific and artistic creativity, *Personality and Social Psychology Review*, 2(4), 290–309.

Feist, G. J. and Barron, F. (2003) Predicting creativity from early to late adulthood: intellect, potential and personality, *Journal of Research in Personality* 37, 62–88.

Kaufman, J. C. (2009) *Creativity 101 (Psych 101)*. New York: Springer Publishing, p. 22.

Kaufman J. C. and Baer, J. (2004) The Amusement Park Theoretical (APT) Model of creativity, *Korean Journal of Thinking and Problem Solving*, 14, 15–25.

Kaufman, J. C. and Sternberg R. J. (2010) *The Cambridge Handbook of Creativity*. Cambridge: Cambridge University Press.

Readman, M. (2010) *What's in a Word? The Discursive Construction of Creativity*, Bournemouth University Phd Thesis. Accessed 12/10/15, http://eprints.bournemouth.ac.uk/17755/1/Readman,Mark_Ph.D._2010.pdf.

Rhodes, M. (1961) An analysis of creativity, *Phi Delta Kappan*, 42, 305–11.

Chapter 2

Time and place – how we got to here

Human beings are complex, what they do is complex and it's impossible to separate the person from the context, environment and time in which they live (Law, Cooper, Strong, Stewart, Rigby and Letts 1997). With creativity, this is especially true.

In an attempt to simplify things, it is helpful to look at the historical, cultural and social context of creativity; particularly the arts and how they shape norms, values and beliefs, all important in coaching.

It is necessary to mention terminology again at this point, as the term 'the arts' – meaning mostly the visual arts, music, poetry and so forth – is often used interchangeably with the term creativity. In this book I may also talk about the arts, especially if referring to creativity, in historical terms, rather than a more modern conceptualisation of creativity, which means something different.

I also find myself using the terms 'context' and 'environment' interchangeably. My background as an occupational therapist (let's forget I was an artist first, it's easier) leads me to consider these differences:

> *Context: the relationship between the environment, personal factors and events that influence the meaning of a task, activity or occupation for the performer*
>
> *Environment: External physical and socio-cultural and temporal factors that demand and shape occupational performance (what we do)*
>
> (Creek 2010)

Simply put, the surrounding context shapes the meaning of an activity. The environment demands, presses and shapes what is actually done.

In relation to creativity, it's easy to see how an individual's socio-cultural norms have been formed and, every day in your coaching work, I imagine you will see how these impact on your clients at many levels.

Take some time to think about where your own opinions and beliefs about creativity and the arts have come from. Take a critical stance acknowledging where you live, what you do, what you read or watch, who you socialise with and how this has shaped what you believe about creativity and the arts.

During my initial coach training, I was coached about my painting, my creativity and the story of Jen to date. This was the first opportunity I had ever had to explore and make sense of what happened and why I chose a pathway away from painting as an eighteen-year old. Through the coaching, it quickly became clear how the context and environment in which I grew up had such great influence on my beliefs and subsequent actions in relation to 'creative' Jen.

At that time, I firmly believed that if you pursued art as a career, the only future job option was to become an art teacher. I definitely didn't want that! (This is not a reflection on my brilliant art teacher Patrick, who is still a close and valued friend.) I just didn't believe that studying art would lead to a 'proper' career, partly because I had never really been exposed to adults with a creative background. We lived in middle England. Mum was a nurse and Dad was an engineer – both very practical, grounded jobs. Whilst my mum started to develop her own writing later in life, it stayed firmly as a hobby.

At eighteen I believed that all artists were poor and, by their choices, were condemning themselves to a life of struggle. I also didn't believe Patrick who said I could paint really well – how could little me become a painter and what did that mean anyway?

I must also acknowledge that at eighteen years old, I wanted a job, to leave home and to live with my boyfriend. Going to art college or university was not on the menu – I wanted to get a real job and perhaps come back to painting later in life. However, beyond that, deeper down, I really didn't believe that a creative life was of value or could earn you a monthly wage. Clearly I have had many years to think about why I held those beliefs and what other factors were at play in my choice making, but even today, thirty years later, these beliefs, and that story, are not uncommon and they don't just belong to me.

You'll see these beliefs and constructs lurking in all sorts of stories, myths and discussions about creative industries and the arts. Listen and you will hear them playing out in education, social policy, at home and in the work place:

Being an artist/writer/poet/musician is not a real job is it?

Creative activities and creative people are rarely valued as highly as other pursuits or types of work, except perhaps those who reach the dizzy heights of fame and fortune. Despite this overt lack of value attributed to creative activities, we need to remind ourselves that without creativity most of the 'real work' out there wouldn't exist. Without creativity there would be no internet, iPhones, medicine or other modern essentials.

I'm not creative. I can't even draw a straight line and was rubbish at art at school.

When you talk to people, there often seems to be a default link between what it means to be creative and our artistic abilities as a child. Ironically, the notion of the ability to 'draw a straight line' being linked to creativity is absurd as we know that wiggles, mistakes and wonky lines are often essential characteristics of the creative process.

> *I'll do something creative when I retire.*
>
> or
>
> *Get a real job first, then you can have a creative hobby outside work.*

Often creative activities are perceived as a luxury, hobby or 'time off' real work. Again, creativity is seen as a luxury, rather than a necessity, which – in light of recent research showing that creative activities are crucial to human wellbeing – is at best ironic, and at worst damaging to our health and happiness. ('Research' in this sense being an activity that often tells us what we have known for years!)

> *Oh I'm not a real artist/writer – it's just a hobby.*

The word 'hobby' clearly presses my buttons. Apparently, you can determine whether an artist is professional or not, whether they are serious about their work, by asking if they earn at least 50% of their income from selling their work (industry standard for being a 'professional' artist!). Now where would that have left Van Gogh, Turner and the hundreds of other Big C creatives who never sold much work in their lifetime?

> *You have to be a bit weird and whacky to be creative, don't you.*

Films, books and television have carefully crafted the archetypal artist who struggles for years, faces financial doom, mental illness and rejection and finally 'makes it' or just dies unfulfilled. However, there are many creative people who are quiet, methodical, measured, sound of mind and so on. This is rarely shown in the media, probably because it doesn't make such good television.

> *Art GCSE isn't worth doing – I need to pass my GCSE Maths and English, or I won't get into any colleges or get a job.*

Creativity is becoming increasingly marginalised in education. Sadly, upon reaching the grand age of seven and entering junior school, my children rarely came home with mucky hands. Most colleges and workplaces see gaining basic levels of maths, English and science as a prerequisite for entry. I wonder what sort of human beings we would find in the adult work force if universities or graduate programmes insisted on the applicant having a creative 'A' level or element to their study. As Ken Robinson says:

> *We don't grow into creativity; we grow out of it... Young children enter pre-school alive with creative confidence; by the time they leave high school many have lost that confidence entirely... if creativity is to become central to our futures, it first has to move to the heart of education.*
>
> (Robinson 2011, p. 49)

Many businesses are not comfortable with the word 'creativity', yet without creative thought, playfulness, making mistakes and so on there is no innovation. Creativity doesn't just belong in creative departments or development teams; it needs to be in every part of an organisation. However, when there seems to be an overriding desire to tighten procedure, reduce mistake making and streamline production, creative thought and action is very difficult. Later on we will ponder whether organisations really want creativity and, if so, what sort of creativity and why.

> *We welcome innovation – it's crucial to our business success.*

These archetypal beliefs or universal stories are built into our culture today. They exist in conversations we have with others and many conversations we have with ourselves internally. They build the foundations of the belief systems that affect our coaching clients both consciously and unconsciously. Of course, as coaches, we too bring a multitude of beliefs and stances about creativity, which in turn affect how we coach. What we believe as coaches will colour our listening, the questions we ask and, of course, how we choose to work with our clients.

Naturally, it is worth thinking about how our current beliefs as a society and our personal constructs regarding creativity have been shaped over time. Where did these universal 'stories' and 'myths' about creativity originate?

A smidgen of history

Our capacity for what we now consider to be creative *thinking* and creative *behaviour* can be tracked through the early development of human beings. A great leap in human development occurred around 40,000 years ago, after which human beings started to behave more creatively – they began to wear clothes, cook food, make marks and produce images. We know that early human beings started mark making and creating visual representations of symbols for a variety of reasons.

In *Man and His Symbols*, Carl Gustav Jung (1979) explained how, outside of the written and spoken word, man's language and communication is full of signs and images, that are not strictly descriptive. A symbol, rather than signs such as badges and logos, possesses 'specific connotations in addition to its conventional meaning. It implies something vague, unknown or hidden from us'. Whilst Jung acknowledged the symbols we use consciously, it was the unconscious symbols and the relationship to our psychology that interested him greatly. His subsequent work provides the bedrock for so many psychotherapeutic, transformational and creative approaches we use today.

The use of symbols and totems can still be seen today. Many indigenous Australians refer to creation time as 'The Dreaming'. In 'Dreamtime', the entire ancestry exists as one: humans, animals, plants, landscape and elements such as wind or fire are temporary incarnations of spirits. Indigenous Australians use totems to symbolise a specific 'Dreaming'. For example, 'Shark Dreaming', where a totem may represent the person, the spirit of the shark or an artistic representation used for magical purposes.

Creation, the Dreamtime, is the time before time. Creation is believed to be the work of cultural heroes in spirit form who travelled across the formless land, creating landscapes, features and sacred sites as they went.

We are talking about the notion of creation here, rather than the word creativity, which we know was coined during the 1950s. Prior to this, we were concerned with the creation of things – be it the world, rivers, humans, animals and later a pot, a house or maybe a wall hanging or a painting.

Some early cultures associate this ability to create with the concept of a spirit, which inhabits places and things not people. 'Jinn' (or genie) are spiritual entities or energies hidden from sight as mentioned in many religious and spiritual texts. Their mystical energy or power inhabits an unseen world beyond the visible universe of humans. Genie is also the root of the word 'genius'. This word is currently used to describe a clever or gifted person, but its origin was the description of the energy of a place or object, not a person.

The Greek Mythologies, composed around 800–900BC and mostly recorded by and credited to Hesiod, introduce vivid stories, which guided the spiritual and daily lives of many people around this time. A number of the myths and stories are of interest to our exploration into creativity, particularly the muses – the many daughters of Zeus and Mnemosyne.

There were nine muses, each with her own specialty: Clio (history), Urania (astronomy), Melpomene (tragedy), Thalia (comedy), Terpsichore (dance), Calliope (epic poetry), Erato (love poetry), Polyhymnia (songs to the gods), Euterpe (lyric poetry), but no muse for the visual arts. Apparently, Plato felt that the visual arts, drawing and painting, were imitation and not pure creation, so, therefore, a muse was not necessary!

This move to emphasise an individual's daimon or muse marked a distancing from the concept of Jinn – the force or energy that existed everywhere and in all things. This started to turn the focus of creativity towards the individual – to people's abilities, skills and drives. Clearly if you needed help from a muse, perhaps you were lacking something. It marks a significant shift towards how we view creativity and the arts today.

This shift was furthered by the Roman Xenophanes, who began rejecting the mythology (mythos) of the Greek gods. This marked a time when people were beginning to lose belief in stories and imaginary worlds, preferring reason and logic (logos), which hastened during the Enlightenment.

This separation and the development of opposing stances are important to note, as polarities seem to exist within creativity; such as the left-brain, right-brain metaphor and extroversion and introversion. The underlying message is that you can't be both or that you must believe one or the other.

The Romans continued to influence thoughts about creativity. Cicero (44BC), Roman philosopher, politician and orator, introduced the term 'afflatus', which literally means inspiration – the gathering of a new idea. The word afflatus also means to be blown upon or toward, which again indicates another party is involved; an unknown source is providing the inspiration.

In the West, as we entered the Christian era, we saw God becoming the 'creator' and man having to develop his personal creativity through a kinship with God. He has to be given the gift of creativity by God, rather than being naturally creative.

It is at this point that Western and Eastern thinking about creativity seem to diverge. In the West, creativity was viewed as a special gift, trait or ability – something to be gained, used or expressed. Creations or ideas are something created from nothing (*creatio ex nihlio*) or perhaps divinely inspired by an external being such as God (Niu 2013). In the West, creativity is a novelty (not natural) and this starts to give us clues as to why we view creative activities in certain ways.

In the East, things are different. In Eastern culture and religions such as Hinduism, Confucianism, Buddhism and Taoism creativity is not seen as a novelty – creation is at most 'a kind of discovery or mimicry'. The concept *'creatio in situ'* (Niu 2013) reflects the belief in natural creativity, and that creation occurs continually, as a result of interactions between one and many, or between the creator (artist, inventor, writer) and the context (everything around us).

Creation out of nothing, *ex-nihilo*, has no place in a universe of Yin and Yang (Boorstin 1992). Creativity naturally happens all the time; therefore, it is not sought or exalted as a special human achievement.

I found it very challenging to get my head round those two diverging philosophies and have reflected on both viewpoints for several years. Over time I started to see how important those historical and cultural positions were and how they led to our current Western stereotypes, myths and stories regarding creativity, which show up in coaching all the time.

Thus, the basis of modern creativity in the West was being formed – it's about being gifted, talented and working very, very hard. With this tenet entrenched in our culture and history, it follows that we start to question and doubt ourselves: 'Is it good enough?', 'Am I good enough?', 'I am not skilled enough to be a painter', 'You have to train for years to be a real writer', 'He has a special gift you know', 'I'm not a real artist'.

Bridging the fourteenth to seventeenth centuries, the Renaissance (period of rebirth) produced many 'great men' and the idea of the 'polymath'. A polymath is a person who excels in multiple fields, someone such as Leonardo da Vinci, who was not only an artist but also a scientist, engineer, architect and botanist. This period served to solidify the concept of the 'great man', with creativity not being spiritually, divinely or naturally influenced, but defined by learning, intelligence and skill.

During this re-birth, literature, painting, sculpture and other arts flourished. Education was reformed and innovations in engineering and science developed, laying the foundations for the industrial revolution and the revolution of communication through printing, which was to follow. 'Humanism' as an educational approach started to strengthen, focussing on poetry, grammar, history and philosophy and asserted the genius of the man, his abilities and his extraordinary mind.

One of the most influential thinkers during the Enlightenment (late Renaissance) was John Locke. In 'An Essay Concerning Human Understanding' (1690) Locke proposed that human beings are born as a blank slate, a 'tabular rasa', and that knowledge and ideas were shaped purely by experience and perception. This essay was highly influential at its time, and even impacted on the US Declaration of Independence. It served to further build the belief systems and conceptual systems around creativity, which still exist today.

The transformation in Western consciousness from the middle of the fifteenth century to the Industrial Revolution was earth shaking, profound and expanded human horizons dramatically in a way that changed the previous worldview. The paradigm shift undermined the 'imaginal' worldview of earlier times where human beings in the West had seen themselves as part of nature, in which man was centred and strongly rooted. Such a loss of 'roots' and past certainties led to a search for meaning that found resolution in science and ultimately offered a view of a more certain, logical and reasonable world.

> *The new image of the Creator was thus of a divine architect, a master mathematician and clock maker, while the universe was viewed as a uniformly regulated and fundamentally impersonal phenomenon.*
>
> (Tarnas 1991)

This period of time seems to have been characterised by 'separation' and a desire to create logic and reason by dividing things into their component parts or categorising their differences, rather than embracing wholeness and mystery.

Another separation of note took place in 1770, when the Royal Academy decided to separate *craft* from *art*. Crafts such as weaving, needlepoint and other forms of 'making' were mostly undertaken at home by women. This served to further the image of the 'fine arts' as being the remit of great men and home crafts, mostly practiced by women, were no longer exhibited alongside painting and sculpture.

It's easy to see how social, industrial, technological and medical advances have impacted on theories of creativity and on creative practice and production. During the twentieth century, massive developments in technology and neuroscience continued to affect our knowledge regarding creativity, including the emergent field of quantum physics. Suffice to say we really don't want to get lost in a 'black hole', but there are a couple of key concepts that add an important dimension to our discussions on creativity.

Quantum mechanics is the study of matter at an atomic level and has brought into question some aspects of traditional physics. Very basically, quantum physicists assert that particles also exist as waves and therefore must be considered as part of an interconnected system (wave–particle duality). Everything is connected – there is no boundary between energy and material (matter). If everything exists as a wave, there are multiple possibilities/potentialities available at any one time. This gives rise to two realms of reality: potentiality and actuality.

It's easy to start seeing how this relates to ideas about creativity. Multiple, creative ideas exist all at once, but only those that are acted upon become actualised. As Goswami (2014) puts it, 'Creativity involves the causal power of consciousness choosing from quantum possibilities' (p. 10).

The principle of 'discontinuity' or 'quantum jumping' (when an electron 'jumps' from one place to another without travelling through the intervening space) is offered by Goswami as a way of understanding creative insight, a Gestalt or those 'aha' moments we value so highly in coaching.

What next?

Modern day living in the West is currently experiencing a massive explosion of creativity. Technology has developed so rapidly in the last thirty years and we are living in an increasingly connected and virtual world.

If I wanted to, I could plug myself into my phone or tablet and watch, read and absorb a vast quantity of freely available information, all day long. I can talk to people all round the world and find out anything I need to know. The raw materials for creativity are at my fingertips – images, music, concepts, inspiration and enormous vaults of free knowledge. I wonder what Jung would make of all this information feeding into what he called the supra-personal or the collective unconscious?

Today, writing a book is no longer the remit of professional authors – if you have access to a computer, a mobile phone or a library with internet access you can start a blog or self-publish books and stories online, instantly.

If you want to learn to paint, you can go online and buy some materials, which will be delivered the next day. You can sit down, find a video on the web that will teach you some painting techniques or you can sign up to an online art course – all without leaving your house.

Creativity, especially in the day to day practice of arts and crafts, has been democratised, but old beliefs and institutions still remain. In fact, the dichotomy between creativity and 'high arts' or daily creativity and 'successful creative people' can sometimes seem wider than ever.

We should also note what could be described as the 'hijacking of creativity by entrepreneurial capitalism' (Fox 2013). Creativity and innovation may be seen as capitalist devices – one of the keys to capital production and wealth creation. On a local level, we see people wanting to turn their creative products into home businesses. On a macro level, large companies know that creativity and the resultant 'must have' new product is the key to worldwide sales and massive wealth. One way or another, creativity is big business. One wonders what might happen next, or indeed, what is already happening.

How might the sustainability movement, the re-emergence of home crafts and up-cycling change the future of creative activities? How has the 'networked society' and our ability to share ideas and resources instantly impacted on human creativity?

So many people are creating; creating through daily journaling, off and online, be it morning pages or a crafted blog, making home videos and writing fiction using their mobile phones. Past creations too are shared on all sorts of professional, academic and social media sites.

The notion of copyright and the increasingly grey area of intellectual property is being challenged in many ways too. Creative Commons licensing allows people to share and distribute what would have otherwise been a copyrighted work. The speed and rate of knowledge generation and mass sharing online will undoubtedly cause interesting challenges in the future in terms of who created what.

Learning points

- The terms the arts and creativity are often used interchangeably, but modern day creativity is much broader.
- High art is culturally ascribed and has been valued more than the crafts and daily home art practices.
- Societal beliefs about creativity differ vastly between the East and West.
- The history and the stories we have about creativity still impact on our clients' beliefs and our beliefs as coaches too.
- Creativity is a social phenomenon as much as an individual one.
- Technology and our modern, networked society have radically changed creativity and the arts today.

References

Boorstin, D. J. (1992) The creators: A history of heroes of the imagination, in Kaufman, J. C. and Sternberg, R. J. (eds) *The Cambridge Handbook of Creativity*. Cambridge: Cambridge University Press, p. 5.

Cicero (44 BC) *De Natura Deorum* (The Nature of the Gods).

Creek, J. (2010) *The Core Concepts of Occupational Therapy*. London: Jessica Kingsley Publishers.

Fox, N. (2013) Creativity, anti-humanism and the 'new sociology of art', *Journal of Sociology* 0(0), 1–15. doi: 10.1177/1440783313498947

Goswami, A. (2014) *Quantum Creativity*. London: Hay House.

Jung, C. G. (1979) *Man and His Symbols*. London: Aldus Books Ltd.

Kaufman, A. B. et al (2010) The neurobiological foundation of creative cognition, in Kaufman, J. C. and Sternberg, R. J. (eds) *The Cambridge Handbook of Creativity*. Cambridge: Cambridge University Press, pp. 216–32.

Law, M. et al (1996) The person-environment-occupation model: a transactive approach to occupational performance, *Canadian Journal of Occupational Therapy*, 63(1), 9–23.

Locke, J. (1690) *An Essay Concerning Human Understanding*.

Nui, W. (2013) Confucian ideology and creativity, *The Journal of Creative Behaviour*, 46(4), 274–84.

Readman, M. (2010) *What's in a Word? The Discursive Construction of Creativity*. Bournemouth University Phd Thesis. Accessed 12/10/15, http://eprints.bournemouth.ac.uk/17755/1/Readman,Mark_Ph.D._2010.pdf.

Robinson, K. (2011) *Out of Our Minds*. Chichester: Capstone Publishing Ltd.

Tarnas, R. (1991) *Passion of the Western*. Pimlico: Mind, UK.

Part II

Creative human

The story of coaching mostly focuses on the person – the individual who appears at their coaching practice, desiring some sort of change. However, the coaching profession acknowledge that coaching is not all about the individual. As we have seen, in relation to creativity, personal awareness and actions that spring forth from coaching are a complex interaction of the person, the context, the environment and on-going 'doing'. This book seeks to explore these complex interactions, so rather than immediately focussing on the individual, we should lend an ear to a different perspective and see what the sociology of creativity has to say.

The dominant paradigm here in the West, the story which persists, is one that continues to privilege the outcome or article produced by an individual. However, Professor Nick Fox (2013), sets out an anti-humanist 'sociology' of creativity, which de-privileges humans as central to creation. He conceptualises creativity as a flow of affect between bodies, things and ideas. This, perhaps, is more allied to the Eastern notion of creation in situ.

Secondly, Fox proposes that 'Creative production is the on-going "becoming other"'. He asserts that 'the body is creative and engaged both biologically and socially, not a passive vehicle for the environment and social context to mould'. Creativity is not just about 'bringing something new into being' (creating other) but is also, just as importantly, about 'becoming other'. Excitingly, both align with coaching's overarching core philosophy and aims and we will return to those ideas as we continue this journey.

For now, though, we will turn our attention back to the 'individual' as in most Western cultures, creativity is seen as springing from the individual. We must also acknowledge that working with individual clients is the starting place of most coach training and professional socialisation.

Holding a lengthy discussion on what constitutes 'the individual' or 'a person' would open a huge can of worms and subject us to yet another massive range of perspectives, theories and philosophies, so I will take some large liberties for the sake of us all.

We have a psyche, which could be argued is purely generated by various systems including our nervous and limbic systems and other biological structures. Clearly, our psyche is shaped by years of external and internal influences.

We have a physical body, a broader biological structure comprising of many complex systems including, neurological, musculoskeletal, endocrine, circulatory and sensory-perceptual systems, to name just a few, which enable us to engage and participate in activity, which in turn help to shape mind and psyche.

Depending on what you believe, we also have a soul or spirit. Whilst some might argue this is produced by our physical brain structures and our mind, most people I have met and work with believe in something beyond their 'self' that cannot be purely explained by neurology and biology alone.

Undoubtedly, these separate parts do not work in isolation and are not static. In recent years we have started to acknowledge and remember age old wisdom, which knew clearly the integration of mind, psyche, body and soul/spirit.

These broad ideas of mind, body and soul are also reflected in the development of coaching. We could say coaching started by looking at the psyche, springing from the world of psychology and the need to mend the 'wounded self' (Western 2012). We could then see the 'mind' entering the coaching ring as we grappled with cognitive concepts. We could then say that the 'body' and the science of its neurological and somatic systems entered the 'coaching' ring. These players in the coaching ring all have something different to say about creativity.

Perhaps there is another player entering the field. One that is trying to integrate a messy, complex, interconnected whole that is not purely about 'I'; one that embraces the soulful, spiritual nature of human beings and their human doings; one that also embraces the failures, traumas, losses and uncertainty of normal life.

Some recognise and are happy to work with this messy, chaotic, uncertain, emerging paradigm. Some find it difficult and are perhaps reluctant or unable to acknowledge it; possibly because outcomes are difficult to demonstrate, name, predict and trust, or maybe we just don't like to acknowledge risk, failure and loss. Interestingly, here, in the muddy, messy depths, the richness and gems of both coaching and creativity are found.

References

Fox, N. (2013) Creativity, anti-humanism and the 'new sociology of art', *Journal of Sociology* 0(0), 1–15. doi: 10.1177/1440783313498947

Western, S. (2012) *Coaching and Mentoring*. London: Sage.

Chapter 3

Creativity and the psyche

There is a vast and still expanding body of knowledge focussing on 'mind' and 'psyche'. Coaching has looked to, and indeed borrowed much of its knowledge base from, these psychologies and the psychotherapeutic approaches springing from them (Western 2012). David Rock explains clearly how developmental, behavioural, evolutionary and cognitive psychologies have also provided a 'bedrock' for the coaching profession (Rock 2009).

The aim of this part of the book is not to map the entirety of coaching's psychological roots, but to start bringing to light the source of some of coaching's main constructs about creativity and society as a whole. I know that many of you will have significant experience and in-depth training in a particular psychological approach. As you read this section, it might feel like I am 'glossing over' or even missing some elements that you find crucial. Please know that what coaching can learn about creativity from this domain is also vast and would easily fill several books.

Whilst many of us have a leaning towards one psychology or another, we must acknowledge that most fields of psychological thought postulate about creativity in some way or another. Personally, I am seeking to take a bird's eye view and try to hone in on what appears to be most relevant to this thing we call creativity in relation to coaching practice.

Finding a way to take this 'bird's eye view' over creativity and theories of psyche was easier said than done. Lively discussions with coach, psychotherapist and life-long friend, Maggie Jeffery, yielded some pragmatic clarity:

'Trust me Jen, it all changed after Woodstock'.

So it seemed natural to divide this complex evolution of psychological thought regarding creativity into pre Woodstock (pre 1969) and post Woodstock (1970s onwards). Happily this also seemed to fit with Simon Western's conceptualisation of a shift from working with the 'wounded self' to working with the 'celebrated self'. Western notes the emergence of coaching and the shift that started to hasten after the 1960s:

Inspired by Emerson, the transcendalists and the Beat generation, the human potential movement of Carl Rogers, Maslow and others, influenced the celebrated self to come to the fore, highlighting an innate human desire to self-actualize.

(Western 2012 p. 7)

Pre Woodstock

Before we delve into 'pre-Woodstockian' psychology and its ideas regarding creativity, we should remember that creativity as a word, wasn't really used until the 1950s. Before the 1950s, people talked of creating, inventing, making or designing something. So whilst I will use the term 'creativity', it didn't exist at the time!

Psychology as a discipline started to emerge around 1875 with Wilhelm Wundt founding the first experimental psychology lab in Germany. In the early days there was a preoccupation with the function and purpose of the physical brain – what parts of the brain did what. At that time there was only one way to find out, remove a part or at least prod it, see what happens, label it, repeat.

Freud appeared on the psychological scene shortly after and started to develop Psychoanalysis around 1886. In studying and interpreting dreams, Freud showed some interest in the 'creative' mind, seeing it as 'a defence mechanism protecting against neurosis, leading thus to the production of a socially acceptable source of entertainment and pleasure for the public. For the artist has the ability of turning his fantasies into artistic creations instead of into symptoms' (Drobot undated). In essence, creativity's purpose was to maximise personal gratification and minimise punishment and guilt (Woodman 1981).

In Freud's opinion, creative behaviours and thoughts were a result of conflicting, denied, sublimated or repressed forces in the unconscious mind. I realise I am presenting a very simplistic view of Freud's thoughts on creativity, and acknowledge that he does leave us with some important thoughts regarding creative practice.

Whilst Freud was busy exploring unconscious drives, dogs start barking and bells start ringing around 1903, with the Behaviouralists doing their thing from around the 1920s. I am not overly concerned with what Behaviourism lends to our exploration, except perhaps that we might treat ourselves with a chocolate biscuit after we finally finish writing a book chapter, or perhaps adjust our subsequent painting activities based on the lack of sales from an exhibition. Skinner (1974) describes the way that operant reinforcement theory (Behaviourism) combines with evolutionary theory, resulting in creativity being behavioural 'mutations'. Personally, I prefer the chocolate biscuit explanation.

The work of Carl Gustav Jung, psychiatrist and cultural philosopher, is well known to many coaches. Jung proposed four principal psychological functions or types by which humans experience the world: sensation, intuition, feeling and thinking. These form the basis of the Myers-Briggs Type Indicator (Myers and Myers 1995) used by many executive coaches, however, Jung's work also provides us with so much more. Here we find rich insights and opinion on the 'how' of art, the experience of art, the source of creativity and the creative process.

Whilst Jung felt that psychology was the best discipline to study creativity, he was also aware of its limitations. He believed that the secret of the creative process was rooted in the unconscious and therefore out of reach of the mainstream psychological methods used at the time, hence using dream analysis.

Van den Berk (2012) outlines the main themes of Jung's work in relation to art and creativity that include:

1 Cryptomnesia – the psychic process of hidden memories; 'one thinks one is presenting something new, when in fact it is an old and forgotten truth'. This 'forgetting' can be an individual or collective 'forgetting'. Jung felt that artists in particular were sensitive to cryptomnesia.
2 The complex – the driving force behind these hidden memories (not a sexually sublimating complex as Freud believed).
3 The participation mystique – the collision of the psychic and physical, the subjective and objective, which results in a work of art. True art is something 'supra-personal', a force that has 'escaped from the limitations of the personal and has soared beyond the personal concerns of its creator.'
4 The 'symbol' – connecting the unconscious and the conscious psyche, the symbol is a unit of transfer or the connecting chain from dream to reality. Record your dreams, draw your dreams and 'unlock the symbolism of your unconscious'

Clearly this is all of interest to us as coaches and as we seek to understand creativity, but there is one more powerful insight from Jung that made me sit up and ponder further, both professional and personally.

To Jung, the raw materials and birthplace of creativity is the same birthplace of 'neuroses' (anxious, unhelpful thoughts and ideas). Our ability to generate multiple thoughts, realities and possibilities is helpful in terms of creativity, but the same innate human ability also fuels anxiety and psychosis. This is not a bland statement supporting the myth of the 'mad artist' but an acknowledgement that the same process that helps us generate ten possible routes to market for a business, or ten possible uses for a ping pong ball, also helps us generate ten possible reasons why our daughter has not come home on time or ten tangible reasons why we believe we are being followed home by a wheelie bin.

If this is indeed the case, its worth pondering the effect of the mass injection of hidden memories into Jung's cryptomnesia via the internet, on us individually and collectively, especially younger people, who have been 'connected' online since birth.

Around the same time as Jung and others were working away developing psychodynamic psychotherapy, Graham Wallas, a social psychologist and educationalist, was also proposing an early model of creativity. In *The Art of Thought* (1926) he described the process of creating something new as a linear progression through the stages of preparation, incubation, intimation, illumination and verification. Much of his language and concepts are still with us today. We talk about 'incubating ideas' and often try to define creativity as a linear process, with a definite start and an end point with some verification of the work, concept or product. As a visual artist and writer, I am doubtful whether there is ever a real starting point and very rarely an end point; my personal experience suggests it's much more messy and complex than that, but I do have close artist friends whose processes appear more linear and contained than mine!

Whilst a contemporary of Freud, Alfred Adler shifted psychological work in several ways: he took a more holistic approach and attempted to be more egalitarian, using chairs instead of the couch; he also viewed people as being motivated by social influence and therefore capable of striving for superiority and success. Adler also felt that behaviour is shaped by an individual's perception and vision of the future and that people are usually aware of what they are doing and why they are doing it. Style of life, to Adler was moulded by people's creative powering. Creativity therefore allows us to freely shape and compensate for a perceived deficiency, be it real or imagined (Ansbacher and Ansbacher 1964).

Around the same time that Adler moved away from Freud, a rumbling could be heard in the Gestalt corner, as Max Wertheimer (1945) published research on the perception of movement. A 'gestalt' is generated as the result of our brain's capability to generate whole forms, from separate and numerous perceptual inputs. This is the founding principle upon which Gestalt theory is built. Fritz Perls (1951), together with his wife Laura, developed the Gestalt therapy process, which involves developing an enhanced awareness of one's sensations, perceptions, physical feelings and emotions in relationship with itself, its environment and 'other'. As we will see, the Gestalt rumble continues to grow today, influencing both creativity theory and coaching practice.

Guilford produced his landmark study in 'The Structure of Intellect' (1956), proposing a model of creativity and conceptualising the familiar term 'divergent thinking'. It describes the thought process that generates creative ideas by exploring many possible solutions and is often used to describe how we respond to questions that have no set answer. It is a helpful construct but many feel it is overused, and frequently used as a blanket term to describe 'creativity' as whole. Creativity is clearly so much more than just a thinking process, but Guilford does provide us with some helpful concepts to ponder as coaches.

Divergent Thinking has four key components:

- *Fluency* – referring to the number and frequency of ideas or thoughts.
- *Flexibility* – the types of ideas.
- *Originality* – production of the most unusual/unique ideas.
- *Elaboration* – the ability to develop the ideas.

> Take some time to ponder how the coaching process already impacts on these four components:
>
> ***How do you see fluency, flexibility, originality and elaboration showing up in the coaching process?***
>
> ***As coaches how do we evoke and develop fluency of thought, promote flexibility, evaluate originality and help them to elaborate their ideas?***
>
> One such example I can think of is how we often use iterative coaching processes to help clients think of multiple solutions and numerous standpoints. A simple question can become iterative in nature, by adding the words 'and what else?' after the client seems to have finished answering the question. According to Harland (2009) and others working with 'emergent approaches', it's only after the fifth or sixth iterations that new knowledge and insight is generated.
>
> Whilst I believe that coaching naturally helps those processes of fluency, flexibility, originality and elaboration, greater awareness of these processes can help you hone in or amplify certain parts of your coaching that are related to these areas, it can also help you to use questions differently. This is particularly relevant if your clients need help in one particular area, such as flexibility or elaboration.

Around the same time that Guilford published 'The Structure of Intellect', George Kelly was exploring creativity through personal construct theory. Personality, in this way, serves to predict and control events, and hence the constructs, that contribute to our personal view of reality. Of great interest here is Kelly's understanding of creativity as a movement between loose constructs and tight constructs (1955):

> *A person who always uses tight constructions may be productive – that is he may turn out a lot of things – but he cannot be creative; he cannot produce anything which has not already been blueprinted . . . so a person who uses loose constructions exclusively cannot be creative either . . . He would never get round to setting up a hypothesis for crucial testing.*
>
> (Kelly 1955 quoted in Woodman 1981).

This is such an important idea for coaches to consider. Whilst Kelly felt that some people could only perform half of this cycle, as coaches we often find ourselves enabling both loose and tight 'thinking' and facilitating our clients' ability to move between the two.

Very recently at a meeting of artists, scientist and educators at the Santa Fe Institute Working Group (Santa Fe, N M 2014), Robert Bilder reasserted the importance of this idea, beacuse it achieves:

> *A clear balance of (the human brain's) stable and flexible regimes. Those states involve high generativity, flexible memory combination and the successful inhibition of intrusive habits or fixed ways of thinking, and they enable us to connect more clearly to drive action or perception.*

Whilst we are starting to veer into the neuroscience of creativity, away from the 'psyche', there is no separation really. Thankfully, individual professionals from the arts, theatre, psychology, education and neuroscience, to name but a few, seem to have started to work together to share crucial learning and develop integrated knowledge. This is an essential piece of understanding for coaches to really take on board and Bilder has another few gems for us later.

Of course, modern research is now starting to illustrate the impact of shifting states of consciousness and the effect this has on the mind. Back in the 1950s, Milton Erickson's work in hypnotherapy and hypnosis was already exploring this within psychotherapy. The unconscious mind and all its creative, solution-generating capacities could, according to Erickson, be accessed through a hypnogogic state (Haley 1993).

So in the years that preceded Woodstock, a time when the moon was still made of cheese, Abraham Maslow, Rollo May, Carl Rogers and Roberto Assagioli and many others, were beavering away looking at the psyche, soul and what it means to be a creative human. Others in psychology were beavering away exploring the more rational and cognitive side to creativity. Both mark the awakening of a new psychological and scientific era.

Post Woodstock

I imagine that those who unzipped their tents and stepped onto the dewy morning grass after the first Woodstock did not suddenly possess radical new insights into the 'ology' of the 'psyche'. Nor did they open their rucksacks to find it stuffed full of colourful, new, creative ideas (then again perhaps they did). The energy of the 1960s and early 1970s was radical, transformative and still makes itself known today, but it emerged from what came before – with all new and shiny things, we must always remember that.

Emphasising free will, potential and creativity, these new approaches moved away from separation towards wholeness. There is a focus on self-exploration, growth and the journey towards integration. Here we find ideas such as free will, empathy, self-help and the 'ideal self' gaining ground against purely cognitive and rational approaches that seem to separate.

Humanistic and transpersonal psychologies were emerging, lending fresh eyes to how the human condition was viewed. Maslow (1968) was exploring the notion of self-actualisation and saw creativity as a key to reaching it. In fact, Maslow made an interesting distinction between primary creativity, new discoveries coming from the unconscious and secondary creativity – the rational, productive creativity, coming from capable people. Maslow felt that everyone has an innate capacity for creativity. Carl Rogers had been talking about the 'conditions for creativity' since the mid-1950s. What he teaches us about the importance of setting up an environment of 'psychological safety and freedom' cannot be understated and will be explored later.

In *The Courage to Create* (1975) Rollo May makes a significant contribution to the discussion about creativity. En route, he notes the inadequacy of some of psychology's theories of creativity. He refutes Adler's 'Compensatory Theory of Creativity', which suggests that human beings produce art, science and other creative forms to compensate for their inadequacies. May felt strongly that psychoanalytical processes were inadequate in dealing with the creative process. How artists and other creative people encounter and interrelate with their world was of the upmost importance to May. He illustrated this through discussing the progression of Picasso's work in relation to the times in which he lived.

He suggests, 'in this sense, genuine artists are so bound up with their age, that they cannot communicate separated from it . . . [creativity] is the encounter of the intensively conscious human being with his or her world' (May 1975, p. 56).

Psychosynthesis developed by Roberto Assagioli in the 1960s, is a transpersonal approach. The focus is on identifying and working creatively with 'sub-personalities'. These are roles and ways of being that might have served the individual well in childhood but that still manifest in the present unconsciously and unhelpfully in adulthood. Once recognised, accepted and integrated, development is towards discovery and synthesis around the 'core' or centre. Growth is towards the super consciousness where the personality discovers and connects with qualities including love, trust and creativity.

In psychosynthesis, creative techniques such as visualisation, free writing and free drawing (Ferruci 1982) are frequently used with clients. John Whitmore, who has made significant contributions to behavioural coaching in the UK, now advocates for a transpersonal approach to coaching (Passmore 2007).

The idea of sub-personalities, archetypes or differing selves has quite a history and is used in many forms of therapy and coaching nowadays (Adson 2004, Bachkirova 2011). The 'artist-scientist' is one of the classic archetypes developed by Jung. Here, Jung does not make a tertiary, unhelpful distinction between left-brain and right-brain people. He acknowledges the similarities between of the rational, logical but creative scientist, engineer, inventor or builder and the artist, seeker, dreamer or thinker.

In exploring this archetypal artist-scientist we find some lovely descriptions:

- Often distracted by their own thoughts and needing frequently to be pulled in out of the rain.
- An ability to focus on a single item or idea, in spite of the surrounding activity (absorption).
- An ability to improvise novel solutions to problems, which, while they may not turn out as intended, somehow are made to work anyway.
- A distaste for simple solutions.
- Being simultaneously vastly knowledgeable and yet innocent.
- Being impulsive yet cautious.
- An outer self-confidence masking an inner fear of failure.

- Naivety about the world and others, in spite of their vast understanding of the academic and philosophical world.
- An inner childlike emotional side intertwined with a staggering logical mind.

(Segal 1998)

Despite the new, transpersonal, energy of the sixties and seventies, cognitive approaches strengthened and contributed significantly to our understanding of creativity. Having started to explore and define creativity in the 1950s, the need to quantify and measure it quickly arose. Following the strong cognitive lead of Guilford, Torrance published his 'Tests of Creative Thinking' in 1966. This is still used in creativity research to this day.

Lateral thinking, a term coined by Edward De Bono and often used interchangeably with divergent thinking, is still used today and can be seen in action in his *Six Thinking Hats* (1985). This approach encourages cognitive and perceptual shifting by asking people to imagine they are wearing different hats. The donning of a 'white hat' helps us to elicit the neutral, objective facts of a situation or problem; a 'red hat' promotes thinking of an emotional, intuitive nature; a 'black hat' encourages us to take a critical, analytical stance; a 'yellow hat' asks us to think optimistically; a 'green hat' allows for creative possibilities and ideas; lastly, a 'blue hat' invites us to take a cool overview of the whole and make a decision.

The concept of 'personality' is still hotly debated in psychology and psychiatry, and colloquially you often hear people refer to having a 'creative personality'. When exploring the concept of personality and trait theories, you will quickly discover the commonly accepted, 'big five' traits: openness to experience, conscientiousness, extroversion, agreeableness and neuroticism. Of these, it is only *openness to experience* that has been shown to strongly correlate with creativity.

According to McCrae (1990) openness to experience includes:

- An *openness* to fantasy.
- *Aesthetics* – artistic interests.
- *Feelings* – experiencing and valuing things.
- *Active* – trying out new things.
- *Ideas* – curious, smart, likes challenges.
- *Values* – unconventional and liberal.

In his meta-analysis, Feist (1998) elaborates further on these traits, showing the creative personality to be 'less conventional and less conscientious, more self-confident, self-accepting, driven, ambitious, dominant, hostile, and impulsive'.

As for the other 'big five' traits, conscientiousness, extroversion, agreeableness and neuroticism, there is no strong correlation with creativity. You may disagree, but many creative types, such as writers, composers, artists and software programmers, are very clearly quiet introverts. We should regularly challenge our assumptions about people, otherwise we bring those assumptions and stereotypes to our coaching and that can be hugely detrimental to the process.

As I write this, I am making some internal judgement calls. Out of these traits, some would be more open to coaching and certainly more ethical; namely self-confidence, self-acceptance and, to a certain degree, impulsiveness. We often find these themes naturally fall out of coaching, but 'openness to experience' has a particular place in coaching creativity.

How can we foster this openness to experience with our coaching clients, knowing that it really helps creativity? We often ask curious questions that invite our clients to fantasise and experience, and the coaching process naturally enables people to try different ways, take action and reflect.

The extent to which you are willing to encourage this openness to experience will largely depend on your personal coaching style and approach. As mentioned before, if your approach is very 'clean' or non-directive, it wouldn't be appropriate to steer the conversation in a particular direction. However, in other approaches, actively promoting and encouraging openness to experience is a defining feature.

Within Kaizen Muse Creativity Coaching, coaches encourage their clients, as does Julia Cameron, to go on 'artist's dates' to feed their creativity and be receptive to new experiences. An artist's date could involve doing something at home or perhaps taking yourself to a different environment or surrounding yourself with different visual stimuli. It might mean taking yourself to a place you would never usually go. As a coach, you might actually consider going on a 'date' with your client and 'coach' them to gain greater benefit from the experience, embedding the learning and capturing any actions or insights.

Perhaps this helps to feed the creative void or access Jung's collective unconscious?

We know that there is much more to creativity than intellectual and cognitive capacity, which can be measured and quantified. An ability to *think* divergently does not determine one's creativity. Stepping back into the emergent psychologies, such as Gestalt, we see a more helpful picture of creativity, which illuminates the process of coaching greatly.

One of my personal joys as a coach is providing the space and environment for emergent thought to flourish and hearing those light bulb moments as they start to occur. These 'a-has' are also seen in Gestalt psychotherapy: when perception and awareness shifts, insight emerges and the whole picture or new picture is suddenly seen. Gestalt psychotherapy has much to offer coaches wishing to understand the creativity process as a natural event, starting with sensory awareness and ending with some sort of satisfaction, awareness or completion.

Congram and Bently (undated), describe the Gestalt Cycle of Experience using the metaphor of a wave:

> *The wave form starts with sensations that emerge out of 'sea depths', otherwise known as the fertile void in Gestalt. The notion of the sea implies a wealth of riches, many untapped, which inform and are informed by our life experiences. Sensations, needs and unfinished feelings seeking attention eventually reach our awareness. As awareness increases so energy increases.*

This wave starts to move upwards through 'energy' into 'action', which forms the peak of the wave. As it begins its descent, it moves into 'full contact' then 'completion' and finally 'withdrawal', returning to the trough point of the wave. Then it starts again as sensations begin to emerge once more.

The process is one of completeness and also involves forward movement – otherwise it just goes round in circles and no progression is made. Returning to the fertile void is necessary so that new information, ideas and content continue to 'fertilise' and grow the process.

A story: Jung's, creative, fertile void?

A few years ago I was on a train to Scotland from Bristol. I don't fly and find the time on a train hugely productive, so it suits me in many ways. I enjoy taking my netbook or old school notebook and writing blogs or exploring ideas. 'Journeying' seems to allow ideas to flow and gives me the space to empty my head onto paper.

This particular rail journey had seen me travel to Edinburgh for a women's Dragon's Den, not for funding, but for feedback and advice on a business idea that I had been exploring for years. The event was superb and the following day I got back on the train for the seven-hour return journey to Bristol. What happened next can only be described as both exhilarating and exhausting but was simply quite magical.

Over those seven hours I wrote and wrote and wrote and could barely stop. Ideas for branding, marketing, tools and unique games for the parties, were just flooding in. I could not and did not want to stop it. The hours passed and I filled nearly two large spiral bound notebooks.

Regardless of personal and spiritual beliefs, I can only say that this felt like a state of 'bliss'. It felt like I was travelling through this rich, connected source of ideas and inspiration. The speeding train literally helped me access this vast soup of raw materials, grabbing hold of ideas, which I pieced together on route.

It felt as if I had 'downloaded' the entire business in the space of seven hours. Clearly I hadn't, as much of the structure, skills and knowledge were already inside me, but they had somehow connected and transformed into something new and original, something incredibly creative.

The download may have been very fast, but the coaching to translate the ideas into reality still continues to this day. As coaches, we understand how a creative idea can take seconds to appear but years to put into practice!

The fertile void talked about in Gestalt theory, is perhaps a creative void. A void of uncertainty, complete chaos and a lack of recognisable form. The void is not empty at all, but chock full of stuff – ideas, thoughts and possibilities. To me, it's like the concept of quantum or primordial soup.

Quantum soup is the term often given to describe the first moments of the universe, where a 'soup' of particles (quarks and gluons) existed, in a vacuum. From this quantum soup, matter and energy were formed. Skip forward a few million years and we have primordial soup, which is often used to describe the origins of life on our earth. Here, a soup of organic compounds gathered at shorelines and in protected pockets developing into the first life on earth.

> Both these mimic a creative process but also remind me of my train journey! It's like I was travelling through this soup of ideas, knowledge and possibilities and I was able to 'catch' ideas as we sped along. Recognising them, playing with them and knitting them together as the journey continued, using my natural strengths and passions. Perhaps I was travelling through the collective unconscious described by Jung, with the help of Virgin Trains.
>
> A few months later I found a lovely TED video of Elizabeth Gilbert, author of *Eat, Pray, Love*, talking about creativity. She quotes the American Poet, Ruth Stone, who described her process as a poet. She says she hears a poem coming over the landscape and has to run to house to get a pencil and paper whilst being 'chased' by the poem. She has to catch the poem and write it down and sometimes only just catches it by the tail, pulling it into herself, backwards!
>
> This is just how my experience on the train felt – like I was catching ideas as I sped through the countryside, back to Bristol. I was gathering a pool of ideas, previous learning, current insights and stimuli from the environment. Sometimes when I am being coached or I am coaching others, similar things seem to occur. As coaches we often help people develop a rich, diverse soup of ingredients and ideas, help them generate new ones, surface and spot the best ones, test them out and bring them into form.

I find the concept of the fertile void particularly fascinating – this void is the birth place of creativity – the quantum soup of possibility, where random ideas jostle and concepts bump into each other while discarded projects decompose into component parts; a dark and chaotic but rich environment.

To me, this fertile void in coaching is recognisable as the place where our clients suddenly feel or think that they feel emptiness or don't know or understand anything. Sometimes it might be a place of overwhelm and confusion. Anger or frustration might be experienced as a result of this confusion and stress of being overwhelmed. Silence often occurs as our client sits with this experience of not knowing. Sometimes it's quite uncomfortable for both parties, but rushing out of the void may be really unhelpful. As coaches, we can learn to sit with silence and wait for the 'a-ha' that often follows.

Longhurst (2006) helpfully described how these delicious moments of insights or 'a-has' are experienced in co-active coaching. We could explain these insights away using cognitive neuroscience (Sawyer 2011), but Longhurst (2006) asserts that these moments are experienced in feelings, thoughts, body and soul, and at a spiritual level. These types of 'a-ha' moments are very different from solving a problem at purely a conscious, rational, cognitive level. Much of creativity's current research is seeking to understand the anatomy of the 'a-ha' (Santa Fe Institute Working Group Report 2015).

Acknowledging this complexity and drawing on learning from Erickson and Perls, amongst others, the somewhat contentious field of neuro linguistic programming (NLP) is defined as 'a system of alternative therapy intended to educate people in self-awareness and effective communication, and to model and change their patterns of mental and emotional behaviour' (Oxford Dictionaries Online 2015). Developed during the 1970s through the work of Bandler and Grinder (1975), NLP uses a variety of different techniques, including hypnosis. Labelled as an NLP creativity tool, the Disney method (Dilts 1994) aims to evoke creative thinking by asking people to take different perspectives or stances, similarly to de Bono's Thinking Hats. Modelling is another NLP tool and would ask us to research and emulate the successful behaviours, thoughts, language and mind-sets of highly creative people, should we desire similar success.

A positive approach to psychology emerged during the late 1990s and with it some new postulates regarding the impact of affect and emotion on creativity. Building on the research into creativity of Csikszentmihalyi (1995), Fredrickson (2001) explored the role of positive emotions, developing the Broaden and Build Theory:

> *The positive emotions of joy, interest, contentment, pride, and love appear to have a complementary effect: They broaden people's momentary thought-action repertoires, widening the array of the thoughts and actions that come to mind . . . Joy, for instance, broadens by creating the urge to play, push the limits, and be creative . . . Interest, a phenomenologically distinct positive emotion, broadens by creating the urge to explore, take in new information and experiences, and expand the self in the process . . . Contentment, a third distinct positive emotion, broadens by creating the urge to savour current life circumstances and integrate these circumstances into new views of self and of the world . . . Pride, a fourth distinct positive emotion that follows personal achievements, broadens by creating the urge to share news of the achievement with others and to envision even greater achievements in the future.*
>
> (Fredrickson 2001)

This 'broadened thought' approach fits with much of the research and approaches mentioned before, and it gives much needed evidence to what we intuitively know: creativity responds to a fun, a relaxed approach, broad-based thinking and perceptual shifting.

In tracking the main psychological frames of thought in relation to creativity, I am aware that we could have just followed the main coaching psychology approaches that are currently accepted and formally developed, including behavioural coaching, cognitive behavioural coaching, solution focussed coaching and so on. However, this book seeks to look beyond the currently ascribed coaching frameworks and into the broader world of the arts, crafts and the 'doing' of creativity in many realms of life. Otherwise we risk just inventing a 'coaching of creativity' from what is currently formally expressed and will have missed out on a great opportunity.

The dark side

A cultural story, a myth that is still prevalent in Western society today, is the link between mental illness and creativity. It is a story that has served the film industry well over the years and I can think of many books and films about the turbulent lives of artists and poets that often end in tragedy. This myth has had weight added to it in recent years, with high profile celebrities opening talking about their mental health problems and discussing how without their problems, they doubt they would be as creative or talented as they are.

Challenging these long held societal stories is crucial at this time with the increase in mental health problems.

In a recent, large, longitudinal study Kyaga et al (2013) found that full blown mental illness did not increase the probability of entering a creative profession (interestingly, the exception is bipolar disorder). However, the first degree, psychologically healthy relatives of patients with mental health problems (schizophrenia, bipolar disorder and anorexia) were significantly over-represented in creative professions.

James Kaufman, one of our experts in creativity, considers whether the relatives inherited a watered-down version of the mental illness, conducive to creativity, whilst possessing 'protective factors'. These protective factors are identified by Carson (2011) as good working memory, high IQ and cognitive flexibility.

Conversely, a recent study supports the idea of a genetic link between creativity and psychosis. Power et al (2015) note that:

> *The results of the study should not have come as a surprise because to be creative you have to think differently from the crowd and we had previously shown that carriers of genetic factors that pre-dispose to schizophrenia do so.*

There is complex, contradictory evidence emerging all the time from various fields and, as always, what you glean from them is highly dependent on what you read, how it's presented and what you personally believe. Prominent creativity researcher Scott Barry Kaufman, a different Kaufman to the previously mentioned one, notes 'there is very little evidence suggesting that clinical, debilitating mental illness is conducive to productivity and innovation' (2013). He bases this opinion on many years of study into the complex facets of creativity, but this doesn't feel like an answer to the questions we are exploring here.

Scott Barry Kaufman's statement refers to productivity and innovation, both outputs from the creative mind. We could say that highly creative thought exists in those individuals with mental health problems, but perhaps our own ability to see the validity and value of their creativity is perhaps impaired. The social construction mental illness, and the context in which an individual lives, often determines how their creativity is perceived and what they are able or supported to produce or create.

Away from formal diagnoses, I often wonder about the relationship between creative thinking and anxiety. Being able to produce a fluency of ideas and having the ability to elaborate on an idea, can also feed ruminating, anxious thoughts. This is present in most mental illness but also apparent in many 'healthy' individuals. I am reminded of Jung's statement:

> *The undeniable fact that a work of art arises from much the same psychic conditions as a neurosis. This is only natural because certain of these conditions are present in every individual whether in the case of a nervous intellectual, a poet or a normal human being.*
>
> (Jung in Van de Berk p1)

Ask a worrier how many reasons they can generate as to why a relative might be late home and you will certainly get an abundance of ideas and some quite amazingly creative thinking. I imagine there is research exploring this, but for someone who has creativity as a top personal strength, I am well aware that the flip side of my creativity is an amazing ability to think around a situation. This often results in the generation of unhelpful, anxiety provoking thoughts. I am also aware that creativity of thought can stretch our idea of what is real or imagined to the limits.

If we hold a strong belief, we often seek evidence to support that belief and a highly creative mind can generate all sorts of compelling evidence. Paranoia can easily be generated when mechanisms such as attentional blindness and hyper-vigilance become out of balance and start skewing perception. We start seeing, perceiving and creating what we believe.

Learning points

- Several psychotherapeutic approaches acknowledge an imaginary space in which creativity takes place or a place where the raw materials of creativity may be found.
- Moments of insight, magical synthesis or 'a-has' are seen in the creative process and the coaching process.
- Divergence, including fluency, flexibility, originality and elaboration are intrinsic to the creative process, but creativity is not just divergent thinking.
- Openness to experience is the only personality trait related to creativity.
- Broadened thought and positive emotions help shift perceptual thinking and impact positively on creativity.
- It is widely acknowledged that there needs to be a movement between loose and tight constructs, a balance of stability and flexibility, a cycle of engagement and withdraw.
- Creativity is involved in 'creating other', such as an item or product and 'becoming other', the evolving self. Both are of interest to coaching.
- The link between mental illness and creativity is misrepresented.
- Strong cultural myths, judgements and assumptions about creativity, creative people and the creative process, impact on us as coaches and our clients.

References

Adson, P. (2004) *Depth Coaching: Discovering Archetypes for Empowerment, Growth and Balance*. Florida: CAPT.
Ansbacher, H. L. and Ansbacher, R. R. (eds) (1964) *The Individual Psychology of Alfred Adler*. New York: Harper Torchbooks.
Assagioli, R. (1977) *The Act of Will*. London: Penguin Books.
Bachkirova, T. (2011) *Developmental Coaching: Working with the Self Maidenhead*. London: Open University Press.
Bandler, R. and Grinder, J. (1975) *The Structure of Magic I: A Book About Language and Therapy*. Palo Alto, CA: Science & Behavior Books.
Bently, T. and Congram, S. (undated) *Gestalt: A Philosophy for Change*. Accessed 12/10/15, http://www.leaderfulwomen.org/sue/03_Downloads/papers/Gestalt_Philosophy.pdf.
Berk, T. van Den (2012) *Jung On Art*. London: Routledge.
Carson, S. H. (2011) Creativity and psychopathology: a shared vulnerability model, *Canadian Journal of Psychiatry*, 56(3),144–53.
Csikszentmihalyi, M. (2008) *Flow: The Psychology of Optimal Experience*. New York: HarperCollins Publishers.
Dilts, R. (1994) *Strategies of Genius: Vol 1*. Soquel, CA: Meta Publications.
De Bono, E. (1985) *Six Thinking Hats*. London: Penguin Books.
Drobot, A. (undated) The psychoanalyst's image in literature and movies. Accessed 13/10/15, http://www.freudfile.org/psychoanalysis/papers_15.html.
Fox, N. (2013) Creativity, anti-humanism and the 'new sociology of art', *Journal of Sociology* 0(0), 1–15. doi: 10.1177/1440783313498947
Guilford, J. P. (1956) The structure of intellect, *Psychological Bulletin*, 53(4), 267–93.
Haley, J. (1993) *Uncommon Therapy: The Psychiatric Techniques of Milton H. Erickson*. London: W. W. Norton & Company.
Feist, G. (1998) A meta-analysis of personality in scientific and artistic creativity, *Personality and Social Psychology Review*, 2(4) 290–309.
Ferruci, P. (1982) *What We May be: Visions and Techniques of Psychosynthesis*. New York: Tarcher/Putnam.
Frederickson, B. (2001) The role of positive emotions in positive psychology: the broaden-and-build theory of positive emotions, *American Psychologist* 56(3), 218–26.
Harland, P. (2009) *The Power of Six*. London: Wayfinder Press.
Kaufman, S. B. (2013) The real link between creativity and mental illness, *Scientific American*, 3 October. Accessed 12/10/15, http://blogs.scientificamerican.com/beautiful-minds/the-real-link-between-creativity-and-mental-illness/.
Kelly, G. A. (1955) *The Psychology of Personal Constructs Volume 1: A Theory of Personality Volume 2: Clinical Diagnosis and Psychotherapy*. New York: Norton.
Kyaga, S. et al (2013) Mental illness, suicide and creativity: 40-year prospective total population study, *Journal of Psychiatric Research*, 47(1), 83–90.
Longhurst, L. (2006) The 'aha' moment in co-active coaching and its effects on belief and behavioural changes, *International Journal of Evidence Based Coaching and Mentoring*, 4(2), 61.
Oxford Dictionaries (2015) Accessed 12/10/15, http://www.oxforddictionaries.com/definition/english/neurolinguistic-programming.
Maslow, A. H. (1968) *Toward a Psychology of Being*. New York: John Wiley & Sons.
May, R. (1976) *The Courage to Create*. New York: Bantam Books.
McCrae, J. O. R. and Oliver, P. J. (1990) An introduction to the five-factor model and its applications, *Personality: Critical Concepts in Psychology*, 60(1998), 295.

Myers, I. and Myers, P. (1995) *Gifts Differing: Understanding Personality Type*. Mountain View, CA: Davies-Black Publishing.
Passmore, J. (2007) *Excellence in Coaching*. London: Kogan Page Ltd.
Perls, F, Hefferline, R, and Goodman, P. (1951) *Gestalt Therapy: Excitement and Growth in the Human Personality* (reprinted 2006). London: Souvenir Press.
Power, R.A. (2015) Polygenic risk scores for schizophrenia and bipolar disorder predict creativity, *Nature Neuroscience*, 18, 953–5.
Rock, D. and Page, J. (2009) *Coaching with the Brain in Mind: Foundations for Practice*. Hoboken, NJ: John Wiley & Sons.
Santa Fe Institute Working Group Report (2015) Prepared by D. and G. Gute, *How Creativity Works in the Brain*.
Sawyer, K. (2011) The cognitive neuroscience of creativity: a critical review, *Creativity Research Journal* 23(2), 137–54.
Segal, R. (1998) *Jung on Mythology*. Princeton, NJ: Princeton University Press.
Skinner, B. F. (1974) *About Behaviourism*. London: Vintage Books.
Torrance, E. P. (1966) *Torrance Tests of Creative Thinking*. Lexington, MA: Personnel Press.
Wallas, G. (1926) *The Art of Thought*. New York: Harcourt Brace.
Wertheimer, M. (1945) *Productive Thinking*. New York: Harper.
Western, S. (2012) *Coaching and Mentoring*. London: Sage.
Woodman, R. W. (1981) Creativity as a construct in personality theory, *The Journal of Creative Behaviour* 15(1), 43–66.

Chapter 4

Creativity, neurology and the physical body

Interest in creativity in the last fifty years or so has led to an ever-increasing amount of research and a desire to really unpick what is happening in the brain and body during creative thoughts and tasks.

The neurosciences, alongside studies in psychology, psychotherapy and the arts, are helping to build a large body of knowledge, from which coaches can draw. Imaging technology, including functional magnetic resonance imaging (FMRI), has developed rapidly in recent years, enabling us to 'see into' the brain and other areas of the body, during specific activities. At the same time, the findings of these enquiries now have the means to be disseminated widely and quickly; enabling sharing, discussion and debate such as never before. This isn't only due to the internet, but also the relative ease with which we can now print books, send material through the post and gather in groups to meet and discuss.

Exploring the neuroscience behind creativity (and behind coaching) is like opening Pandora's Box; an explosion of complexity flies out and eludes most attempts to measure, name, conceptualise, organise and explain this thing we call creativity. It feels at times like the more we discover about creativity, the less we know. The more generalisations are picked to pieces and myths de-bunked, the more laser focussed the research is, the more complexity arises. Add in the jargon and language used by scientists and researcher in the literature and 'creativity' as a topic, becomes a reflection of its innate self: complexity in action.

Whilst the neurosciences are revealing helpful knowledge concerning creativity, what you choose to take from this field of science depends on what you read and how you decide to interpret it. Robert Bilder from the Tennenbaum Family Center for Biology and Creativity at UCLA helpfully noted at a recent meeting that neuro and cognitive science has finally 'managed to isolate some plausible components of creativity. They include *memory, divergent thinking, convergent thinking* and *flow*' (Santa Fe Institute Working Group Report 2015).

In this chapter, I could have just looked at those four components but there are other considerations regarding the 'physical body' that we understand and use in coaching – it's not all about the brain. I also wanted to structure this knowledge in a way that coaches might see in their practice and intuitively recognise. Hopefully this will unpick and simplify some of the main findings that inform and further support our work as coaches.

We know, from a brain development point of view, that the modern human brain is quite different to that of early man. Puccio, in his TED talk (2012), notes the great changes in creative thinking that arose and enabled humans to develop from using simple hand tools alone to throwing spears. This shift, known as the great leap, that happened about 40,000 years ago, also saw humans start to wear clothes and paint caves; acts that were beyond the merely functional. Puccio's argument is that we humans are innately creative and we can enhance this through deliberate practice and priming.

What I find fascinating about this evolutionary view is wondering how much our actual behaviours and our daily acts shaped this evolving brain and changed it, thus enabling more creative thought to occur. Just how much did we create our creative brain by using creative thought and action?

Clearly, it's a two-way street – this is one of the main lessons we can take from studies in neuroscience – thought and action both change neurology just as much as neurology affects thought and action. So let's start looking at some of this research and knowledge that is growing daily.

Whole brain

I love science and have a medical background, but early on I realised the inherent danger in seeing research and its interpretations as gospel. There are also pitfalls in generalising research results and using them to whitewash over the much more complicated and subtle relationships that exist when trying to make sense of things. For example, I love talking about the left-brain, right-brain concept. It shortcuts a complex topic into something quick and easy to conceptualise, but it is just a glorious metaphor that lends itself to some lovely visual images.

Apparently, there is not a lot of empirical evidence in neuroscience to support the left-brain, right-brain metaphor (Sawyer 2011). Research findings from the neuroscience of creativity show that it does not involve a single brain region or single side of the brain (Kauffman, B. S. 2013). The whole brain is active during creative thinking and creative activities. Creative thought and actions, result from interactions between several large-scale networks in the brain. It depends on what you are trying to do. If you are trying to move or rotate an image in your mind, you might need the Visio-Spatial Network. This network involves both sides communicating between the posterior parietal cortex and frontal visual cortex. However, if the task is language based, then Wernicke's and Broca's areas will be used.

In a short, but helpful article entitled 'The Real Neuroscience of Creativity', B. S. Kauffman (2013) describes three large networks involved particularly in creative cognition (creative thought): the Attentional Control Network, Imagination Network and Attentional Flexibility Network.

The Attentional Control Network helps when active focus or concentration is required when engaging, for example, in complex problem solving and reasoning. The Imagination Network (also called the Default Network) is involved in constructing mental simulations, scenarios and alternative perspectives. It's also involved in social cognition, which is important in understanding metaphor, and helps us to try to imagine what someone else is thinking. The Attentional Flexibility Network monitors external and internal events/consciousness passing information to the other two networks, depending on what it finds most salient and then acting as a dynamic switch.

These networks are activated or deactivated during different stages of the creative process, for example, if we want our minds to wander, which can be helpful when imagining new ideas, the Attentional Control Network needs to let go of too much focus so that the Imagination Network can become more active.

Memory

Vartanian (2013) in *The Neuroscience of Creativity*, advises us to view creativity as being comprised of three main components: motivation (task commitment), ability (domain expertise) and creative thinking skills. He explores how improving our working memory and fluid intelligence (part of the Thinking Skills component) plays an important part in helping creativity. Working memory involves the ability to maintain and manipulate information. He suggests that brain training for working memory does improve general cognitive function, including what is required for creativity.

Neurologist Jagan Pillai (2014) supports this further by saying that working memory can be enhanced in many ways, but particularly through engaging fully in an activity. Anything from playing 3D computer games, to pottery, to learning to play an instrument, to cooking an interesting meal. Although preparing a microwave meal does not have the same benefits as cooking a complex recipe from scratch, it still requires attention, concentration and problem solving to a certain degree!

In *Learning, Arts and the Brain* (2008) the Dana Foundation explored the impact of the arts on cognition and higher academic performance. As well as increased motivation and genetic influences, there are specific links between high levels of music training and improved cognition, particularly working and long-term memory. The studies also showed that the links extend beyond the domain of music training – if you engage in music practice, it will help your memory function in general.

Fuster (2013) provides us with one of the clearest and simplest summaries of what can seem like a very complex neural picture of creativity:

> *Creative intelligence is the ability to form unique new relations in perceptual memory and knowledge, as well as unique new relations in executive memory and knowledge.*

For Fuster, creativity involves associations or links being formed by our brains so that stored items from our memory can be retrieved; therefore, good working memory is important for creativity. Representations (perceptual memories) get encoded or memorised in overlapping regions and they can be evoked by stimuli that are the same or similar in some way (Gabora and Ranjan 2013). This is critical for creativity as it allows new/novel associations to be forged.

Another interesting feature of the architecture involved in storing memories means that we don't actually retrieve memories, it's more like they are reconstructed (Edelman 2000). A memory is never re-experienced in exactly the form it was first experienced. We all perceive events so differently in the first place, therefore the memory is a perceptual memory and it is also reconstructed upon retrieval – no wonder we all have such different views and opinions about the same event!

Fuster (2013) presents quite a different model, whereby creativity is presented as a memory of the future. Ideas are just cognitions (or created memories) based on future possibilities. This should be of great interest to coaches. In Fuster's 'PA model', 'P' is the past (experiences, memories, ethics, emotions, instincts) and 'A' represents the many possible alternative actions, generated via the executive systems of the brain. He represents this as two cones, touching each other at an apex, the left cone converging from the past, the right cone diverging out from the right. The present decision/moment is a point of convergence from the inputs from the right and divergence of possible outputs/actions to the future.

Fuster's model also reminds me of Jung's idea of cryptomnesia (Berk 2012) and the notion of the fertile void in Gestalt: drawing on a place that contains a rich mass of memories of all kinds, sensory inputs, thoughts, feelings, emotions, memories, sounds and ideas – the raw components of creativity.

So memory function and creativity have an important relationship. With this in mind, significant studies have been carried out looking at art and creativity in relation to dementia. The parts of the brain affected by dementia can be clearly identified, and the impact of the varying creative abilities thus evaluated.

Viskontas and Miller (2013) note that progressive neurodegenerative disease disrupts creativity in a myriad of ways. Diminished language function can lead to the emergence of visual and musical creativity, possibly by facilitating function in posterior brain regions. Conversely, reduced regulation of frontal function may enable creative, spontaneous insights. However, as these frontal lobes also help with organisation, monitoring and other executive functions implementing the insight or idea could be tricky.

As we saw earlier, there is a long held societal belief that creativity and poor mental health sit together. Carson's (2011) model of 'shared vulnerability' helps us to understand the greater importance of memory function in relation to psychopathology. Carson suggests that both creative people and those with psychopathological problems share some middle ground, some 'vulnerability factors', namely a preference for novelty, hyper-connectivity and reduced latent inhibition. The protective factors that enable creative people to be productive include having a high IQ, good working memory and cognitive flexibility, whilst the risk factors include having a low IQ, poor working memory and perseveration (persistent, repetitious thoughts/behaviours).

Loosening and wandering

In a recent critical review of the cognitive neuroscience of creativity (in other words a piece of research that evaluates lots of other pieces of research around a specific topic), Sawyer (2011) describes the main insights:

- The entire brain is active during creative tasks.
- Mind wandering helps incubate ideas (and brief, micro-incubations occur even when we don't know it's happening).
- Patterns of brain activity related to moments of insight are complicated.
- Training the brain appears to result in different patterns of activation, for example, you can train your brain to increase its creative abilities, although long-term studies are needed.
- No one agrees on or can define creativity anyway.

The notion of a looser, wandering mind and how it enables creativity is not a new one. Many creative people say that it is when they are not thinking about anything in particular – for example, when they are walking the dog or taking a shower – that a new idea or insight pops up. Mark Runco, Professor of Creative Studies at the University of Georgia (Santa Fe Institute Working Group Report 2015) knows well the challenges of the opposite problem through his work with older adults who suffer from functional fixity, rigid thinking and a tendency towards routine. Runco cites ways of reducing the rigidity, including the practice of mindfulness.

So a wandering mind is good for creativity as it allows new ideas, which are often weaker synaptic connections, to get a look in. That has several implications, especially in education, as unstructured time and daydreaming isn't often encouraged!

Whilst being able to loosen up and allow our minds to wander is helpful, it needs to be balanced with the ability to focus or tighten up. With this in mind, the Reticular Activating System (RAS) is also notable. This clever system filters out sensory inputs, enabling focus to be possible. This system is the one that makes us start seeing lots of blue Ford Fiestas just after we have been talking about them! This system is invoked when we have positively stated goals and we use our imagination to visualise ourselves actually doing or achieving our intended outcome. This creates new neural pathways that allow us to see new opportunities and to focus, despite sometimes overwhelming input – something that the highly creative mind can often struggle with.

Sculpting

Your brain is changed physically by the conversations you have, the events you witness and the love you receive.

(Robertson, 1999)

These days it is generally acknowledged that the brain is plastic, not rigid as believed for many years. You can train and sculpt your brain to a certain extent. In his very practical text *Mind Sculpture*, Ian Robertson discusses the vitally important Hebbian principle: 'cells that fire together, wire together'. This means that our brains change through repeatedly learning or experiencing a sensation or thought.

This principle has been accepted for some time, but in recent years more attention has been given to the actual structure of neurons, not just the chemical neurotransmitters. In his brilliant book *The Talent Code*, Daniel Coyle (2009) brings a new player to the attention of those of us seeking to understand how peak performance is achieved. Around our nerves is a sheath of white material called myelin. Myelin is known to help insulate the neurons and speed up transmission. Often myelin is discussed in relation to certain neurological disorders. In cases of Multiple Sclerosis (MS), plaques (patches) of de-myelination can be seen on brain scans. This is known to relate to the sensory, motor and cognitive problems that people with MS have.

Coyle is particularly interested in how 'deep practice' promotes myelin growth, which in turn allows for greater speed in neurotransmission and enhanced abilities. The concept of deep practice is very interesting and he uses it to explain how people reach peak performance in the fields of sports and the arts.

One example he gives is how Brazilian footballers are brought up playing a game called futsal, which requires many more frequent touches of the ball than regular football. It is also played in a very small space, requiring much greater accuracy as well as speed and constant adjustments. Coyle describes this deep practice zone as involving 'making and correcting errors (at speed), constantly generating solutions to vivid problems'. Constantly firing the same neural pathway all the time, making adjustments, enables myelin to grow faster and thicker; thus making the neural pathway quicker and more efficient. Struggle and mistake making are not optional in peak performance – to Coyle they are a 'biological requirement'.

Whilst we mustn't reduce creativity purely to discussions about ability, many of our coaching clients will be seeking ways to improve their skills and performance in relation to their chosen creative field.

Noticing

In their comprehensive book *Coaching with the Brain in Mind* (2009), David Rock and Linda Page provide an illustration of the whole coaching paradigm and it's foundations from the sciences. Three important discoveries are noted for their importance in relation to coaching:

- Neuroplasticity (the sculpting just discussed).
- How the human brain is different to other species and how humans create, learn and use language.
- The helpful effects of psychotherapy and mindfulness practice on brain function and structure, as well as social and mental wellbeing.

These foundations have become clear from our previous explorations but we haven't paid much attention to the concept of mindfulness.

Originating in the Buddhist tradition of 'mindfulness as meditation', mindfulness has received much attention in recent years as a practice for mental wellbeing and stress reduction. Evidence supporting its use for a variety of conditions is growing.

Mindfulness implies being present, moment to moment, with awareness, curiosity and kindness. It helps us access what is possible in each and every moment. Briefly, mindfulness practice involves tuning in fully to sensory input: what you hear, see, smell, taste and feel. But instead of analysing the input or letting your mind wander off into endless chatter, you just notice that you have become distracted and bring yourself back to being aware of your full sensory state. Sometimes paying attention to one sensory experience helps, such as focusing on the journey of a complete breath, or the eating of a bite of apple, from picking it up, through to smelling it, holding it, biting it and so on.

Mindfulness practice has been shown to reduce cognitive rigidity, something that hinders the flexibility and openness needed for creativity, (Greenberg, Reiner and Meiran 2012, Runco in Santa Fe Institute Working Group Report 2015). It also helps overcome attentional blindness – not seeing the obvious as we are excessively focussed on something else.

> Tuning into sensory input and sharpening our awareness to the colours, shapes, sounds and patterns around us, can be nothing but helpful in terms of creativity. I had first-hand experience of this during a silent retreat, following an eight-week mindfulness training course. The silence was a challenge, to say the least, but during one afternoon, we went on a mindful walk in the grounds of the retreat centre.
>
> Having practiced mindfulness all morning and eating mindfully at lunchtime, I was very attuned to my surroundings and sensory input. Walking round the grounds, observing the trees, grass, shapes of leaves, buildings and shapes in the landscape, everything seemed very alive; the colours seemed brighter, the patterns interesting and the relationship between elements in the landscape intrigued me. I remember thinking 'If all I did was to stand on this spot and paint for the rest of my life, there is inspiration here for a thousand paintings'. Being in a hyper-vigilant state might also describe it, but this moment was accompanied by complete calm.

As a recognised way to reduce stress, mindfulness has been developed into a specific approach called mindfulness-based stress reduction (MBSR), which is proving highly effective in health and wellbeing services. As we are just about to see, stress and pressure are among the top enemies of creativity. So knowing that mindfulness aids cognitive flexibility as well as reducing stress, we can see mindfulness as a big ally in enabling creativity as it also tunes up our sensory perception.

Whole body, sensory body

Since the 1970s, the mind, body and indeed spirit connection has been moved from just a wacky theory to an accepted wisdom, even if our health and medicine fields seem to be slow to catch up. With this in mind, there can be little doubt as to the importance of the individual senses, the integration of the sensory system, the formation of perception and how this impacts on creativity.

The main things that stand out to me in relation to coaching and creativity are: the application of sensory and body psychotherapy knowledge in coaching; our understanding of highly sensory people and sensory integration disorders; synaesthesia and its relationship to creativity; the body's reaction to *real* and *imagined* events.

In psychotherapy and coaching, the importance of the body, movement and sensory systems are starting to be understood and used. The field of somatic coaching has developed rapidly in recent years, acknowledging the important part the body plays in change and transformation, rather than just focusing on the mind (Strozzi-Heckler 2014). The importance of living an embodied life and listening to the wisdom and knowledge that our bodies hold is fundamental to somatic coaching (ibid). This has been known in Eastern cultures for hundreds of years and practiced in the internal arts such as Aikido.

Coaches often refer to people as more auditory, visual or kinaesthetic, in relation to their communication and learning style, but it is rather more complex than this. We are learning more and more each day about how our mind and body react to sensory input from our internal and external environment. Just to clarify, sensory input refers to input from the eyes (visual input), the nose (olfactory input), the skin/muscles/bones (kinaesthetic input), the ears (auditory input) and the mouth/taste (gustatory input). However, the sense of touch is actually comprised of several somatic senses, including perception of pressure, pain and heat. Internal receptive senses also exist that analyse information from within the body such as balance and alignment, hunger or thirst and proprioception (the brain's knowledge of relative positions of body parts). These internal senses are known collectively as interoception.

Processing the input from our senses results in how we perceive our world. This can be anything from our perception of an image, a task, the clothing we wear or the emotion/meaning we glean from a communication. Sensory processing is highly complex and the integration and regulation of our many senses is vital to human functioning (Ayres, 2005). These days it is even more so, as our world involves very different sensory input than it did a few hundred years ago. Jean Ayres likened sensory processing disorders to a 'neurological traffic jam' that disrupts how parts of the brain receive the information they need.

Awareness of sensory processing disorders is increasing, but these are now being shown to contribute to many commonly known problems such as autism, motor coordination problems, behavioural problems, depression, anger and anxiety problems (Dawson and Watling 2000, Kinnealey and Fuick 1999). However, there also seems to be a link with creativity. The term 'highly sensitive' has been used to describe people who process information much deeper than usual. Creative people have often been labelled as more sensitive than others and our learning from sensory processing disorders and other studies now suggest this, there is a 'relationship between higher sensory processing sensitivity, introversion, ectomorphism and creativity' (Rizzo-Sierra, Leon-Sarmiento and Leon-Sarmiento 2012). This also further dispels the myth about creative people being extroverts. (By the way, ectomorphic refers to the body's degree of slenderness, angularity and fragility).

The other fascinating thing regarding our sensory system as human beings is the strange condition of 'synaesthesia', where people experience two sensory modalities simultaneously; for example, being able to smell the colour green or hear the sound of circles. This 'rare' phenomenon is often seen in creative people, but its occurrence in the general population is not really known. Bilder sees synaesthesia as a great illustration of the brain's connectivity and a prerequisite for creativity (Bilder 2015)

The mechanisms that synaesthesia utilises might also help explain why our bodies and minds react to events, real or imagined, in a similar way. Imagining an event can produce the same feelings and response from the body as the event itself. This is easily illustrated when thinking about something we are scared of: a thought or memory alone can evoke the fear response, without the presence of the actual threat. Once a fear is perceived, the thalamus and amygdala are activated within eight milliseconds and the mind and body are both alerted to whatever is coming, be it real or imagined. The sympathetic nervous system (SNS) is then activated and in turn produces the well-known 'fight or flight' or stress response.

The stress response is a normal reaction and helps us function every day, but whilst it is activated several unhelpful things occur, including:

- Reduced immune function.
- Reduced cognitive abilities.
- Reduced creativity.
- Reduced neurogenesis (brain tissue growth/regrowth).

This goes some way to explaining why creative action can be really hindered by stress and fear! Long-term stress is not great news for creativity; our amygdala is rather too effective in spotting fearful activities or thoughts that can include the mere thought of doing something new and creative – let alone the actual participation and engagement in long-term creative pursuits. It also explains why pressure and stress, often associated with high performance or the need to come up with solutions and ideas, actually hinder creative thought. It might also explain why 'big goals' generated by certain styles of coaching, can hinder progress as the flight or fight response kicks in, often resulting in complete avoidance or self-sabotage.

The parasympathetic nervous system (PNS) does the opposite of the flight or fight response and it is through this that we rebuild and bounce back after stressful events or thoughts. Activities or thoughts that promote feelings like, for example, calmness, joy, flow, relaxation, hope, compassion, laughter and playfulness activate the PNS and help the brain to renew, therefore enabling you to be your cognitive and creative best (Boyatzis and McKee 2009, Fredrickson 2001).

Some stress and other pressures in life are unavoidable and some can be seen as necessary, especially a deadline like the final editing of a book or perhaps finishing work for an exhibition. However, the most creative parts of those activities have already passed. It's during the early parts of the creative journey – getting started on writing a book or beginning to paint – and during the deeply creative phase that stress and fear can be really unhelpful. Jill Badonsky (2010) and Bob Maurer (2004) introduced me to the idea of 'tip toeing around the amygdala' so it doesn't induce the flight or fight response. To me, Jill and Bob are the king and queen of kaizen (continuous small step approach) and we will explore that in the context of coaching later on.

Reducing fear can also be aided by experiential simulation. We know that the brain struggles to discern whether a sensory input is real or imagined. For example, Wicker et al (2003) showed how observing someone's facial expression triggers the same brain regions in the observer as it does for the person actually performing the expressions. Mirror neurons are one of the clever types of neurons at work here, but this has broader and very helpful implications in our endeavours to help our clients tackle fear. Experiential simulation can also provide a window to the possible states of others or a means to practice a different state, perhaps a new creative state we desire (Hass-Cohen and Carr 2008). Both have many uses within coaching as simulating and practicing a different state can reduce anticipated fear, making avoidance less likely and participation more likely.

Expanding perception, creating action and magical synthesis

A different way of thinking about how the brain and its various structures and networks work together to facilitate creativity, is 'adaptive resonance theory' (ART). Put simply this is fundamental to how the brain co-ordinates a unified perception–action cycle. We looked at this earlier in Fuster's PA model – how we draw from perceptual memories at the same time as forming possible outputs and actions. This encapsulates the principles of divergence and convergence but in a much less linear way – we don't just diverge first and then converge second. The present moment is formed at the point at which past memories and future outcomes meet to form action.

This is a continuous cycle and might occur quite quickly for some actions and thoughts but take longer for others, such as making difficult decisions, longer creative processes or the generation of an important insight/awareness. This cycle involves learning, thinking, remembering, exploring and the a-ha moments, such as we often see in coaching, at the same time as we take action. This has been described as 'magical synthesis' by Arieti (1976) and is well known to practicing artists – their brain has to be convergent and divergent *at the same time*, to be creative and do creative.

In coaching, I feel we are really supporting the flow between perception and action, between looseness and structure, between expansion and contraction.

'Coaching' feels like it is positioned between the two cones that Fuster describes: the one that encourages expansion and integrates perception, and the one that draws on and integrates future possible memories. The result is the creation of a node of activity, an action or an insight – one of Lacan's quilting points, a 'pont du capiton' the point of convergence (Zizek 1991).

It is this ability to stand with our clients between these two opposing states, states that often feel paradoxical or confusing, and help our clients integrate and gain synthesis that is so important in coaching creativity.

Learning points

- Creativity is an innate human capacity.
- The left-brain, right-brain concept is only a metaphor – the whole brain, in fact the whole body, is involved in creative thought and action.
- Stress, competition, pressure, evaluation and comparison all hinder creativity, including the cognitive abilities required.
- Positive emotions such as joy, relaxation and hope aid creativity; small rewards help creativity.
- Working memory and cognitive flexibility are central to creativity.
- Memories are perceptions that are reconstructed, not recalled.
- Providing a real or simulated experience for the whole body may reduce fear.
- Brains change through repeatedly learning or experiencing a thought or sensation – they are plastic and can be sculpted (this includes using our imagination!).
- Making and correcting errors helps build neural pathways quicker.
- Mind wandering helps ideas and insights form.
- A mixture of loose and tight states are in play during creative tasks.
- Mindfulness improves cognitive flexibility, openness, reduces attentional blindness, heightens sensory awareness and reduces stress – all helpful for creativity.
- Creativity can be seen as a memory of the future; ideas are created based on future possibilities.

References

Arieti, S. (1976) *Creativity: The Magic Synthesis.* New York: Basic Books.
Ayres, J. (2005) *Sensory Integration and the Child.* Torrance, CA: Western Psychological Services.
Badonsky, J. (2010) *The Nine Modern Day Muses (and a Bodyguard).* San Diego, CA: Renegade Muses Publishing House.
Berk, T. van den (2012) *Jung On Art.* London: Routledge.
Bilder, R. (2015) in Gute, D. and G. (2015) *How Creativity Works in the Brain*, Santa Fe Institute Working Group Report.
Boyatzis, R. and McKee, A. (2005) *Resonant Leadership.* Boston, MA: Harvard Business School Press.

Carson, S. H. (2011) Creativity and psychopathology: a shared vulnerability model, *Can. J. Psychiatry*, 56(3), 144–53.
Coyle, D. (2009) *The Talent Code*. London: Random House Books.
Dana Foundation (2008) *Learning, Arts and the Brain*. New York: Dana Press. Accessed 16/05/16, http://www.hewlett.org/uploads/files/Learning_Arts_and_the_Brain.pdf.
Dawson, G. and Watling, R. (2000) Interventions to facilitate auditory, visual, and motor integration in autism: a review of the evidence, *Journal of Autism and Developmental Disorders*,30(5), 415–21.
Edelman, G. (2000) *Bright Air, Brilliant Fire: On the Matter of the Mind*. New York: Basic Books.
Fuster, J. M. (2013) *The Neuroscience of Creativity and Freedom*. Cambridge: Cambridge University Press.
Frederickson, B. (2001) The role of positive emotions in positive psychology: the broaden-and-build theory of positive emotions, *American Psychologist* 56(3), 218–26.
Gabora, L. and Ranjan, A. (2013) How insight emerges in a distributed, content-addressable memory, in Vartanian, O., Bristol, A. and Kauffman, J. (2013) *Neuroscience of Creativity*. Cambridge, MA: MIT Press, chapter 2.
Greenberg, J., Reiner, K. and Meiran, N. (2012) 'Mind the trap': mindfulness practice reduces cognitive rigidity, *Plos One*: Epub, 15 May. Accessed 12/10/15, http://www.ncbi.nlm.nih.gov/pmc/articles/PMC3352909/.
Hass-Cohen, N. and Carr, R. (eds) (2008) *Art Therapy and Clinical Neuroscience*. London: Jessica Kingsley Publishers.
Kauffman, B. S. (2013) The real neuroscience of creativity, *Scientific American* 19 August. Accessed 12/10/15, http://blogs.scientificamerican.com/beautiful-minds/the-real-neuroscience-of-creativity/.
Kinnealey, M. and Fuiek, M. (1999) The relationship between sensory defensiveness, anxiety, depression and perception of pain in adults, *Occupational Therapy International*, 6(3), 195–206.
Maurer, R. (2004) *One Small Step Can Change Your Life: The Kaizen Way* New York: Workman Publishing.
Pillai, J. (2014) You can strengthen your brain power, *Health Essentials* online blog January. Accessed 16/05/16, http://health.clevelandclinic.org/2014/01/you-can-strengthen-your-brain-power/.
Puccio, G. (2012) Creativity as a life skill, TED talk. Accessed 16/05/16, https://www.youtube.com/watch?v=ltPAsp71rmI.
Rizzo-Sierra, C. V., Leon-S Martha and Leon-Sarmiento, F. E. (2012) Higher sensory processing sensitivity, introversion and ectomorphism: new biomarkers for human creativity in developing rural areas, *Journal of Neurosciences in Rural Practice*,3(2), 159–62.
Robertson, I. (1999) *Mind Sculpture: Unleashing your Brains Potential*. London: Bantam Press.
Rock, D. and Page, J. (2009) *Coaching with the Brain in Mind: Foundations for Practice*. Hoboken, NJ: John Wiley & Sons.
Runco, M. (2015) in Gute, D. and G. (2015) *How Creativity Works in the Brain*, Santa Fe Institute Working Group Report.
Sawyer, K. (2011) The cognitive neuroscience of creativity: a critical review, *Creativity Research Journal*, 23(2), 137–54.

Strozzi-Heckler, R. (2014) *The Art of Somatic Coaching*. Berkley, CA: North Atlantic Books.
Vartanian, O., Bristol, A. and Kauffman, J. (2013) *Neuroscience of Creativity*. Cambridge, MA: MIT Press.
Viskontas, I. V. and Miller, B. L. (2013) Arts and dementia: how degeneration of some brain regions can lead to new creative impulses, in Vartanian, O., Bristol, A. and Kauffman, J. (2013) *Neuroscience of Creativity*. Cambridge, MA: MIT Press, chapter 6.
Wicker, B., Keysers. C., Plailly, J., Royet, J. P., Gallese. V. and Rizzolatti. G. (2003) 'Both of us disgusted in My insula': the common neural basis of seeing and feeling disgust, *Neuron*, 40(3), 655–64.
Zizek, S. (1991) *Looking Awry*. Cambridge, MA: MIT Press.

Chapter 5

Creativity and human 'doing'?

Having explored the psychology and biology of creativity, we turn to the 'doing' of creativity: the doing of creativity in everyday life, the doing of arts and crafts and the doing of creativity at work.

Pretty much everything human beings do requires the capacity for creative thought and a process of experiment, action, reflection and adaptation. With some daily tasks, such as making a meal, that cycle mostly occurs quickly, but with other activities, such as producing a painting or sculpture, it takes longer. We also need creativity at work – something of increasing interest to employers and organisations around the world.

'Doing' – it's our nature

We are human *doings*, as much, if not more so, than human *beings*. As a species, we have occupational needs. That is, we have a desire to participate in activities that have meaning beyond just survival; it's one of the things that distinguish us from being a merely instinctive animal. The way in which our human brain has developed, enables us to be exceptionally adaptive and provides the necessary means for us to be creative. As we have evolved, this has opened up many more avenues for the ways we use our time each day.

> *Among humans... perceptions of depth and direction, a central nervous representation of space, Gestalt perception and the capacity for abstraction, insight and learning, voluntary movement, curiosity... exploratory behaviour (and) imitation... are more strongly developed that any of... animal species.*
> (Lorenz, 1987)

Whilst this gives humans a strong drive and the ability to engage in new, daily, creative activities, it also enables us to undertake the practical and sometimes less enjoyable activities that our social and cultural backgrounds expect (Wilcock 1998). Every day we are therefore faced with a pull between creative, playful, expressive urges and the need to do the washing up!

We know that what we *do* each day, shapes us. Participating and engaging in activities we find meaningful, is intrinsic to our health and wellbeing and has an impact on others. In 1922 Adolf Meyer wrote:

> *What people do with their time, their occupation, is crucially important for their well-being. It is a person's occupation that makes life ultimately meaningful.*
>
> (Christiansen and Townsend 2004)

We have known this for centuries – that what we do each day, shapes our wellbeing and our identity – and science is now proving this. Advances in the neurosciences and the use of functional magnetic resonance imaging (FMRI) and other imaging systems have enabled us to see into the brain during activity, showing us the broader effects of that activity on our whole system, our minds and our wellbeing.

Whether you constitute them as creative or not, certain activities, those that result in a state of engagement and flow, can help people manage pain, fatigue, depression and anxiety (Reynolds 2000, Prior and Reynolds 2006). Purposeful, 'flow' activities are powerful, natural medicines and we will explore flow and flow activities later in this chapter.

Knowing that the need to do, to create, to use our hands, be inventive, playful and adventurous is innate goes a long way to explain why more people are coming to coaching in recent years. In life coaching especially, we frequently hear people say 'there must be more to life than this' and 'I want to start doing my own thing'. It also helps explain why there has been a resurgence of people's desire to be creative; perhaps as a natural response to today's high pressure, technically driven life that sometimes feels devoid of soulful, creative connection?

A hierarchy of creative doing

Regardless of the personal meaning and life enhancing benefits that we get from our creative activities, society seems to like to label and categorise our efforts and activities!

One such system labels creative human doings according to the size, impact and societal importance of their creative activity – its either big or little creativity (Kaufman and Sternberg 2010).

The term 'big-C' creativity is used to describe the work of eminent creators, such as the poetry of Dickinson or the paintings of Kandinsky. In this category, we find the famous polymaths; people who excelled in more than one field, such as Leonardo da Vinci who was exceptional in engineering, sculpture and painting. Modern day polymaths could include Chomsky, Hofstadter and Brian May – rock legend and astrophysicist!

'Little-c' creativity describes everyday creativity – the more subjective creativity that occurs when we cook in a novel way or when we enjoy exploring the colours, shapes and qualities of watercolours for personal enjoyment. This type of creativity has boomed in recent years with a surge of knitting groups, craft fairs, and workshops, fuelled by the increased range and availability of materials and information on the internet.

After a few years, Kaufman and Sternberg acknowledged that this was a bit limited so they later added 'mini-c' creativity, which involves the more personal/subjective, internal, mental or emotional forms of creativity, and 'pro-c', which acknowledges the professional creative who has not yet attained eminent status, or may never do, but who is well beyond the weekend watercolourist.

I have to say, whilst I initially enjoyed Kaufman and Sternberg's 'big-C, little-c' idea, I quickly found myself getting rather irritated as it feels like it serves to somehow devalue certain types of creativity and overvalue others. Maybe some interesting buttons in me were pressed? Perhaps buttons around my own painting and whether I consider myself a mere 'hobbyist' just because I don't want to work my way up the art establishment ladder through exhibiting and membership of exclusive bodies. As I mentioned in Chapter 2, many organisations only consider you to be a professional artist if you earn at least 50% of your annual income from selling your art, but I wonder how that would have been seen by famous artists such as Van Gogh who struggled to sell work at all?

How society constructs the value of art and creative products is a hot topic and beyond the scope of this text, but it does impact on whether our coaching clients feel that something creative is worth doing or whether they feel it could be just a waste of time and money.

Engagement and flow: towards mastery

Turning a conscious choice into actually doing something can be an uphill struggle. We all know too well how challenging it can be starting a new creative hobby or getting around to writing. Away from lengthy discussions about creative blocks, motivation or procrastination, we should first consider the importance of participation itself, as a stepping stone to deeper engagement and subsequent mastery and flow.

I am writing this as someone who lives with two people at either ends of the engagement spectrum! Even as a toddler, my eldest daughter preferred socialising and chatting: sustained engagement in a task was often a challenge for her. At the other end of the engagement spectrum, my husband never stops doing. I can't remember the last time he watched television or sat without purpose – he just can't. He always has projects on the go, lists of jobs in his mind and something to work on. He can engage instantly and sustain focus for hours and hours. He forgets all else while in this state of flow.

Initial engagement in a task is more likely if it's made easy. Then, after even a tiny engagement, we often observe that the task we are involved in captures our attention, starts to take over, enabling us to attend more and, possibly, later immerse us.

For some people conscious choice or a desire to engage in an activity is enough. For others, including my daughter, different ways are needed. I need to come alongside her and invite engagement, leave things around that could be picked up and explored, perhaps ask for her help with something. I have to make engagement as easy and natural as I can.

It's important to ponder this: as coaches we often need to work with our clients to find different routes to engagement. A direct approach such as 'buy pencils and sit down on Tuesday and draw' is not going to work for everyone. Sometimes we might need to almost 'trick' ourselves into doing something or try something that might result in unexpected creative outcomes. Perhaps placing ourselves in a different environment or a situation that presses us to act in a different way. Sometimes we could do with someone just coming alongside us and doing at the same time – not teaching us, just being alongside us. Sometimes we might need to change the environment in which we are trying to operate.

If we can become sufficiently engaged in a creative task, we might enter a state of what is known as flow. The concept of flow was coined by Mihaly Csikszentmihayli, a psychologist who became interested in creativity early in his career. In early research, he studied artists and noted that when their works were going well and they were deep in creative flow, they were unaware of hunger, pain and fatigue (Getzels and Csikszentmihayli 1976). In 1990 he published his seminal work, *Flow: The Psychology of Optimal Experience*.

Flow refers to a state characterised by 'intense concentration and full involvement in an activity'. There is a focus on the 'extended present' and perceptions of time alter, seemingly passing more slowly or more quickly during the flow state (Nakamura and Csikszentmihalyi 2002, p. 90). Nine distinct coexisting factors are necessary to create flow:

1 Goals are clear, attainable and in alignment with skill set and abilities.
2 A high degree of concentration on a limited number of items.
3 A distorted sense of subjective time.
4 Self-consciousness disappears.
5 Awareness emerges from action – feedback is gained, making clear the need for adjustments.
6 A 'just right' level of challenge is needed, because excessive task difficulty creates anxiety (Rebeiro and Polgar 1999).
7 A sense of personal control develops over the activity – there is no fear of failure.
8 The activity is intrinsically rewarding.
9 The activity is all encompassing (Csikszentmihalyi 1990).

For me, a life-long artist, coach, occupational therapist and mother who aims to support people's creative activities and endeavours, whatever they may be, Csikszentmihalyi's work is crucial.

I believe that what he teaches us about the circumstances and environments needed to achieve a state of flow should be taught as a basic life skill. It helps us understand our basic human needs, as much as knowing we need to exercise and eat decent food. We really should teach our children this at school – how to maximise their innate human capacity for engagement, creativity and flow, so essential for peak performance in all areas of life and work.

However, my natural criticality kicks in and wants to take Csikszentmihalyi to task on a couple of points. Coaching understands that goals are emergent – they shift and change as we work around and towards them. So while some clarity of purpose is needed at the outset, goals change as the process develops, and in the creative process we can never guarantee the outcome.

Consideration should also be given to the role of mastery in creative pursuits. Practice, failures and disasters are all essential to both skill development and creativity itself. This currently feels somewhat absent from our sometimes romanticised view of creativity and perhaps doesn't help our clients understand the challenges of craftsmanship. It's not just about donning a smock, grabbing some paint and expecting a masterpiece to emerge.

The tricky subject of motivation

The word 'motivation' is laden with huge cultural meaning and is often used to berate ourselves or others for not doing something we say is important. This word is a language short cut and is often used harshly, thus expressing a lack of understanding of the complex factors surrounding a creative goal or activity. It's an umbrella term, just like 'procrastination' and needs unpicking, so that the factors that contribute to motivation can be better understood. Reward and competition have quite a clear impact on creativity. The research messages about these factors are fairly conclusive:

> *The promise of a reward, made contingent on task engagement often serves to undermine intrinsic task motivation and qualitative aspects of performance, including creativity.*
>
> (Hennessey 2012)

Hennessey goes on to say that aspects of competition often include killers of creativity including *reward* and *expected evaluation*. The 'Intrinsic Motivation Principle of Creativity' states that intrinsic motivation is conducive to creativity and extrinsic motivation is almost always detrimental (Amabile 1996). This principle seems fairly undisputed, but it is just one component affecting creativity (Boden 2004). Kaufman also notes the impact of the levels of autonomy and choice in relation to creativity:

> *Autonomy is good for creativity and its development, but too much autonomy, and there may be no direction, no focus (Albert & Runco 1989). The same can be said about competition, challenges, constraints, attention, experience,*

and many other potential influences on creativity (Runco, 2001; Runco & Samamoto, 1996).

(Kaufman 2010)

Neuroscientist Oshin Vartanian (2013) offers a helpful framework to consider creativity. Viewing it as componential (meaning fostering one part should benefit creativity as a whole) he describes the three main components as:

- Motivation (task commitment).
- Ability (domain expertise).
- Creative Thinking Skills.

So, if you improve intrinsic motivation, it should enhance creativity. If you improve your actual ability (and, I would add, how you perceive your ability), that should also help creativity. If you improve creative thinking skills these may well help. A potent mixture of each would be ideal.

Making stuff: what we can learn from the artists and makers

Becoming 'other', not just creating 'other'

As I was nearing the completion of this book, as if completion is something ever attained in a creative activity such as writing, I was given a marvellous book by Peter Korn, a woodworker and furniture maker. The book, *Why People Make Things and Why it Matters: The Education of a Craftsman* (Korn 2015) had just been published and felt like one of the missing pieces I had been waiting for.

Korn reminds us that 'object making' remains a constant throughout the emergence and decline of human civilisation. He reminds us that we currently label object making as 'art', 'craft' and 'design' but they are new ways of describing age old human activities. His personal story also reminds us of the many years of skill building, sweat, tears and perseverance we know is required to become a craftsperson.

Importantly, Korn also describes how he created his adult identity through the process of becoming a craftsman – the process of 'becoming other through doing'. To his mind, all people engaged in creative, self-expressive work, be they visual artists, writers or craftspeople, go to the studio and expect to emerge from the creative process as different people.

> *For a craftsman, making is a lifelong project of self-construction and self-determination . . . we think with materials and objects at least as much as we think with words, perhaps far more.*
>
> (Korn 2015 p. 68)

Through a life dedicated to furniture making, Korn found personal understanding about how life should be lived. He expresses them as three aspects: discovery, embodiment and communication: discovery – the process of coming up with new ideas and implementing them decision by decision; embodiment – the object is made, it has a physical presence; communication – the object communicates meaning to the maker, but more so to the people seeing it and using it.

Many ideas expressed here interest me as a coach, but mostly the idea that participating in a creative activity doesn't just create other (a painting or pot) but we also become other in that process. We also met this idea earlier, when considering the work of sociologist Nick Fox (2013). These two notions really seem to cover both outcomes that coaching works towards; that is, clients either want to be something different (become other) or they want to produce something, maybe a business, project, or book (create other).

The art of seeing: observation and perception in action

> *The real voyage of discovery consists not in seeking new landscapes but in having new eyes.*
>
> (Proust 1923)

Another aspect of interest to coaches when considering what they can learn from artists is their strong observation skills and ability to work with shifting perceptions. Visual artists undertake significant training, which enables them to see very differently to other people. Observational drawing, such as drawing from life, whether a plant or a body, allows you to see everything much clearer – the texture of skin, the subtle shifting tones, the soft downy hairs, how the image changes from second to second as the light changes. Photography is extremely helpful to artists, but photographs only capture a small moment, not the dynamic changing object in front of us. Photographs often exclude subtleties and don't enable us to see the depth and richness that drawing in the moment offers. Drawing and the observation skills that naturally develop allow us to see the broader image, including the absence of things and the negative spaces created in between objects. We start seeing things we never noticed before, we see from different perspectives and begin relating to the subject differently as a result.

Training the eyes and other systems involved helps artists observe familiar things, often things they look at every day, and see them anew every time. This helps overcome attentional blindness and literally opens our eyes to new ways of seeing. In the same way that verbal dialogue in coaching aims to help our client see familiar situations, thoughts and feelings differently, so drawing and visual observation do the same, just through a different medium and with different results.

Artist as coach: in conversation with Peter Moolan Feroze

I met Peter on a creativity coaching day that he was facilitating. Although I had been working with creativity in coaching for a while, speaking with Peter stimulated lots of further questions - ones in which he was happy to answer.

The word creativity is a very popular word these days, what does 'creativity' mean to you?

For me creativity is a state of mind, a way of being in relation to context or environment. An innovation is what results from creativity, a useful form or idea that is realised. In that state of mind, I look for flow that can come from a heightened sense of experience or through the discipline of applying ones' self, practice and concentration.

Why do artists see things differently to other people?

Many subjects are specialised, which results in people being more conscious of boundaries, the more specialised the subject the more difficult it becomes to see connections with another subject. Artists don't see limits to subject matter or material, order is there to be disordered and organised again into something new. Artists chase the form of something that doesn't yet exist so generally they see connections, infinite opportunities rather than boundaries or divisions. It's about discipline within total openness that can seem at odds in a work context where job definitions, routines and structures shape and monitor the way people think and perform.

What is it as a life-long visual artist that you personally bring to the coaching arena?

I currently sketch but I've also taught myself to write songs and sing them. As a visual artist my nature is more introverted but in finding the confidence to sing its drawn out a more extrovert expression. Exploring the world of art has made me more philosophical. I help leaders and teams to question reality, identity and mental and creative perspectives. For example, on the Proteus programme at the London Business School a CEO questioned the validity of drawing a white cup, first just as he and the group instinctively saw it and without instruction from myself. Later they were asked to see the cup through a lens, as 'an excitable character with a name or as being shy'. The leader stated that the exercise had little purpose, but a year later the course director told me he had sent her an email telling her that he had taken the white cup home and has it on his mantle-piece as a reminder to be more open minded about how he sees and interprets the world around him.

When you, Peter, engage in 'making' something, what happens inside? How does it change you as well as change the thing you are making?

For me making a picture, creating a song is about an emotional experience, as I mentioned it's about heightened experience. In a painting you are not copying the

(continued)

(continued)

subject you're trying to give form to what you find fascinating or magical. If you paint a picture of a person nude or clothed you become more and more aware of their presence, their nature or spirit; you're trying to capture that. I remember a friend at the Royal Academy of Arts painting a still life set up with a blue cloth. One morning he rushed out into the corridor of classical casts looking for me and explained that something amazing had happened in his picture. I returned with him to the studio to see the familiar blue cloth but in his picture it had become the most dramatic deep purple. The relationship between what you see and what you feel is a fascinating conundrum! I think wonderful art is born of a strong, passionate feeling.

How does using creative media and visual language, help people in a way that talking might not be able to do?

Art work releases the subconscious, it takes you inside and you are released for that period of time from the often onerous task of having to verbally articulate yourself to others through words. When we talk we are trying to make ourselves clearly understood by others and if we think about it, it can be a struggle. A good example is the question, 'what exactly do you mean?'

When you create a picture the colours and shapes might suggest many things, there doesn't have to be one clear meaning, some artists would say it's less about meaning than experience. That is part of the value of business clients making pictures in one to one coaching, by drawing they are exploring different interpretations around the issue being discussed and the imagery comes more from intuition than logic or reasoning. In addition, making pictures allows for ambiguity and capitalising on unanticipated opportunities, the drawer can often be surprised by what they create and by how significant ideas emerge in the picture without conscious thought. So while drawing we can dwell in feelings over a period of time but in conversation much of our effort is often spent on understanding, listening, tracking what is being said over time, thinking, disagreeing or getting our thoughts in order. It's unusual to be party to a meeting at work in which there are substantial breaks of silence for people to dwell in their feelings over the issues being explored before continuing. God forbid, that would mostly be seen as bizarre or a waste of meeting and agenda time.

Research in neuroscience has proven that when people are exposed to regular gallery visits and paint themselves regardless of artistic ability it increases introspective capability and resilience. Words and literature are every bit as wonderful and revealing as visual art but for me it's the relationship and journeys between the two languages that are so valuable to managers and teams.

A group of engineers at a high performance car company recently commented that while making a picture in silence as a team they felt greater empathy, clarity and collaborative spirit than when they discuss work objectives around a table. A team painting together in silence is more aware of subtle energies, body movement, sensing colleagues, empathising with the paint marks made by others, and with silence more aware that words are not the only way that we communicate. By going away from words to pictures we make a journey and when we return to discussing the issue we may see it in a new light.

The creative process

Artists, writers, musicians, mathematicians, programmers, creative entrepreneurs and other practicing creatives, understand the nature of the creative process all too well.

Brewster Ghiselin captured the thoughts and reflections of many creative people, ranging from Van Gogh to Yeats, from Henry James to D. H. Lawrence, in a brilliant anthology in 1952. In the Foreword to the 1985 edition, in which Ghiselin changed very little, he re-stated his position:

> *The creative process... in the arts and in thought is part of the invention of life, ... essentially a single process.*

Ghiselin notes some of the core features of the creative process, commonly expressed by the creative people. Many talk of the horrible feeling of 'I don't know what this is all for': this uncertainty of purpose often exists alongside the somewhat opposite feeling of 'something in me is alive'. Many of those he studied also speak of their work creating them, rather than them creating the work.

Ghiselin also identifies the chaos and disorder of the creative life:

> *It is organic, dynamic, full of tension and tendency.... it is a working sea of indecision.*
> (Ghiselin 1985, p. 4)

He describes how the chaos and confusion eventually condenses into form but the creator needs to sit with the formlessness, with the 'invention' rarely appearing complete:

> *production by a process of purely conscious calculation seems never to occur.*
> (Ghiselin 1985, p. 5)

This reminds me of the arrival of an 'a-ha' moment, or a gestalt – the moment of insight in coaching or therapy when something falls into place for a client, they gain some clarity or a plan starts to form.

The importance of the pre-verbal in opening up people to a broader range and variety of activity is highlighted by Ghiselin, with significant reference to Jung's work. He goes on to state an important point, a paradox perhaps, that both automatic (unconscious) and conscious production exist and occur together throughout the creative process. Many other creatives discuss the creative process in a similar way. Nick Cave (2014), musician, writer and speaker, says:

> *I think the creative process is an altered state in itself.*

but then he continues further, saying:

> *The artistic process is mythologized quite a lot into something far greater than it actually is. It is just hard labor.*

To me it is clearly both – switching between an altered state of consciousness and some kind of activity or doing. Through my personal creative work and my work with all kinds of clients, I see the constant interweaving of creative thought and ongoing doing or activity. I know that a creative idea can take milliseconds to arrive, but years to produce. During the doing or activity phases, I have to revisit that loose, unconscious, creative space frequently – I have to dance, often not gracefully, between doing and being.

During the unconscious stages, Ghiselin notes the importance of holding the ideas loosely, without 'forcing a pattern' too early. This waiting can be difficult especially if there is a desire to plan or create structure too early. Plans must come as part of 'organic development', notes Virginia Woolf (Ghiselin 1985).

Grief and loss

> *Painting is like a war in your head . . . you have to decide this way, this way and you lose 99% of the possibilities because you can only use one possibility, one option, so it's always a war in your head to do the right thing.*
>
> Anselm Keifer (undated)

Making decisions always means we have to let go of other options and ideas. This happens in every creative process, not just during the creation of an image in paint as Keifer describes. In life too, we may have to park an idea or project until later, but in doing so we have to face the fact that we might never get round to it.

For some highly creative people, this can be a real problem, as they find it difficult to let go of some ideas in order for others to be developed more fully. This can then lead to lack of focus, stress in trying to tackle too many things and a general lack of accomplishment and fulfilment – trust me, I know this one well.

Discernment, figuring out what to go with, what to dump and the subsequent need to grieve the loss of ideas, can be challenging and is not often talked about in creative activities or coaching. Whilst grief may sound like a rather strong word, I do feel that this sense of loss is rather ignored in the coaching domain and this might be detrimental to creative, sensitive types who are struggling to understand why they feel the way they do. Grieving is often seen as more in the domain of counselling, but perhaps coaching would benefit from revisiting this basic human process.

Something else I struggle with in painting, but also in the development and creation of my business, is the need to accept that I can rarely create the exact image that I am able to imagine so vividly. I am able to develop such a clear image in my head of a painting or how the business could be, but nothing ever turns out the way I imagine – nothing. This is not a lack of skill or ability – any painter will say the same. In terms of the business, it might, however, be a case of unrealistic expectations, but of course that is the thing about creativity and imagination – no one ever taught it to be realistic.

Work: creativity and innovation

There is a loud, frequent and sometimes frantic cry for innovation from many workplaces and organisations, but the term creativity is rarely used. Perhaps innovation is less fluffy and messy or perhaps it sits more comfortably with income creation and business growth. But without this fluffy, messy, uncertain thing called creativity, there is no innovation. Innovation, like creativity, is both a product and process. As a process, innovation is a cycle between creativity (ideas), action/doing, ongoing reflection, adjustment and refinement. Creativity is necessary at all these stages in the innovation cycle.

This text was never intended to be an 'innovation at work' text, a book on 'creativity in organisational development' or a 'treatise on the subversive nature of creativity and capitalist wealth creation', although all of these do entice me. There are some fab publications out there, which can help you with these issues, but this book is about creativity – the messy, fluffy heart of innovation, which is very misunderstood in the context of work.

Unpicking creativity in the context of a work environment is helpful, regardless of whether it's a small business, public sector organisation, large blue-chip company or the self-employed, lone worker. As we saw earlier, the academic world of creativity really enjoys classifying creativity and, in relation to the world of work, I find the work of Boden very helpful (2004). She classifies creativity as either *combinational, exploratory* or *transformational*.

Combinational creativity is the type most investigated by researchers. It describes new ideas generated from combinations of familiar ideas, taking two known things and combining them to make something new; for example, Marmite flavoured chocolate (yes it does exist) or headphones with a built in MP3 player.

Exploratory creativity involves using existing styles or rules to generate novel 'twists' not previously realised before the exploration took place. An example of this would be the new way of painting (existing) that was explored and developed by the Impressionists. It may also be seen in the changes made to internal processes in an organisation following an audit!

Transformational creativity is more radical. The creation or idea or thing is not merely new but may seem impossible and shocking; the rulebook is thrown away. The 'conceptual space' is changed so that completely new things can be generated (Boden 2004).

Within organisations, combinational creativity leads to new products and income streams. Exploratory creativity can help companies understand and improve their processes and systems and is essential in research and development. However, deep and radical transformational creativity at work is a different kettle of fish. Transformational creativity is just that – it's not just about jiggling things around a little or re-shaping what's already there. It can lead to radically transform and change things at all levels, therefore all parties need to consider whether transformation is really desired, and if so, by whom and to what ends.

In all organisations there is an ongoing dance between maintaining the status quo and the desire for change: 'we want innovation/change/radical reform and we also want stability/predictability and things to just tick along as they are, thank you'. Those of you that coach within organisations will know this well and the story that follows is not an uncommon one.

I was invited to run some short creativity sessions by a very keen development manager of a large, established, well-known technology company. Despite creativity being a core value of the organisation, she perceived a clear lack of creativity in the staff as a whole and held a desire for the new graduates to not lose their creativity! We explored what she meant by creativity and decided that the sessions would focus on raising awareness, understanding barriers to creativity and some ideas for enabling creativity at work. I ran the sessions, but quickly became aware of three things:

1   A desire for creativity may be voiced by organisations, but clearly only certain types of creativity.
2   What is desired from creativity by senior leaders, might not be desired by middle management or those managing grass root teams.
3   The concept of creativity might not have the same meaning to different generations.
4   Creativity and expressing new ideas is perhaps not a priority for newly recruited graduates.

Looking at these new graduates in front of me I also became aware of what their current priorities were: fit in, be accepted, learn the ropes, minimise risk. This is the primary concern of human beings in many situations 'I want to be loved and accepted', 'I want to belong', 'I want to feel secure'. While we sometimes think that fresh new graduates will be full of ideas, brimming with creativity and bring juicy new learning from university, that's not what I saw. I saw a group of mostly young people trying to fit in, wear the right clothes and not rock the boat.

During this event, a combination of empathy and irritation kicked in for me, at the same time. Why aren't they up for changing things? Why aren't they enticed by doing things differently? But then again perhaps expecting creativity from them at this point in their career might be a little unfair? Expressing ideas requires vulnerability and the risk of rejection, exactly the opposite of their priorities at present. At this point, their basic human needs of safety and survival were most important.

I started to also remember what I was like as a new graduate in a large organisation. As a rather creative and probably annoyingly visionary person, I could often see how things could be different or better in the places I worked. I would frequently question the status quo and often ask 'why is it done like this?' I would generate ideas for creative change; everything from service redesign to new techniques or ways of working. I intuitively could see the big blocks and the desperate need for systemic change, but I was a junior member of staff suggesting transformational ideas. Whilst Mintzberg (2008) expresses the value of disruption in innovation, it wasn't what my organisation, the NHS, wanted from me. Perhaps some gentle exploratory or combinational creativity would have been more warmly welcomed. I was rather too creative and perhaps people like me working in non-creative environments need to be supported differently?

Learning points

- Humans beings are occupational beings: we do stuff.
- Mastery of skill is different to creativity.
- Creativity can be seen as combinational, exploratory or transformational.
- Creativity could be seen as comprising motivation, ability and creative thinking.
- Participation in a craft or art doesn't just produce other; it changes us and we become other.
- Participation in a craft or art, helps us see and think differently.
- The creative process is a fluctuating state, alternating between unconscious and conscious states, between reflecting and doing.
- Artists and seasoned creatives seem to understand and manage the fluxing nature of creativity.
- The nature of creativity at work is often poorly understood.
- At work, disruption can help creativity, but is rarely encouraged!
- Intrinsic motivation outweighs extrinsic forces, so we need to be clear about for whom the creative task/goal is truly important.
- Small rewards given to oneself upon finishing a project often have more value than large rewards.

References

Amabile, T. (1996) *The Motivation for Creativity in Organizations*. Boston, MA: Harvard Business School, 23 January. Accessed 14/10/15, https://xa.yimg.com/kq/groups/13791546/147358703/name/creativity.pdf.

Badonsky, J. (2010) *The Nine Modern Day Muses (and a Bodyguard)*. San Diego, CA: Renegade Muses Publishing House.

Boden, M. A. (2004) *The Creative Mind: Myths & Mechanisms*. London: Routledge.

Cave, N. (2014) The creative process is an altered state in itself. Assessed 20/10/14, http://www.npr.org/2014/09/16/348727370/nick-cave-the-creative-process-is-an-altered-state-in-itself.

Fox, N. (2013) Creativity, anti-humanism and the 'new sociology of art', *Journal of Sociology*, 0(0), 1–15. doi: 10.1177/1440783313498947

Getzels, J. W. and Csikszentmihalyi, M. (1976) *The Creative Vision: Longitudinal Study of Problem Finding in Art*. Hoboken, NJ: John Wiley & Sons, p. 73.

Ghiselin, B. (ed.) (1985) *The Creative Process*. Berkley, CA: University of California Press.

Hennessey, B. (2010) The creativity-motivation connection, in Kaufman, J. C. and Sternberg, R. J. (eds) (2010). *The Cambridge Handbook of Creativity*. New York: Cambridge University Press, chapter 18.

Kaufman, J. C. and Sternberg, R. J. (eds) (2010) *The Cambridge Handbook of Creativity*. New York: Cambridge University Press.
Keifer, A. (undated) Speaking on an audio guide at the 2014 Royal Academy exhibition, London.
Korn, P. (2015) *Why We Make Things and Why it Matters: The Education of a Craftsman*. London: Vintage Books.
Lorenz, K. (1987) *The Waning of Humaneness*. Boston, MA: Little, Brown and Co.
Mintzberg, H. (2008) *Mintzberg on Management*. London: Simon & Schuster.
Nakamura, J. and Csikszentmihalyi, M. (2002) The construction of meaning through vital engagement, in Keyes, C. L. M. and Haidt, J. (eds) *Flourishing: Positive Psychology and the Life Well-lived*. Washington: American Psychological Association.
Proust, M. (1923) La Prisonnière, *Remembrance of Things Past*, Volume 5.
Robeiro, K. and Polgar, J. M. (1999) Enabling occupational performance: optimal experiences in therapy, *Canadian Journal of Occupational Therapy* 66(1), 14–22.
Runco, M. and Albert, R. (2010) *Creativity Research: A Historical View*, in Kaufman, J. C. and Sternberg, R. J. (eds) (2010). *The Cambridge Handbook of Creativity*. New York: Cambridge University Press, chapter 1.
Vartanian, O., Bristol A. and Kauffman, J. (2013) *Neuroscience of Creativity*. Cambridge, MA: MIT Press.
Wilcock, A. (1998) *An Occupational Perspective of Health*. New Jersey, NJ: Slack.

Part III

Creativity as a means and also as an end

We know that this thing we call coaching is just one part of a range of professions that help people transform their lives, albeit from different perspectives, using different approaches and perhaps with differing outcomes in mind. Whilst it builds its own body of knowledge through research, scholarly works and of course practice, as a younger profession, coaching can look to other professions and allied fields for a wealth of knowledge regarding using and enabling creativity. So much knowledge, wisdom and research and so many practices and techniques already exist that can inform us as coaches.

Chapter 6

Creative therapy

Art therapy

The mind never thinks without a mental picture.

Aristotle

According to the British Association of Art Therapists (BAAT), art therapy is a form of psychotherapy that uses art media as its primary mode of communication (BAAT 2015), so as a coach interested in creativity this seems a natural starting point to me.

Historically psychiatric hospitals were the incubators of art therapy (Vick undated) but now art therapists work in rehabilitation, cardiac medicine, autism support, AIDS services and other settings such as schools. Just as traditional psychotherapy shifted focus in the 1960s and 1970s, art therapy appears to have emerged, perhaps as a more humane, inclusive and responsive treatment to mental distress. Whilst it is now an accepted discipline, McNiff (1992) notes that he had to blaze a trail for art therapy in the 1970s amid huge scepticism.

Early art therapy interventions may have evolved using creative activity as a means to an end; the rationale being that this activity is gratifying and purposeful. However, a different focus developed, which was the principle of projecting an inner experience into the world using media such as drawing or painting. This was consolidated by subsequent analysis and exploration of the meaning of the projection. This follows the psychoanalytical tradition that was prevalent in psychology at that time, but as art therapy developed it also drew in other approaches from Jungian, developmental and humanistic sources.

These days, art therapy looks quite different and, just as other helping professions have taken on board new learning, so has art therapy, including a strong influence from clinical neuroscience (Hass and Cohen 2008), family therapy and mindfulness (Rappaport 2013).

Congdon (1990) contends that contemporary art therapy promotes mental health beyond diagnosing and treating illness, as it operates at numerous levels that include: giving people a sense of identity and place; conferring status; expanding and directing thought processes; and utilizing the security of the rhythmic 'takeover' phenomenon (flow). McNiff (1992) adds weight to this by stating that 'virtually every person who uses art in psychotherapy believes in the ability of the image to expand communication and offer insight, outside the scope of the reasoning mind' (p. 3).

The opinions of these art therapists identify strong reasons why coaches would benefit from seeking to understand creativity and using creative techniques in their practice. However, I am reminded that coaches are often fearful of delving into the psyche in case they get drawn into using overly therapeutic techniques.

When I started to train and practice as a coach, there was, and probably still is, debate raging about coaching not being counselling and warning coaches of the dangers of stepping over this boundary. Outside of the obvious areas of acute and significant psychiatric illness, this implies that a neat, orderly boundary between 'well' person and 'ill' person exists. Those of us that have been around a while, know that this is not a tidy boundary. If we continue to 'not go there' as coaches, I feel we may sometimes be in danger of doing our clients a real disservice. I am also mindful that current predictions infer that by the time the majority of us reach our late forties we will have experienced a period of mental distress that requires some sort of medical treatment: future projections regarding the mental health of the whole population are actually more worrying (Barnett et al 2012).

Promoting mental wellbeing and working with the psyche and mind is not confined to the medical professions. Like it or not, our interventions as coaches impact on mental wellbeing – we know this well. As I read Congdon's contentions above, I notice the blurring of the boundary further – using art as therapy is not necessarily about expressing dark, repressed trauma. It uses art to work with natural, human needs such as developing a sense of identity, helping thought processes, expanding communication and raising insight.

Whilst I think we need to take lessons from art therapy on-board, I am aware that, just as counsellors or psychotherapists might look at a process coaching session and question the difference, an art therapist might look at a coaching session using creative media and raise similar questions. But does that really matter?

Occupational therapy

The occupational therapy (OT) profession, the name of which always confuses people, sprung from the knowledge that participation in meaningful activities helps to promote wellbeing, restore skill, and improve participation and engagement in daily life. While it was one of the earliest professional groups to recognise the value of creative activities, OT itself was built with a history including Tukes moral treatment principles, Quakerism and the Arts and Crafts Movement. Interestingly, many OT departments included art therapy until around the 1970s when art therapy became a profession in its own right.

Occupational science, the science of what human beings do, and one of the foundations of the OT profession, holds rich learning for coaches. Of course I am biased, but I often feel that coaching looks too much to psychology for answers and not enough to understanding people as 'human doings'.

One example is the Model of Human Occupation (MOHO) (Keilhofner 2002), which provides a way of linking our knowledge of the psyche, mind and the physical body, including all its neurology, with the doing side of human activities. This model takes a systems approach that can be helpful for us to understand what makes optimal performance and engagement possible, including creative activities.

In the MOHO, people are conceptualised as an open system, comprising volitional, habituation and performance sub-systems. This system operates within a complex social and environmental system. The volitional system (thoughts and feelings) includes: competence and effectiveness – our sense of personal causation; what is important and of meaning to us – values; what we find enjoyable and satisfying – our interests. The habituation system (semi-autonomous patterning of behaviour) includes: our temporal, physical and social habits; the usual patterns or ways we encounter others; how we perform tasks in a routine, repetitive fashion; all our automatic habits and roles – chosen and ascribed. The performance system: this is comprised of the objective components of capacity, physical, cognitive, social and psychological phenomena.

In this model, change in one area will affect the whole. This, as we know, is the premise of a systems approach. So in terms of creativity, if someone focused on just making a small new creative habit (habituation) or a small change to support creative thinking, it would have an impact on their whole system including a change in volition (beliefs and thoughts), our performance system (body, mind, brain) and, subsequently, the environment around us.

So let's think a little further about this model of human doing in relation to creativity and what that might mean for coaching.

> **Volition:** What thoughts, feelings and beliefs do people hold in regard to their creativity and the creative process? How do their personal values impact on their creative process, desires and goals? How do we help our clients raise awareness and increase their sense of personal causation and self-efficacy in relation to creativity? What is important and meaningful for our clients in regard to their creative process and goals? What interests them? What creative activities give them a real buzz, sense of flow or make them laugh? What motivates and rewards people in relation to creativity? What are valued activities for that person?
>
> **Habituation:** What role do habits play in relation to creativity? How might their roles (mother, worker, spouse, sister, church goer, volunteer, carer) impact on their creative desires? How might new habits or roles help creative pursuits? How do we help people develop useful habits and routines? How might small, habitual practice be integrated into the coaching intervention? How are practice, risk and failure – all necessary for true creativity – viewed by our client?
>
> **Performance capacity:** Does our client have any physical, cognitive, psychological or sensory problems that might impact on the doing of creativity

or the creative goal? How does their subjective experience of their skill or ability impact on the rest of their system (e.g. self-belief, interests)? How might body and sensory awareness help develop creativity? How could cognitive flexibility that is known to help creativity be developed? How can the coaching or the activity engaged in enhance working memory functions, which we know to be important in creativity?

Environment: Does our client's social environment impact on their creative desires/process? Are there supportive people around? Do friends/family somehow criticise their efforts? Is the physical environment restrictive in relation to their goals? Is creativity cultivated/supported by their culture and social surroundings?

Taking a systems approach, this model of human activity emphasizes how, in terms of creativity, a change, even a small one, will make an impact throughout the whole system, not just at the personal level. Small changes, small bits of doing, small actions, should never be underestimated in coaching, therapy or any other change-enabling process.

Writing as therapy and self-help

Post-structuralism, a way of thinking and studying how knowledge is produced and critiqued, explores the relationships between people, their worlds and what they do to make meaning through language. This can include all sorts of forms: spoken, written, crafted, performed or envisioned through other media.

Writing is used by all sorts of people in all sorts of arenas and is not confined to use in therapy: in education and learning we use reflective writing to help our development; creative writing is used in schools and education to explore a subject or historical context or develop an idea; we might write a letter to a loved one to express our feelings; we may write things down informally to just clear our heads or take notes at a conference; a poet will use writing in different ways as will a writer of a film, book or play.

Like all stories, the origin of using writing specifically as therapy is hard to uncover. During the 1960s, Dr Progoff, a humanistic and Jungian psychologist, advocated for the use of structured journaling, using a colour-coded system, depending on the topic/issue (Progoff 1992). Formal research into using writing in individual and group therapy was carried out by James Pennebaker in the 1980s and 1990s (Pennebaker and Segal 1999). His basic writing assignment was as follows: 'write down your deepest feelings about an emotional upheaval in your life for 15 or 20 minutes a day for four consecutive days'. Subjects were told to write whatever arises and not to worry about the spelling or grammar. Pennebaker's research showed that doing this for even three or four days had a positive effect on immune system functioning.

While Speedy, in 2005, noted that counselling was lagging behind other professions, such as education and sociology, in developing and using writing, organisations such as Lapidus have since emerged to support and train therapists in the use of writing as therapy. More recently, Pauline Cooper has developed UWaT (Using Writing as Therapy), which is an accredited training programme through Oxleas NHS Foundation Trust. The use of writing as a method of inquiry in qualitative research has also gathered speed and is used in many fields of study (Richardson, L. 2000).

Regular, daily journaling as a form of self-support gained steam in the early 1990s after the publication of *The Artist's Way* (Cameron 1995). Aiming at all sorts of creative people, not just writers, Cameron introduced the practice of 'morning pages' where by one writes at least three pages every morning, regardless of content. Incidentally, Cameron originally self-published *The Artist's Way*, after being turned down by formal publishers; however, it went on to sell millions of copies world-wide and is still seen as a 'bible' for creative souls. Today websites like 750words.com provide a free, online platform to help people journal on a daily basis and find personal support through writing. Free online tools, such as these, are available for our clients to support their individual coaching and, of course, we might want to use them too.

Writing poetry to facilitate self-expression, inquiry and healing has also grown in popularity amongst ordinary people. A lovely introduction to this can be found in the works of David Richo, particularly in his easy to use book *Being True to Life: Poetic Paths to Personal Growth* (2009).

Many of you will already encourage your clients to write a reflection following a coaching session or use regular journaling alongside the coaching journey (Doherty, in Megginson and Clutterbuck 2009). To me, there is so much potential to use writing creatively as a coaching activity – be it stories, poetry, songs, plays or structured, analytical writing. Writing naturally encourages the expansion and flow that are both helpful in the creative and coaching process.

The new world of creative enablement

Before Cameron's success with *The Artist's Way* in the early 1990s, other landmark texts had already appeared, marking the emergence of a new paradigm of creative enablement. Work such as Rollo May's *Courage to Create* (1975) and Betty Edwards' *Drawing on the Right Side of the Brain* (1986) added to the weight of feeling that human beings have a need to create something and gain meaning through that creating. These explorations started to unearth the challenges inherent in trying to be creative and also highlighted the broader benefits that working with the creative self could yield, such as insight, clearer thinking, wellbeing and greater creativity.

Focussing on the emerging field of what has been labelled 'creativity coaching' leads us to the work of Eric Maisel. He appears to have coined this term and his numerous publications are well worth exploring, particularly *Making your Creative Mark: Nine Keys to Achieving Your Artistic Goals* (Maisel 2013) and *Coaching the Artist Within* (Maisel 2005). As a psychologist and life-long writer, Maisel has many gems for coaches to explore. Writing from a different background and with a more playful and, to my mind, more rounded approach, Jill Badonsky, founder of Kaizen Muse Creativity Coaching (KMCC), has also authored many books including *Nine Modern Day Muses and a Body Guard* (Badonsky 2010) and *The Muse is In* (Badonsky 2012). (Incidentally, in addition to being a poet and creativity coach, Jill Badonsky's background is in OT.)

Sufficed to say that since the start of the new millennium we have been preoccupied with enabling and using creativity in some way, shape or form. Hundreds of books on creativity have been published, too many to list here. There are books about learning to paint, draw and write. There are books about how to connect with the spirituality of creativity. There are many, many books about how to start a creative business and be successful as an artist. There are also many books on using creative approaches to aid thinking and build wellbeing. The era of self-publishing has exponentially increased the emergence of books in this field and regurgitating summaries of these here feels unhelpful: we need to focus on what coaching can take from this mountain of knowledge, insights, tools and techniques.

How to hold a paradox

Forgetting this thing we call coaching for a little longer, two main streams regarding creativity seem to have emerged over the last fifty years or so:

1   The use of creative activities to gain insight, awareness, learning and wellbeing for personal development (becoming other).
2   Support and inspiration to understand the uncertain creative process, generate creative ideas and move into action (creating other).

These two ideas, that creative practice helps us *become other* and *create other* (Fox 2013, Korn 2015), both resonate with coaching aims and philosophy.

It would be nice for this book on creativity and coaching to simply sum this all up in a 'What helps creativity?' or a neat 'How to' guide or a nice coaching model with natty acronym. However, whenever I try to separate out the factors that help or hinder this complex thing called creativity, I meet equally complex, opposing opinions and what feel like unwieldy paradoxes.

For example:

creativity doesn't like pressure

and/but

great creativity can be generated under pressured circumstances

or,

I want to do something creative

and/but

I want it to end up looking the same as this

another one is:

creativity responds well to habits, routines and containment

and/but

creativity is a free spirit that hates being pinned down and wants to run free

Balance is another quality frequently cited to help productive output but it can lead to a flattening effect. If you asked Van Gogh to moderate his behaviour in favour of a more balanced approach, can you imagine what he might say!

So how can we say that just one set of circumstances or principles enables this diverse, paradoxical process called creativity?

How can we weave together what the biological sciences, psychological sciences, doing sciences and the real life stories of creatives teach us about creativity?

And, how can we identify a set of principles for coaches to work with, given that everyone is different in their creative process and what they desire from participating in it?

How can we frame our coaching activities, knowing that we are aiming to both use creativity and enable it and that creativity both creates other and helps people become other? Perhaps we need to loosen the stranglehold and start acknowledging that creative activities and coaching already do both.

Learning points

- Creative activities are intrinsic to many therapeutic approaches including art therapy, writing as therapy and OT.
- Interest in enabling creativity has increased since the 1970s, with the term creativity coaching arriving in the 1990s.
- Creative processes both *create other* and help people *become other*.
- Making sense of creativity is difficult: many paradoxes exist.

References

BAAT (undated) *What is Art Therapy?* Online resource. Accessed 14/10/15 http://www.baat.org/Assets/Docs/General/ART%20THERAPY%20TRAINING%20July%20%202014.pdf.

Badonsky, J. (2010) *The Nine Modern Day Muses (and a Bodyguard)*. San Diego, CA: Renegade Muses Publishing House.

Badonsky, J. (2013) *The Muse is In*. Philadelphia, PA: Running Press Book Publishers.

Barnett, K. et al (2012) Epidemiology of multimorbidity and implications for health care, research, and medical education: a cross-sectional study, *The Lancet* 380(9836), 37–43, doi: 10.1016/S0140-6736(12)60240-2.380.

Cameron, J. (1995) *The Artist's Way*. London: Pan Books.

Congdon, K. G. (1990) Normalizing art therapy, *Art Education* 43(3), 19–24, 41–3.

Edwards, B. (1986) *Drawing on the Artist Within*. New York: Simon & Schuster.
Fox, N. (2013) Creativity, anti-humanism and the 'new sociology of art', *Journal of Sociology* 0(0), 1–15. doi: 10.1177/1440783313498947
Hass-Cohen, N. and Carr, R. (eds) (2008) *Art Therapy and Clinical Neuroscience*. London: Jessica Kingsley Publishers.
Kielhofner, G. (2002) *Model of Human Occupation*. Maryland, MD and Philadelphia, PA: Lippincott Williams & Wilkins.
Korn, P. (2015) *Why We Make Things and Why it Matters: The Education of a Craftsman*. London: Vintage Books.
Maisel, E. (2005) *Coaching the Artist Within*. California, CA: New World Library.
Maisel, E. (2013) *Making Your Creative Mark*. California, CA: New World Library.
May, R. (1976) *The Courage to Create*. New York: Bantam Books.
McNiff, L. (1992) *Art as Medicine – Creating a Therapy of the Imagination*. Boston, MA: Shambhala Publications Inc.
Progoff, I. (1992) *At a Journal Workshop: Writing to Access the Power of the Unconscious and Evoke Creative Ability*. New York: Jeremy P. Tarcher.
Pennebaker, J. and Segal, J. (1999) Forming a story: the health benefits of narrative, *Journal of Clinical Psychology*, 55(10), 1243–54.
Rappaport, L. (2013) *Mindfulness and the Arts Therapies: Theory and Practice*. London: Jessica Kingsley.
Richardson, L. (2000) Writing: a method of inquiry, in Denzin N.K and Lincoln, Y.S. (eds) (2nd edn) *Handbook Of Qualitative Research*. Thousand Oaks, CA: Sage.
Richo, D. (2009) *Being True to Life*. Boulder, CO: Shambala Publications Inc.
Speedy, J. (2005) Research methods: writing as inquiry: some ideas, practices, opportunities and constraints, *Counselling and Psychotherapy Research*, 5(1) 63–4.
Vick, R. (undated) *A Brief History of Art Therapy*. Accessed 14/10/15 http://areas.fba.ul.pt/jpeneda/Briefhistoryat.pdf.

Chapter 7

This crazy thing called coaching

Coaching is a product of its time. Western (2012) reminds us how it emerged from thousands of years of natural, supportive kinships circles: friends and family supporting each other. As society developed, specific helping roles emerged including 'shamans' and 'sages' who healed and advised, to be historically succeeded by the realm of the Confessional (Church) and the more recent world of Freud and his 'talking cure'. During the middle of the twentieth century, we then see a shift towards working with the 'celebrated self' and the emergence of this practice we call coaching, which is different to the practice we call therapy that focuses on what needs to be cleansed and healed. Rock and Page (2009) also describe the paradigm shift and the differing systemic approach upon which coaching is based: from observer to participant, from passive to active, from negative to positive, from teaching to experiencing, from telling to listening.

At this point in time, coaching is not a protected title (anyone can call themselves a coach) and there are coaching courses that last anything from a day up to several years – for example, if one is pursuing a PhD. There are professional coaches who just coach, there are consultants who coach as part of their role, there are mentors and supervisors who use a coaching approach and there are many therapists and counsellors who are now adopting a coaching method to their work. There are also facilitators and trainers who embed coaching into their work, knowing that it strengthens any learning and development process.

Some coaches adopt a quite purist, non-directive approach that focusses on deep, active listening, intuitive questioning and responding alone. They use skilful reflecting and listening for the unsaid in their client's communications. They are aware how they are being in their coaching relationship and understand their personal motivations and agenda as a coach. They utilise all these skills as well as helping their clients to develop and hold a compelling vision for the future.

Other coaches have a more eclectic practice, with elements of mentoring and advising, and perhaps use particular tools such as a 'Values Elicitation' process or a standardised assessment such as Myers–Briggs Type Inventory.

Regardless of your particular approach, coaching can be defined as:

Partnering with clients in a specific conversation-based, thought-provoking and creative process that inspires them to move from their current state to a more desired future state.
(Stober and Grant 2006; International Coach Federation, 2011)

The reasons people come to coaching, which relate to creativity in some way, are numerous: some people may want to generate more creative thinking or ideas; some may want to produce something creative such as write a book or start a business; others might have a desire to master a creative skill; they may want to gain insight by working differently and creatively with a coach; some may want to regain life balance or wellbeing through their personal connection with creativity; highly creative people may be seeking support to manage the challenges that their creativity brings to work and home life.

The current coaching and creativity texts available seem to either deal with these arenas separately or fail to unpick the complex relationship between coaching and creativity. I feel we need to rethink how we conceptualise this relationship more fully.

To me, there are several ideas running through the current academic literature on creativity, practice examples and personal stories. These seem to cluster in the following ways:

- Coaching itself as a creative process.
- Creative 'doing' as part of coaching.
- Coaching as activating and supporting creativity.

These three themes will be explored as separate issues in the following three chapters.

Learning points

- The term coach is an unprotected title.
- Coaching theories, models, approaches and tools differ widely.
- The coaching process is a creative process.
- Creative activities are sometimes used in coaching.
- Coaching can activate and support the creative process.

References

International Coach Federation (2011) website. Accessed 16 November 2011, http://www.coachfederation.org/about-icf/.

Rock, D. and Page, J. (2009) *Coaching with the Brain in Mind: Foundations for Practice.* Hoboken, NJ: John Wiley & Sons.

Stober, D. and Grant, A. (2006). *Evidence Based Coaching Handbook: Putting Best Practices to Work for Your Clients.* Hoboken, NJ: John Wiley & Sons.

Western, S. (2012) *Coaching and Mentoring.* London: Sage.

Chapter 8

Coaching as 'creative' process

The following exploration arose from an idea I had for a video blog. I had the title 'why painting and coaching are similar', but had no idea as to what to write or why. I sat with it, as you need to do with creative ideas, and something started to emerge. Perhaps what follows represents my desire to make sense of or justify my strange existence as both a coach and an artist. However, over the years I have noticed many similarities between the coaching process and the creative process undertaken by painters, writers and other creative people.

On the surface, painting and coaching may seem miles apart: one of them helps people achieve things they want, move forward with certain goals and understand themselves better; the other involves me indulging myself in paint, turps, colour and canvas. However, there are many parallels when we look closer.

Creating other, becoming other

The creative arts, such as painting and participation in the coaching process, can both involve bringing something tangible into form – 'creating other' (Fox 2011, Korn 2015). Often the output from a coaching process is a newness of idea or perhaps a different approach to an old problem. The desired output might be a new product for a business, a new marketing plan or a new way to improve personal wellbeing. The desired outcome from many creative activities is the production of something tangible and new; perhaps a painting, a book, a piece of music or a tapestry.

Through participating in an art, craft or other creative practice, we also change as a person. We change through our relationship with the creative practice itself. We choose our materials and our methods. We find what works for us and what doesn't. We discover what suits our needs and what doesn't. We make choices based on those discoveries. We become other. Through coaching we also change. We might desire greater confidence, clarity or purpose. We might seek to change who are in our relationships. We might change our life purpose, our careers or the way we do things at home. We 'become other' (Fox 2011, Korn 2015).

Inquiry and experimentation

Coaching constitutes an inquiry into ourselves, our lives, our work and our relating. People come to coaching with many questions and thoughts, sometimes revolving around a desired goal or vision for something different. It's often been bugging them for a while and either sufficient energy has arisen to tackle it or a circumstantial need has presented itself.

Through a coaching inquiry, many questions are asked and answers explored – both new questions and ones that often follow us through life. Awareness, learning and personal resources are explored. Creative thinking is intrinsic to the process as ideas arise, visions created and options generated and evaluated. Experiments take place and actions are reflected upon. Clients test stuff out in the session but also go away and try things out between sessions.

Paul Klee talked about drawing as 'taking a dot for a walk'. I like to think of coaching as 'taking a thought, idea or goal for a walk'. Coaches invite clients to explore different routes and pathways, experiment and test out desired goals and examine prevalent thoughts about a situation.

We often think that eminent artists work to fulfil a clear vision they have or to produce a piece of finished/perfect work. However, if you explore painters lives, their archives, sketch books and letters to friends, you see that it is full of experiment and trial and error. As Picasso once said, 'paintings are but research and experiment. I never do a painting as a work of art. All of them are researches' (1956, cited in Megginson and Clutterbuck 2009).

Indeed, when I paint, I do a lot of playing and often my best work arises from experimentation – 'What happens if I put a figure here or maybe move it over here? What might happen if I lighten this area here or remove this piece of sky?'

Developing a vision, whilst embracing what emerges

As a painter, I usually start with some semblance of a vision in my mind for a piece of work that I would like to produce. Most times, I am unable to create the image that I have in my head, but I do start with a vision for my ideas and endeavours. From this point on, much of my time spent painting is in pursuit of that ideal, envisioned outcome, sometimes at the expense of other interesting creations and discoveries *en route*.

During our coaching work, we spend a lot of time helping clients develop and clarify their vision or the outcome they desire. As the coaching relationship continues, the vision/outcome is often revisited to check that it is still desirable, relevant and congruent with the client's emerging awareness.

Just as I need to embrace the emergence of a painting that always differs from my original intentions, clients too are faced with emerging insights and realisations, which challenge their values and beliefs and, of course, their intended vision for the future.

Other thoughts arise that could apply to both a painting and a coaching outcome, such as:

- Perhaps I need to tear this up and start again.
- Perhaps it just needs tweaking not completely reinventing.
- Perhaps I need to wait; maybe things are yet to emerge?
- Perhaps I need to go away, do some more research or find some different resources.

The notion of a static vision or goal does not exist in either coaching or creating a piece of artwork. Coaching goals are emergent, as are paintings, writings or other creative products.

Resources

Another similarity between painting or creating and coaching involves resources and often becoming more resource-full. Both processes involve the identification of resources, be they existing resources we already have that can be used differently or new resources that we might need to find.

During my own coaching, my painting and my coaching work with clients, I often hear the following thoughts about resources:

- Perhaps I don't need lots of money or a new office space to start this business, maybe I can use what I have.
- Thinking about this, I have most of what I need already, it's just my lack of confidence that tells me I need more! Perhaps I don't need a PhD.
- Actually, I do really need to work towards a qualification/more experience/a work-space.
- In fact, going to the art shop is just a way of procrastinating, I have so many materials at home – I really don't need any more.
- Perhaps I don't need to start with a new canvas for this experiment, perhaps I can paint over a previous experiment or just start on paper rather than committing to canvas at this early stage.

Finding or creating a story

Common to painting a picture, writing a book or working with coaching, are the use of and emergence of narratives and stories. 'Stories' are everywhere. There is a story around why we have come to coaching, a story about why we are painting or writing. There is story contained in the process of coaching and creating – why we started here, changed this, abandoned that, the shocking thing that happened next!

The products of both processes often include a narrative, especially in the case of narrative painting. In the case of coaching, there is often a story about our journey through the coaching process and our successes and failures in pursuit of our goals. There is also a future story that we want to be able to tell about ourselves, which coaching can bear witness to.

Accessing an altered state

Many artists and writers speak of a kind of transcendence or altered state, which they enter into during creative times. For some, this state is induced naturally (Chizentmihayli 2008), for others differing substances including drugs might be involved (Cave 2014). Often habits and routines are used to mark the start of this creative period (Currey 2013). This ritualised behaviour can be seen to induce an altered state – 'the state from which I create'.

So, does this happen in coaching? I would suggest that it does. Entering a coaching space necessitates a shift in state – sometimes one of contemplation and openness or perhaps one of provocation. Personally I have found that through the space and presence created during the coaching session I am able to let go and play with my thoughts. As we know, this condition can be more conducive to insights and a-ha moments than a rigid state of focus and concentration (Runco 2015).

Reality checks, re-framing and learning

Neither a creative process, such as painting, nor a coaching process is linear and neither guarantees an exact outcome.

Throughout a coaching journey, clients will bring reflections, results and insights from their endeavours during the previous weeks. Often this will involve reality checks and sometimes the need to deal with disappointment – perhaps an interview didn't go well, a contract was not won, a product launch went badly. All coaching is different, but usually there will be an evaluation of what went wrong, what went well and why, and clearly some re-framing regarding the learning involved and what could be done differently next time.

Creating something like a painting also involves significant reality checks and many disappointments! Those of you who paint will have quickly learned to get used to how different things are compared to the final results often exhibited on gallery walls. No one tells you about the vast range of disasters and messed up sketchbooks that were produced prior to the production of one solitary decent drawing.

Dealing with disappointment or loss is rarely talked about in coaching or in the creative process and this is something that personally fascinates me. In Western culture, the Heroic[1] paradigm is prevalent. It goes like this: someone decides to tackle an inner demon, difficult situation or do something different, for example, start a business, become a writer, give up their job to become a film star and so on. They start full of ideals and enthusiasm but at some point come up against a challenge that knocks them for six. At this crisis point they want to give in, but, in the Heroic storyline, they find the inner resolve to carry on. They have an epiphany, find inner resolve and decide to fight/work harder to overcome the problems. It all works out rosy. Everyone's happy. The end.

Well, what if it doesn't? What if the idea, business, painting or play just doesn't work? Perhaps the person can't balance the budgets, maybe the business idea wasn't that great or possibly they are not a very good artist or can't act for toffee.

Disappointments like these are quite normal and often confronted in both a coaching journey and a creativity journey, but I feel we are ill equipped to deal with them. I struggle with disappointment every time I fail to create the image for a painting I have in my head. I have had to accept that disappointment is part of the process, learn from it and move through it. I also struggle with my inability to bring all my ideas into form – there are just too many ideas. In some ways, I have to deal with a kind of grief that occurs when I know I have to let go of perhaps 95% of my ideas.

Circling ideas and repeating patterns

I wrote to my painting mentor recently, stating the frustration I feel due to constantly repeating the same mistakes in my painting and circling the same ideas repeatedly over the years. He replied by saying that 'circling ideas' should be an artist's middle name and that my struggle with this was not unique.

In coaching too, this can be seen and felt. When I am being coached I often hear myself saying 'here we go again . . . same old chestnut'. Sometimes this is regarding a pattern of belief or activity that persists and regularly gives me problems, sometimes it is an idea that I keep bringing up in coaching, that seems to want to be heard – again.

Conclusion

The similarities between coaching and painting are strong and allude to them both being a creative process, with uncertain outcomes despite both stating a clear desire at the start, trial and error throughout and, of course, a human element at the heart of it all.

Learning points

- Through participating in a creative process or coaching process, we create something new: *creating other*.
- Through participating in a creative process or a coaching process, we also *become other*.
- Creativity and coaching both involve:
    - inquiring and experimenting,
    - developing a vision,
    - identifying resources,
    - finding or creating a story,
    - accessing an altered state,
    - reality checks and learning,
    - circling ideas and repeating patterns.

Note

1 Such as described by Joseph Campbell in *The Hero with a Thousand Faces* (1993) and many other movie and book plots.

References

Campbell, J. (1993) *The Hero with a Thousand Faces*. Waukegan, IL: Fontana Press.

Cave, N. (2014) The creative process is an altered state in itself. Interview, 16 September. Accessed 14/10/15, http://www.npr.org/2014/09/16/348727370/nick-cave-the-creative-process-is-an-altered-state-in-itself.

Csikszentmihalyi, M. (2008) *Flow: The Psychology of Optimal Experience*. New York: Harper Collins Publishers.

Currey, M. (2013) *Daily Rituals: How Great Minds Make Time, Find Inspiration and Get to Work*. London: Picador.

Fox, N. (2013) Creativity, anti-humanism and the 'new sociology of art', *Journal of Sociology* 0(0), 1–15. doi: 10.1177/1440783313498947

Korn, P. (2015) *Why We Make Things and Why it Matters: The Education of a Craftsman*. London: Vintage Books.

Megginson, D. and Clutterbuck, D. (2009) *Further Techniques for Coaching and Mentoring*. Oxford: Elsevier.

Runco, M. (2015) in Gute, D. and Gute, G. *How Creativity Works in the Brain*, Santa Fe Institute Working Group Report.

Chapter 9

Creative 'doing' as part of coaching

Engaging in a creative activity, as part of a coaching process, may mean quite different things:

- That by choosing to engage in a new activity, hobby, creative pastime, we often see clients build resilience, wellbeing, social inclusion, meaning and purpose. *Through creating other, we become other.*
- That through further mastery of a creative skill and talent or the completion of a long desired creative outcome, such as writing a memoir or holding an exhibition, we see clients further their self-awareness, esteem and perhaps grow in confidence. *We become other and create other.*
- That away from dialogue alone, engagement in doing something creative or engaging with a physical object or process outside of ourselves, we can evoke something new in ourselves – new knowledge, insights, personal awareness and action. *Through creating other, we become other.*

I don't feel we need to explore the first two of these – I think they are fairly obvious ways that creative activities appear in the coaching domain. Through our explorations into the science of creativity, activities and human nature, we have seen the clear benefits of engaging in particular activities, both at a hobbyist and craftsmanship level. If a client brings a desire to increase their skill level or performance capacity, in a creative activity, we tend to know as coaches what to do to help. However, it is the use of creative activities within coaching practice that needs some more discussion and exploration here.

There seem to be three main ways in which using practical, creative activities can contribute to a coaching process:

1 By participating in an activity, we can create a sense of flow. Being in flow changes our brain physiology and somehow enables the loosening required for creativity, insight and ahas in different areas of our life: 'While I was knitting the other day, it suddenly occurred to me what to do about the leaky roof.'

2   Working with a physical object can evoke different thinking and feeling. An evocative object brings together the 'inseparability of thought and feeling in our relationship to things' (Turkle 2007). In confronting this thing, this other, we shape our self (Turkle 2007, Korn 2015). We encourage subject to object shifting, essential in coaching (Bachirova 2011).

3   Exploring ideas through visual, often metaphoric images promotes creative thinking and insight – a basic premise of art therapy (McNiff 1992). Coach and sculptor Vivien Whitaker (2009) extends this by saying that creative coaching techniques take less time than talking: 'a picture is worth a thousand words'. They can create an instant overview. Drawing or creating a model of 'how it is now' can help us see the situation in context and identify all the connections. Complex scenarios can be represented quickly. In coaching, creative methods can also take us away from the limitations and misinterpretations inherent in using language.

In reality, a mix of all this probably takes place: we enjoy the sense of flow in the creative coaching activity, working with a physical object evokes and stirs up different things and through the visual imagery created we gain new insights. Perhaps that is what we should be aiming for when using creative coaching activities – a potent mix of all three, with the intention that insight will be gained through the expansion, synthesis and doing of an activity?

Perhaps the best way to illustrate this is to tell a story.

Wanting to be a fairy

Ever since I became a coach, I have always encouraged my clients to draw their desired goals and then draw their current position in relation to their future goal. I am always stunned by the ease of expression and abundance of insights that fall out of this simple exercise. I have used it with hundreds of clients over the years and can only think of a small handful that couldn't engage with it. It's easier to illustrate this using my own experience of the exercise. I describe the process more fully in the final section of this book.

I was asked to draw a simple image of my future desired outcome in relation to a current issue. For me this was easy: I was bogged down, burnt out and almost penniless, two years into starting my own business. I happily and vigorously drew what this looked and felt like – a person with many pairs of hands, juggling boxes that leaked money, with bent knees sinking into the mud. Above my head I drew two people who were looking down on upon me 'tutting'.

I was then asked to draw how I wanted the future to look, with regard to my business. I immediately drew a fairy, flying gracefully between the flowers while the sunshine and rain were helping the flowers to grow. Nearby on the earth lay small seedlings – my children – yet the fairy could not reach them from where she was flying.

After completing my sketches, my coach then asked me to explain my desired outcome. She asked some simple questions before asking me to identify the difference between the ideal and current images.

There were some obvious insights: I start too many projects, create too much stuff (curse of the creative!). I will always want multiple activities in my business but I need to let go of trying to carry them, I am holding on to things too tightly, taking things too seriously and investing too heavily – both emotionally and financially.

And then came the deeper insights: I feared loss. I didn't want to choose between the things I loved and had created. I feared the loss of my creations. At that moment in their development, my children's needs were mostly physical, but as they grew into teenagers and young adults, they would need more from me. If I am continually flying around in fairyland, how would they be able to get my attention or a piece of my fairy action? There was also the issue of the 'imposter syndrome' – those people who were looking down on me, judging me, seeing through me. Clearly I feared being 'found out'.

It was then easy to generate simple doing actions. I was coached on which projects gave me most joy, which were leaking money and how I could focus yet also simplify things. Of course, the fear of loss and not feeling good enough are a little trickier and are ongoing, recurring challenges.

Learning points

Creative activities in coaching, have a variety of purposes. They can:

- Induce a flow state and enable creative insights and shifting awareness.
- Enable subject to object shifting.
- Create visual images and metaphors to explore complex scenarios.

References

Bachkirova, T. (2011) *Developmental Coaching: Working with the Self.* Maidenhead: Open University Press.
Korn, P. (2015) *Why We Make Things and Why it Matters: The Education of a Craftsman.* London: Vintage Books.
McNiff, L. (1992) *Art as Medicine – Creating a Therapy of the Imagination.* Boston, MA: Shambhala Publications.
Turkle, S. (2007) *Evocative Objects.* Massachusetts Institute of Technology.
Whitaker, V. (2009) Offering creative choices in coaching and mentoring in Megginson, D. and Clutterbuck, D. (2009) *Further Techniques for Coaching and Mentoring.* Oxford: Elsevier, chapter 8.

Chapter 10

Coaching as activating, integrating and supporting creativity

Expansion of ideas, overwhelm and eventual contraction

As a painter, I don't do commissions. I have accepted commissions twice and they took me two years and three years respectively. I just don't do deadlines and I don't like painting something to order. Writing a book therefore presented significant challenges.

I had already finished writing this book – well I thought I had, but my decision to seek formal publishing necessitated a complete rethink. I had to propose an outline of what I would write, have very clear deadlines and expectations. A contract would follow. Both of these were restrictions and required significant focus to allow this book on creativity and coaching to be produced.

This enforced focus, this contract(ion), should have meant that the book could be tidied up, finished, done and dusted. However, this squishing together had a fascinating effect. The opposite occurred; the opposite to the focussing down that was required. The paradoxical nature of creativity seemed to be taking effect. Although I thought I just needed to tweak and reshape the book, I had to 'unpack' what I had already written and see it with fresh and fairly critical eyes. This unpacking caused agitation and ideas and concepts seemed to start moving around and growing. The containment and restriction promoted the opposite and rapid expansion was taking place. In the space of a couple of weeks, I had rich conversations with all sorts of people that yielded new insights, new ideas, new perspectives and theories. All had a relationship to the topic of creativity and coaching and all seemed relevant. Books, yes even more books, gravitated towards me and fed into this cooking pot of creativity. Not just coaching books, but books on social anthropology, spirituality, shamanism, chaos theory, poetry, clinical neuroscience, symbolism, mental illness and, of course, woodwork!

This broadening of thought and expansion of ideas was rapid and many disruptive occurrences and influences happened on a daily basis. Aside from this, I was in danger of slipping into a huge theoretical and philosophical debate on creativity, spirituality and human existence, all of which took me further away from the purpose of the book. Overwhelm and creative chaos had firmly kicked in and the expansion felt like it would go on forever unless it was contained again – unless I could limit this expansion, bring the concepts down and come to a focused or at least an emergent point of action or clarity of insight. I recognised that, although the expansion had been essential and yielding greater creativity and strength to the book, enough was enough – I couldn't stay in this expanding, creative phase for ever.

Enter coaching – a mixture of formal coaching with my long suffering coach Jo, informal coaching with various peers and colleagues, self-coaching and a combination of reflective writing, doodling and drawing.

Integration and assimilation began. Forward energy naturally occurred as I squeezed together, pulled in, discerned, dumped some stuff and created some more focus, structure and action.

Outside of the actual book writing itself I also started to ponder what on earth had happened during this time. Why had the restriction of deadline and the need to be more focused produced the opposite effect? I felt like I had really met the paradox of creativity – the fluxing, oppositional forces that exist in creative processes and practices. The best way I can describe it is like a squeeze and then release – a process of expansion and contraction – a natural 'pump' that provides forward energy.

My belief is that, whatever you deem coaching to be, it engenders the necessary qualities to enable and support the creative process – the ability of our clients to work with this fluxing, paradoxical, uncertain thing we call creativity.

Learning points

- Creativity involves an expansion of ideas, which can lead to overwhelm and chaos.
- Coaching can support this expansion, the integration of ideas and the focus that leads to the actions required.

Chapter 11

Proposing a model for coaching creativity

Theorising is a highly creative activity and new theories are simply the creative formation of ideas, propositions and connections into a new form; a form that helps people explore and make sense of complex ideas. The following ideas have emerged through my personal practice as a coach, therapist and artist, background research and knowledge of creativity and my desire to find a unifying theory with which all coaches can work.

Sorry, but you won't be getting a neat acronym, tidy Venn diagram or a four box model. Please don't get me wrong, I really love theory and find the many ways of presenting theoretical ideas and frameworks very helpful. However, I hope by now you can see just how complex this thing called creativity is and yet paradoxically how simple it is. Finding a way to work with the idea of creativity, which is a highly contentious concept, and integrate it with this thing we call coaching, presents many challenges. It needs a creative response.

Waving hands

A couple of years ago I started a series of discussions with Peter Mayes, a coach who has a very different background to me. Peter was originally an engineer, he then moved into organisational development and eventually coaching. He has been there, done that and owns many brilliant T-shirts. Then there was me, the expansive, creative, haphazard artist, coach and therapist. We seemed so different in every way, in background, knowledge and in our approaches to coaching.

In our lengthy discussions we played with how different we were – the artist and the engineer. We started to explore the similarities between these archetypal characters and how they bring different but helpful qualities to our work.

Peter, the engineer, seemed characterised by process, logic, detail, order and the focused application of sound proven technique. Jen, the artist, was random, creative, fun and perhaps a little disruptive. We initially felt like polar opposites but over time and through letting go of our assumptions we allowed ourselves the freedom to explore how similar we were. More than that, we started to explore what happens in the creative process, both in the arts, sciences and, of course, coaching.

Gradually, I found myself drawing the same little image in my notebook when Peter and I met. I found myself waving my hands in and out, in the same pattern.

> *'It's like this Peter,' I said, 'we need the expansion, the divergence, the risk taking, random thoughts and ideas – the creativity,' I drew my hands wide apart, 'and then get on with actually producing or doing something,' I pulled my hands close together. 'Then', I went on, 'we need to widen it out again, let go of the pressure, embrace creativity, disrupt everything,' I opened my arms wide apart before continuing, 'then once more we need to focus in, nail things down and take actual action.' My hands came close together again. 'This is how creativity and coaching work together,' I explained, 'and it's a natural pumping action; expansion and contraction that provide energy and forward momentum in the creative process.'*

Over time, this random hand-waving exercise and my little sketches provided me with the starting point of a model of creativity and coaching.

Blood vessels, lungs and labour

Of course, I am mindful that this could just sound like convergence and divergence, but it's not. The essence of this fluxing movement between opposites, the point in between and the forces therein, provides us with so much more when we explore it further in the context of creativity and what coaching aims to do.

In proposing a model of coaching creativity, I hope by now that the influences have been made clear: the psychological, neuro, biological, social and occupational sciences, the arts, crafts and creativity literature and a little smatter of quantum theory. However, what seemed to be missing was a look at actual language used by real people, when talking about the creative process. When we start looking, some interesting themes arise that fuel the idea behind my waving arms and the notion of squeeze and release. Please know that this is not based on an intensive, formal discourse analysis, but the language really does correlate with the findings and theories of the sciences that we explored earlier, which is very exciting.

The language of artists and people that create

I feel inspired.

The word inspiration or afflatus seems to have first been used by the Roman orator Cicero to describe an act or expression of creativity. More commonly the word inspiration is used to describe what happens when we breathe in and fill our lungs – our lungs being a flexible container/vessel. Our expanded lungs start to compress, as we exhale, pushing air out. Once our lungs are compressed again, a vacuum is created that automatically draws in air once more. So we inhale and so the cycle repeats.

90 Creativity as a means and also as an end

I feel creativity pumping through my veins.

Think about this highly metaphoric language. Here blood pumping round the veins and arteries is likened to the feeling of heightened creativity. Compare this description, this model of creativity, with our blood. Our blood is contained in veins and arteries (vessels) and pumped round our bodies by the *contraction* of these vessels during systole. The blood is then forced through the narrower, contracted vein. Pressure momentarily increases before the vessel releases and *expands* once more. This process can be seen in Figure 11.1.

Giving birth to an idea.

Nick Cave (2014), famous songwriter and performer, says that 'each song is a difficult and painful birthing experience' alluding to the process of inception, gestation/containment in the womb and the inevitable contractions needed to birth the baby into the world through the narrow cervix. The use of this lovely language metaphor is not unique to artistic activities. We hear this phrase 'to give birth to an idea' used to describe new projects, products and ideas in all sorts of institutions, settings and the natural world.

I feel blocked and need to regain creative flow.

These words are frequently and commonly used to describe our joys and woes with the creative process. If it's going well, we are in *flow*, if it isn't, we are somehow *blocked*. Beyond the perception that something is either working or not, Picasso and many other artists acknowledge that action and non-action are natural

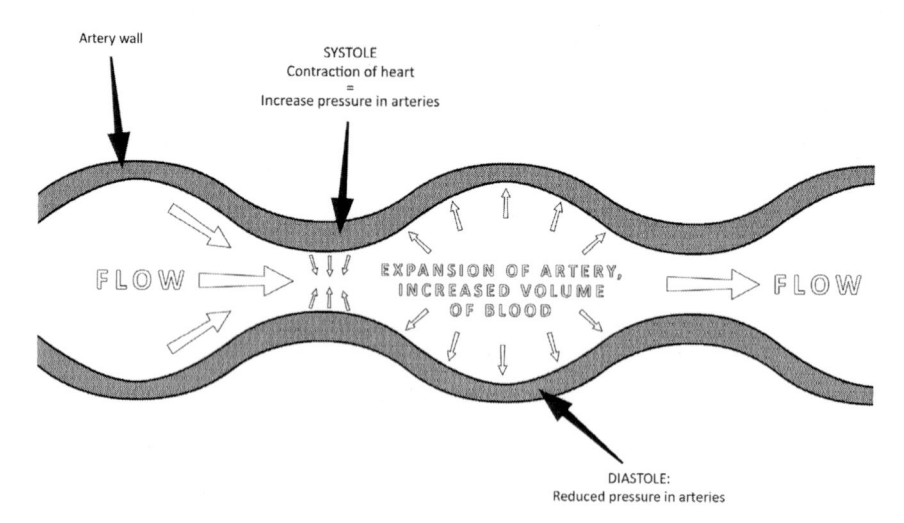

Figure 11.1 Expansion and contraction of the blood vessel creates flow

and necessary: 'the painter passes through a series of fullness and emptying. That is the whole secret of art' (Ghiselin 1985). Keats also famously described this concept as 'negative capability', which means negative in the sense of being empty of specific content, uncertain and unclear (Hebron undated).

The language used to describe creativity is highly metaphoric and offers some universal components:

- The notion of a flexible vessel or containing force.
- Something that expands and contracts.
- There being a fullness followed by an emptying.
- There being a transition point, the extent of contraction.
- Energy and flow being naturally created by the push and pull of the opposing states.
- Movement is created automatically if sufficient expansion is followed by sufficient contraction.[1]

The visual image of the pumping artery provides us with a model that also seems to portray the creative process described by creative people including artists, writers and mathematicians and many others (see Figure 11.2).

It also creates a visual representation of what the various sciences teach us about creativity, including Fuster's PA model in neuroscience (2013) and the Gestalt cycle in psychology, among many others. It unifies what happens in both creativity and coaching, which are both active, dynamic, fluxing and continuous in nature.

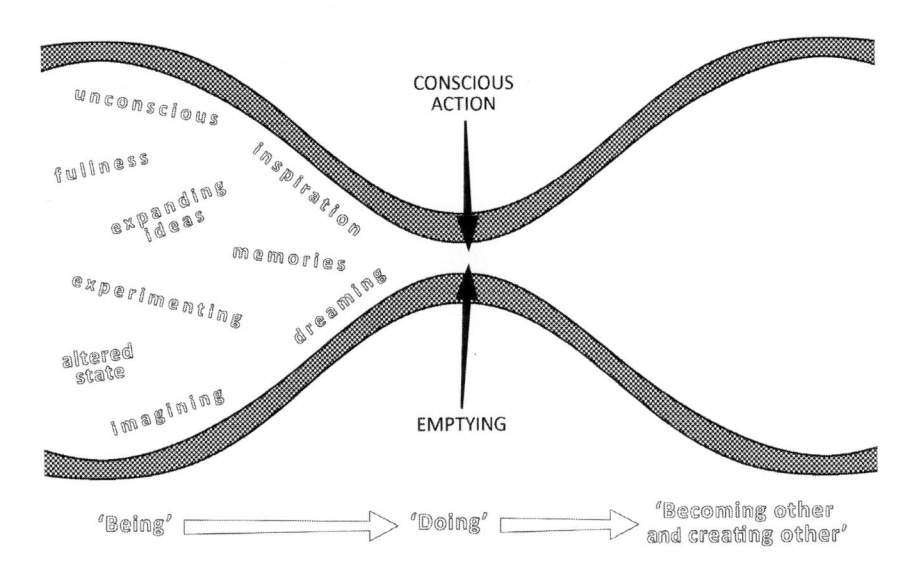

Figure 11.2 The creative process described by artists and creatives

The model also acknowledges the quantum principles of 'discontinuity', particularly how conscious choice (contraction) precipitates the collapse from possibilities (our expansion section) into actualities (our action point). In this way 'creativity involves the causal power of consciousness choosing from quantum possibilities' (Goswami 2014, p. 10).

This unified way of seeing, this model also helps us make sense of often conflicting feelings about creativity; the paradox of creativity and polarities evident. We can hold the polarities and work with them rather than the tertiary separations we are often presented with such as:

'I'm an extrovert, you're an introvert.'

'You are either a left brain thinker or a right brain thinker.'

'Creativity needs to be free' versus *'creativity flourishes within structure.'*

'Artist or scientist.'

This model lets us know that creativity needs both left-brain (contraction) and right-brain (expansion) qualities. We weave deftly between the two constantly during the day, but at times need a conscious period of expansion to help us open up to more creativity. Conversely, contraction needs to occur in order to create energy to move forward.

From the expansive creative places, squashing and focusing down provides energy and ensures that ideas develop and are taken into form. Of course, coaching is just one of many activities that can assist with this process of expansion, containment, integration, contraction, synthesis and the creation of activity, but it is a very helpful one.

This model allows for multiple choice points, multiple nodes and types of activity. It is process based and emergent, expressing the natural flow between the 'creative, expansive phase' and 'nodes of action'.

What does this mean for coaching?

It is very easy to see that coaching involves an opportunity to expand perception, broaden thought, bring to light our past learning and self-awareness and also recruit our intuition and sensory awareness.

We might also see that coaching helps draw things together, contract our ideas and integrate rich learning, insights, ahas and wisdom, thus creating a synthesis. We know very well that coaching helps people create activity or a point of *creative action – creation*.

This expansion, contraction and the point in the centre (action/creation) can occur during a coaching session. This process may also occur over a longer period of time – combining all that happens inside and outside the coaching session.

This model describes how coaching operates in several ways:

Proposing a model for coaching creativity 93

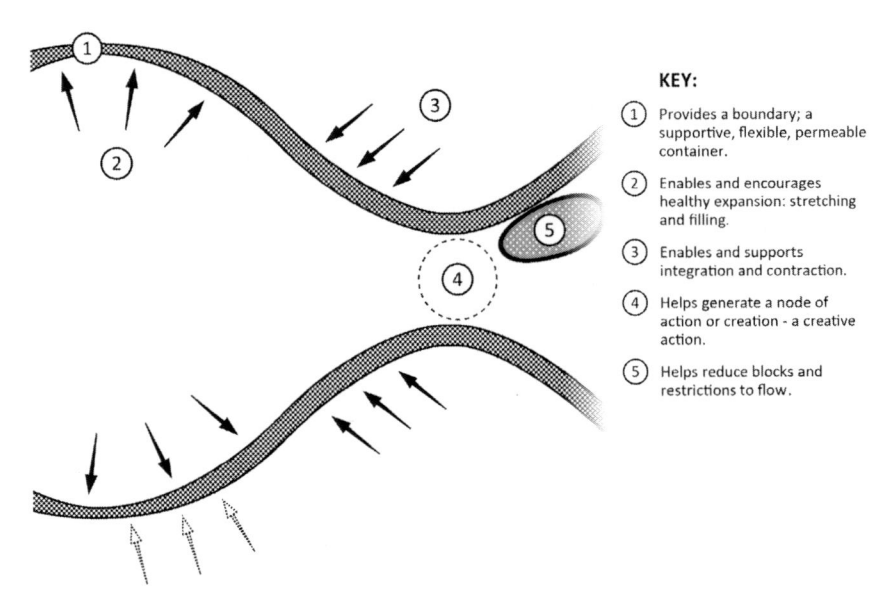

Figure 11.3 How coaching supports and enables the creative process

- Coaching generates and sustains a containing force or vessel.
- Coaching enables expansion – previous learning, memories as well as new input. It also can help ideas stay within helpful limits.
- Coaching can help draw together, contract, integrate, synthesize and move towards the point of action/creation.
- Coaching can subsequently help the process to start again, expand from that action/creation.
- Coaching works to reduce or remove blockages and restrictions.

The coaching model from a neuroscience stance

You will also recall Fuster's model, representing the neuroscience of creativity, and will see that it seems to mirror the shape of this model (Fuster 2013). Remember how Fuster describes a point where the P 'cone' containing past perceptual memories (experiences, memories, ethics, emotions, instincts) converges and meets with the apex of the A 'cone', which expands and projects forward. The A 'cone' represents our future vision and possible alternative future actions.

This intersection also feels like the actual moment of coaching that draws on the past, while holding an image for the future and generating an action in the now. At this point, a creative coaching activity would also enable the expansion of perception and also stimulate existing (past) perception (senses, learning and memories).

In addition, the creative activity can help develop future vision and generate possibilities for action.

The coaching model from a psychological stance

This model, this representation, unites many perspectives and theories from a psychological point of view. You can see the Gestalt cycle of Engagement and Withdrawal and the notion of a Fertile Void. Guilford's idea of convergence and divergence (Guilford 1956) is easily identifiable. You can observe Jung's Collective Unconscious in the expansive vessel, the container of hidden memories (Cryptomnesia). You can also see the movement between 'tight' and 'loose' constructs that many neuroscientists, psychologists and artists cite as intrinsic to creativity. You can also see that expansion beyond normal limits of consciousness/cultural acceptance could result in conditions we might call delusions or hallucinations in the Western medical paradigm.

The coaching model from an arts and creative practice stance

This way of thinking also reflects how artists and creatives commonly talk about their creative process being a fluctuation between conscious and unconscious states. This model also allows us to see the relationship between doing creativity and being creative, with the outcome always being both creating and becoming other. It also encompasses this empty phase, reported as essential by many famous creative people.

Understanding the challenges related to creativity, often seen in coaching

This model of creativity and coaching also helps us identify some of the most common creative challenges that coaches meet when working with clients (Figure 11.4).

Think again about a blood vessel, an artery in the human body. Like a muscle, the wall of a blood vessel needs to be healthy and able to contract and relax when required. What happens if the artery has lost flexibility and can't relax and expand? It remains narrow. In creativity terms, this is like lacking expansive thinking and being unable to shift perception, which is necessary for generating creative ideas (coaching topic *I lack creativity and creative ideas*).

If an artery is unable to expand sufficiently blood pressure will be reduced, because it lacks the natural energy generated by expansion and contraction. It doesn't pump very well (coaching topic *I lack momentum/energy, I procrastinate*).

If a blood vessel is too floppy and too wide it will struggle to contract, which will also reduce flow and the energy to move forward. In creativity terms this is like being too expansive, having too many ideas, too much creativity – resulting in a lack of ability to focus on one idea and generate action (coaching topic *I have too many ideas*).

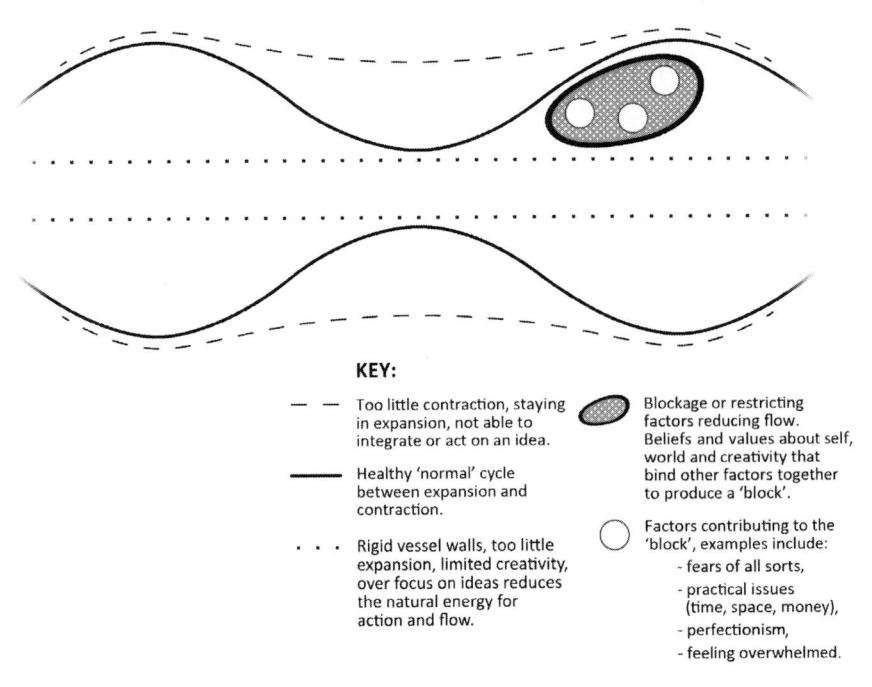

Figure 11.4 Common creative challenges faced in coaching

KEY:

— — Too little contraction, staying in expansion, not able to integrate or act on an idea.

——— Healthy 'normal' cycle between expansion and contraction.

· · · Rigid vessel walls, too little expansion, limited creativity, over focus on ideas reduces the natural energy for action and flow.

Blockage or restricting factors reducing flow. Beliefs and values about self, world and creativity that bind other factors together to produce a 'block'.

Factors contributing to the 'block', examples include:
- fears of all sorts,
- practical issues (time, space, money),
- perfectionism,
- feeling overwhelmed.

We could also talk about blood clots, barriers or creative blocks such as unhelpful beliefs and values, combining with various practical circumstances and specific environments and contexts that together result in blocking energy (coaching topic *I feel blocked or I sabotage myself*).

Like all creative endeavours, this model is in its formative stages and as such I open myself up to discussion and debate, some of which I imagine I might not like and will no doubt disagree with. However, sharing our ideas and enabling discussion is a crucial part of the creative process and the development of theoretical knowledge.

Learning points

- Creativity involves a continuous movement between an expansion of ideas, through integration into a compressed point of action.
- Artists and other creative people often describe their process using language that reflects this expansion and compression, such as a pumping blood vessel or inflating and deflating lungs.
- This language provides the basis of a coaching model for creativity whereby coaching:

- generates and sustains a containing vessel,
- enables expansion, integration and synthesis,
- creates a point of action or creation,
- enables continuation of the process,
- works to reduce or remove blockages and restrictions.

- This proposed model allows the knowledge from neuroscience, psychology and the arts and crafts to be assimilated.
- The model provides a way to understand the recurrent challenges in coaching creativity.

Note

1 Interestingly, the Latin word *flux* also means to flow and in physics 'flux is the rate of flow of fluid, particles, or energy or a quantity expressing the strength of a field of force in a given area' (Collins Online Dictionary).

References

Cave, N. (2014) The creative process is an altered state in itself, online article. Accessed 20/10/14, http://www.npr.org/2014/09/16/348727370/nick-cave-the-creative-process-is-an-altered-state-in-itself.

Fuster, J. (2013) *The Neuroscience of Creativity and Freedom*. Cambridge: Cambridge University Press.

Ghiselin, B. (ed) (1985) *The Creative Process*. Berkley, CA: University of California Press.

Goswami, A. (2014) *Quantum Creativity*. London: Hay House.

Guilford, J. P. (1956) The structure of intellect, *Psychological Bulletin*, 53(4), 267–93.

Hebron, S. (undated blog) John Keats and 'negative capability'. Accessed 8/5/16, http://www.bl.uk/romantics-and-victorians/articles/john-keats-and-negative-capability.

Part IV

Coaching the creative process

How coaching enables and supports the process of creativity

Delving into the sciences, psychology and practice of creativity has led to a conceptual model of creativity and coaching. This model, or way of thinking, is based on the metaphor of a vessel in the body, which expands and contracts to produce movement. Whilst it could have been one of many vessels in the human body, the notion of a blood vessel is familiar to many people and most people can relate to how it expands and contracts to create flow. I will also readily admit that I like thinking of creativity as the life force of the human body beginning and ending with the heart.

When using models based on a metaphor it is accepted that whoever uses the model will interpret and use it in such a way that makes sense to them – it's not set in stone and it's not a set of rules to follow rigidly. Use it, change it and adapt it in ways that you and your clients may gain helpful understanding and insights. Using a natural well-known metaphor also provides a universal language that is understandable and inclusive for our clients; it's not just professional babble. Remember too that whilst this model might seem quite conceptual, it does allow us to integrate the various sciences of creativity discussed earlier.

Working with the metaphor of a pumping blood vessel allows us to consider the different ways that coaching helps the creative process, such that it:

- Provides a supportive, responsive, flexible and permeable vessel or container.
- Enables healthy expansion; stretching, filling and activating the space.
- Enables integration and contraction.
- Generates a point of creative action or creation.
- Reduces blockages and restrictions.

The remaining chapters in this part of the book are based around these five issues, which are key to working with creativity. Whilst explored as separate issues, they clearly interact with and affect each other – that's the strength of an integrative model based on a natural process. Thus, moving into action will also create expansion and learning for future integration and action.

Some of the discussions here may sound familiar – for example, the coaching relationship and ways of enquiring and questioning – however, they will be explored in relation to specific creativity issues. Where relevant, I have included some coaching questions. These come from a variety of sources as well as experiences working with clients in relation to creativity.

Chapter 12

The vessel wall – containing the process

When considering the wall of this 'blood vessel', the notion of a containing energy or force that coaching creates, I initially thought it represented the coach themselves or perhaps the coaching relationship, or maybe the boundaries and characteristics of coaching itself. However, as time went on, I saw that it was the qualities that were produced when these came together during coaching. This containing energy is like the wall of an imaginary vessel and exhibits the following qualities:

- It has a clear purpose and works to clarify the meaning of creativity for the client: the client develops self-awareness about their personal creative process, including what they mean by creativity and what they want from creativity and the coaching process.
- It offers containment but in a flexible way. It's a 'force' to push against and creates a feeling of safety and challenge. The vessel, created by the qualities of the coaching, maintains congruence and coherence while developing greater responsiveness and the ability to move between expansion and contraction.
- It serves the client's creative process in a way that is best for them and strives to ensure continued participation as the process progresses.
- It has a degree of permeability; one which lets ideas and stimulus in but also helps figure out what is real, what is imagined and offers reality checks as needed.

So, what does all this look like in coaching?

> *It has a clear purpose and works to clarify the meaning of creativity for the client: the client develops self-awareness about their personal creative process, including what they mean by creativity and what they want from creativity and the coaching process.*

This vessel wall – and the space it creates for dialogue – needs to have a sense of purpose; in this case it's about creativity and the place creativity has in the client's life. However, creativity also wants to talk about things like a difficult marriage, the problem of a lack of money, coping with a painful hip and so on. While we know that allowing these things into the coaching space is important, the purpose of the coaching may become unclear unless we draw those things back to creative process. The experience of the coach is vital in knowing how much attention to give to these other issues and how much to relate them back to the agenda of creativity. We also know as experienced coaches that working on other issues often results in a change, which impacts on creative goals in some way.

We need to start with clarity of purpose; what the coaching is about and what creativity means to our client. Do they desire meaning from a new hobby? Do they want to produce something to be proud of or perhaps sell – a nice watercolour, a handmade cushion or something else. Perhaps they love getting messy with paint and having fun. Perhaps they enjoy solving complex problems and want to be able to think more creatively.

Conversations to clarify the meaning and purpose of creativity

What is your creative dream?

What does creativity mean to you?

When you say you want to be more creative, what does that mean?

Tell me about a time you were able to be really creative? What was going on at that time that helped you be creative?

What sort of creative desires, dreams or goals do you have?

What will becoming more creative or achieving these goals give you?

What do you believe about creativity? Where does it come from? What is it like?

What expectations do you have from creativity? What are you hoping for?

Conversations to explore the purpose of coaching

How do you feel coaching might help?

What are you expecting from this coaching relationship?

When you were coached in the past, what helped?

What might get in the way of our coaching together?

It offers containment but in a flexible way. It's a 'force' to push against and creates a feeling of safety and challenge. The vessel, created by the qualities of the coaching, maintains congruence and coherence while developing greater responsiveness and the ability to move between expansion and contraction.

Having something to push against, bounce ideas off, to be accountable to, a yielding, flexible force – these are common qualities experienced when being coached. Most experienced coaches, will immediately understand how this intrinsic quality, this flexible containing force is created by both coach and client. As a coach, the basic relationship, resonance and core skills are in play here: deep, active listening; yielding yet challenging; with good boundaries yet pragmatic; grounded but intuitive.

Essentially, your understanding about the nature and diversity of creativity supports this process. You may have helped dispel some of the myths about creativity. Together with your client, you have worked to find out what is needed at this moment in time, to support their creative process. Is further creative expansion needed at this point or integration and grounding? Does intrinsic motivation need to be questioned? Does the coach need to do something specifically to encourage expansion or contraction or do they just allow the process to unfold?

Although I was educated as a non-directive coach, these days I would argue that directed intervention really helps in coaching sometimes. This might include providing snippets of 'learning' about creativity or a language to describe what might be occurring for a client. For example, to the client who is experiencing creative chaos and overwhelm, you might say:

> *This is quite common in the creative process. As your thinking has expanded and you have experimented with different ideas, you might feel confused or in overwhelm. This is creative chaos and is completely natural, sometimes exciting but often a little uncomfortable. It will pass and doing something low pressure and practical might help.*

Offering specific knowledge or learning such as this can help reduce anxiety and upset, by normalising common experiences during the creative process. Knowing that experiences such as creative chaos, overwhelm and perfectionism are very common and indeed sometimes necessary, can really help people let go of the struggle and stress as they try to battle against it.

Other common concepts that I find it helpful to explain and share with clients when appropriate include the normality of:

- Being in the 'gap' or void, when nothing seems to be happening.
- Being in the expansive phase, which can be chaotic.
- Being in the integration phase, which often involves difficult choices.
- Feeling they are procrastinating and avoiding moving into action.
- Often crippling feelings of perfectionism.

Finding a way to offer this type of knowledge succinctly and share the normality of what can feel like a highly difficult set of circumstances can move mountains for people.

> *It serves the client's creative process in a way that is best for them and strives to ensure continued participation as the process.*

Something I underestimated as a novice coach was the importance of keeping my clients engaged and 'in the process'. Actively helping people to stay in the process, in between coaching sessions, was something never discussed in my early coach education, in fact it was actively discouraged. This is what I understood: you do the coaching session, schedule the next one, client goes away and does their stuff. You don't do anything in between because 1) you are not getting paid to do so and 2) that means they are not developing inner motivation and self-accountability.

Those arguments are valid to a certain extent, but in terms of this fun, messy, delicate thing called creativity, this quite harsh line might be worth reconsidering.

Creativity is fickle and often forgets. Creativity is delicate and sometimes gets squashed amongst the weight of other daily tasks. Creativity sometimes needs a bit of a helping hand. Finding ways to help clients remember the 'juicy bits' of awareness, excitement and learning gained during a session and bringing that awareness into daily life can be immensely valuable. That's why I am in favour of sending the odd email saying 'how's the book going' or 'I saw this and thought of you' or sending useful reminders through the post or other things that might inspire, remind or perhaps break habitual thinking! You might have other and different views on this but I have found it can often help strengthen the process and my relationship with my clients.

If clients are worried about showing up to a session for any reason, it can be the start of disengagement. Although some may question client commitment or readiness, we need to consider whether the coaching itself has created barriers to engagement?

Questions for the coach to reflect upon

Is the coaching adding to stress levels? (Is the container too rigid?)

Is the coaching an enhancing experience?

Are the agreed steps too big and adding pressure?

Is the client worried about turning up as they haven't done what they said they would? (There can be a flip side to accountability.)

Are you paying enough attention to what is working well for your client inside the session? Do you ask them what worked and what didn't?

What is likely to make them want to continue to show up?

Has there been a pattern of disengagement in the part? Should the coaching pay attention to that?

> *It has a degree of permeability; one which lets ideas and stimulus in but also helps figure out what is real, what is imagined and offers reality checks as needed.*

This could refer to what is and isn't discussed in the coaching space, such as other life issues, however, I suggest this vessel wall has a much greater function in terms of creativity in that it's a perceptual filter and regulator.

Our perception of the world and how we experience it is a complex mechanism. What we 'believe' about ourselves, the world and this thing called creativity, all impact on how we process and interpret the vast sensory input we receive. We will talk about the role of 'beliefs' in relation to creativity later, but important here is how the vessel contains and serves as a healthy filter for the expansion of our sensory perception and awareness.

We could look at this in a pragmatic way – coaching helps to boundary ideas and provides a safe way to test them out. Coaching helps contain ideas so they remain in the 'real world' while not losing those concepts that are a little mad, but may also hold great potential. (I am thinking of those ground breaking ideas, scientific ideas and inventions that at the time looked implausible but in years to come would prove to be highly influential – like the internet). This vessel 'holds' those ideas long enough for people to decide whether to tweak them, dump them or shelve them for a while.

If we extend this idea further, we could see that this vessel serves to filter out some ideas that we could argue are beyond the realm of normal consciousness. The upper limits of this holding vessel could also represent the fine line between madness and genius. And, of course, ideas that would have been perceived as 'madness' a hundred years ago, are now completely accepted as normal. For example, unseen, disconnected forces that transmit large amounts of information and communication around the world – WIFI!

We can see this coaching vessel, at its maximum point of expansion, as holding multiple possibilities – possibilities that to some people appear completely barmy, but to others might hold great potential. The coaching vessel protects and perhaps may prevent people slipping into grandiose or delusional thought and help to test out perceptual skews, which under certain circumstances lead to hallucinations.[1]

Learning points

The characteristics and boundaries of coaching combine with the coaching relationship to create the qualities of a containing force or vessel. This vessel:

- Has a clear purpose, working to clarify the meaning of creativity for the client and what they want from the coaching process.
- Offers containment in a flexible way. It's a force to push against while at the same time creating a feeling of safety and challenge. It maintains congruence and coherence while developing greater responsiveness, enabling the ability to move between expansion and contraction.

- It serves the client's creative process in a way that is best for them and strives to ensure continued participation as the process unfolds.
- It has a degree of permeability; one that lets ideas and stimulus in but also helps figure out what is real, what is imagined and offers reality checks as needed.

Note

1 Psychosis is defined as thought and emotions that are disordered and that have lost contact with external reality. Hallucinations occur when one sees, hears and feels things that are not there. Delusions are beliefs that are not true. These are accepted definitions in the modern medical paradigm of mental health and of course highly culturally bound.

Chapter 13

Enabling expansion – stretching, filling and activating the space

What does expansion look like? How does expansion take place? What might be already in the creative space that could be activated and what else could be added?

This part of the process is about expanding consciousness, pushing into new areas, opening up to all sorts of new ideas and input, provoking new feelings, thoughts and ways of doing or being, evoking old memories and adding interesting new ingredients too. This process requires the vessel wall to expand outward, create space, accommodate new things and allow movement to take place.

This is where we can draw on the learning from the research we encountered earlier. The neurosciences, psychological sciences and learning from artists and makers, who all cite the importance of activities, practices and processes that:

- Encourage a greater openness to experience.
- Promote disruption and agitation.
- Lower pressure to enable the mind to wander, let go and dream.
- Enable mindful noticing and the activation of a variety of senses, thus expanding perception.
- Develop fluidity of ideas and a healthy working memory.
- Reconnect to existing memories, learning and yearnings.
- Promote a willingness to take risks, be wrong and to fail.
- Develop greater freedom and comfort in this often chaotic place.

As human beings, all of this happens unconsciously and naturally as we participate in daily life. However, in our desire to be more creative or generate creative ideas, we can consciously evoke this process by adding new 'ingredients' and also activate existing or dormant elements. At the risk of mixing metaphors, we can recall the lost ideas, previous learning (failures), half-baked ideas, unconscious memories and so on, so that together they transform into rich, fertile compost.

Gestalt coaching talks about this being 'the fertile ground': a place rich with possibility that we return to after engaging or completing an action fully. The fertile ground is a rich tapestry of learning and experience and Leary-Joyce makes it clear that 'this resource is always available for us to tap into, although in our rush to get

106 Coaching the creative process

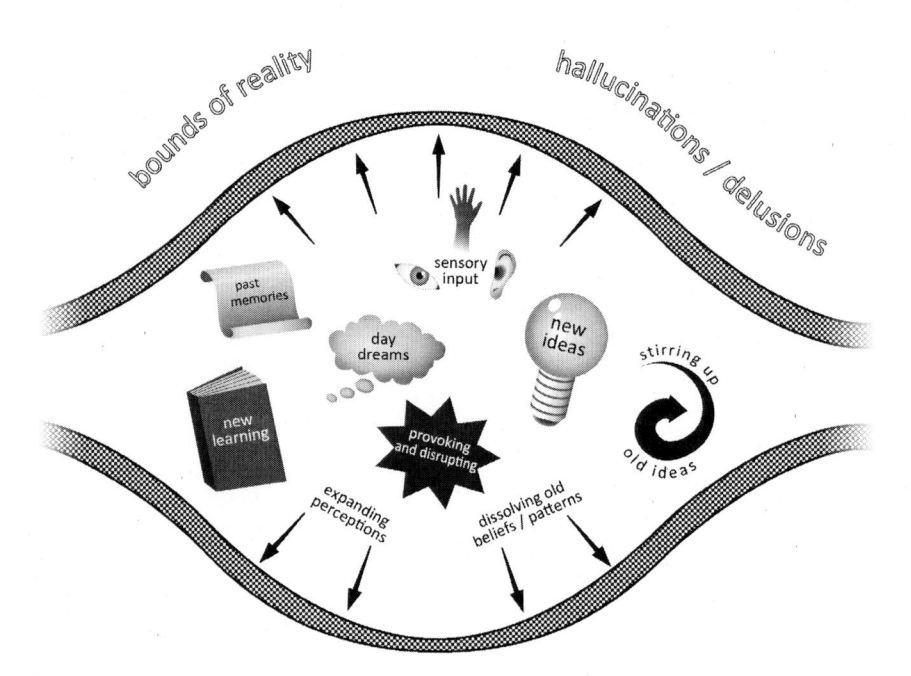

Figure 13.1 Enabling healthy expansion: stretching, filling and activating the space

on and do the next thing we don't allow the space or time to draw on that wealth of experience' (Leary-Joyce 2014, p. 31).

Yet coaching also has a strong part to play in actually creating this fertile space. Coaching helps clients unpack ideas, challenge perceptions, recall previous learning, relive passions and revive interests, so that expansion can occur and a fertile space can develop.

Creative actions, experiencing different environments and participating in different activities help the agitation and expansion of this fertile space and should be considered as part of possible coaching activities. In the final part of the book we look at different activities in coaching but conversation alone can activate this creative space and is our natural starting point.

Conversations to encourage expansion of ideas

At this point, would some expansive, wider thinking be helpful?

Have we become too narrow in our discussion or perhaps a little over focused?

Let's brainstorm this. Without attaching to the ideas or overthinking, quickly come up with seven, twelve, fifteen or more ideas.

What are other possibilities?

What is just one more possibility?

What other angles can you think of?

What else might help encourage ideas to flow?

In the past, what helped you generate ideas?

When in the day or during what times do you get ideas?

How can I look at something normal/familiar and see something different?

What would happen if . . .?

It should be noted that iterative enquiry can be easily encouraged by adding a simple '. . . and what else?' several times, after a question. For more on this principle, read the work of Harland 2009).

Conversations to develop and elaborate ideas

Tell me about your idea/project. What is it about this that really interests and excites you?

How does this idea/project tap into your best strengths and talents?

How does this idea/project relate to other things you are doing or hope to achieve?

What's missing from this idea/project?

What else could you do with this idea/project?

What other ideas do you have about it?

What else could you do to expand this idea?

Will you elaborate . . .?

Tell me more about that . . .?

Is there more?

What else are we conveniently forgetting?

And if we just dump the whole thing, what will happen?

Conversations to promote playfulness

How might a child approach this? How would their thinking change it?

If I was four years old, what ideas would I have and how would I have tackled this?

What if my idea wrote to me about what it wants to do next? (JB)

What are you taking far too seriously about this?

(continued)

(continued)

Conversations to encourage and promote mindful wandering

If you had completely free choice in this, what would you do?

What helps you let go?

What would it take to let your mind wander?

How could you create some space between these ideas, so they could move around a little?

What if I walk, meditate, daydream and pause? (JB)

During what times or activities do I notice ideas and insights popping into my mind

If you took this idea for a walk, where might it go?

Conversations to promote adaptability, flexibility and fluidity

What is it to be fluid/ flexible/ adaptable?

How might that help now?

How might letting go of the end result, help right now?

In what way are you thinking too rigidly about this?

What do you need to let go of?

Conversations to encourage imperfection, mistakes and learning

The following questions and ideas need to be kept in context especially if your clients' creative form requires precision and accuracy!

In what ways is imperfection great?

What did you learn about making mistakes when you were growing up?

What are the benefits of making mistakes?

What might you need to surrender to?

Tell me about a time when you just threw something together and it really went well?

What if you were to dump this project/idea now and let it stagnate for a bit?

> **Conversations to stir up and agitate what already exists**
>
> *Can you recall where this came from? Tell me some more about that...*
>
> *What experiences have you had in the past that could add a different slant to this?*
>
> *If you had to rely only on your existing knowledge and experience, what might present itself here?*
>
> *What life experience or piece of learning has stuck in your mind most? How might that inform this idea?*

Of course, it is often during this phase, that we meet a common challenge to coaching: 'I am not creative enough' or 'I lack creative ideas'. Crucially our focus needs to encourage expansion, different perspectives and a greater openness to experience. This helps put people in a richer, more accessible position from which to 'get ideas'. For naturally expansive thinkers, conversations might be enough, but for people that struggle to let go of tightly held beliefs and perceptions we know we need to work in a different and possibly deeper way. As coaches we also know that there are often conscious or unconscious reasons why people resist being more creative and may sabotage both individual and group ideas.

We will discuss reducing blocks, restrictions and self-sabotage later on, but if conversation based approaches are not working then practical, art-based coaching activities or ones that evoke a different range of sensory experiences can really help – we will also explore lots of those in Part V.

At present, I feel that the coaching profession has a wealth of tools and structures to support focusing and planning action, but things that support expansion of ideas and perception are under-developed. I also feel that the structures such as 'competency frameworks' insufficiently reflect the creative, playful, expansive nature of coaching and, indeed, may restrict it further. Although this is inevitable in some ways, as the nature of regulation is clearly convergent in nature, coaching is naturally an expansive and creative profession. If greater value is not placed on this, coaching risks losing its naturally powerful and creative self.

Learning points

- Coaching supports and enables healthy expansion, filling and activation of the creative space.
- Knowledge from neuroscience, psychology and learning from artists and makers is combined, to provide principles for the expansion, filling and activation of this space, namely:

- encourage a greater 'openness' to experience,
- promote disruption and agitation,
- lower pressure to enable the mind to wander, let go and dream,
- enable mindful noticing and the activation of a variety of senses, thus expanding perception,
- develop fluidity of ideas and a healthy working memory,
- reconnect to existing memories, learning and yearnings,
- promote a willingness to take risks, be wrong and fail,
- develop greater freedom and comfort in this often chaotic place.

References

Harland, P. (2009) *The Power of Six*. Rodgway, CO: Wayfinder Press.

Leary-Joyce, J. (2014) *The Fertile Void: Gestalt Coaching at Work*. London: AOEC Press.

Suggested reading

Drum, J. (2007) A fruitful soil: what coaches can learn from how theatre directors in rehearsal create a learning environment, *International Journal of Evidence Based Coaching and Mentoring* 5(2), 34.

Chapter 14

Enabling contraction and integration

What does contraction look like? What prevents contraction and integration? What helps contraction and integration take place?

In our model there needs to be an eventual shift away from expansive thought and towards integration of ideas and action, otherwise there is no consolidation and we never bring things into form. This downward drop on the curve in our model represents the start of contraction, which promotes an increase in pressure as the vessel narrows.

In coaching, this is the integration of creative ideas that starts to bring together what we have experienced and considered, prior to the point of *crea*tive act*ion* or *creation*. Our intuition and experience as coaches is crucial, but the questions we might consider include:

Is it time to now to condense these ideas down for a while to ensure we maintain forward momentum?

or

What is starting to emerge from our discussion.

or

Are obvious things occurring to you as we speak or do we need things to keep things loose for a bit longer?

Contracting down and consolidating sufficiently before moving into the action phase involves a combination of:

- Integration of multiple input including feelings, intuition and sensory/body awareness, resulting in a felt sense of what action to take.
- Reflection on the insights and 'aha' moments to date with the result of conscious synthesizing.
- Consciously choosing one idea or project and a willingness to let go of others, at least for now.
- Preparing for a move into action.

While conversations are not the only way to help clients integrate their ideas and contract sufficiently to create action, they are a natural starting point.

Conversations to test out ideas

Live this one choice or idea for a moment. Be 'in' the option. What do you notice?

What might it be like when you . . .?

Is the world ready for this?

If you proceed with this, how soon will you reap the benefits?

If you were on Dragons Den, what would they be telling you right now?

Whose opinion might really help at this point?

Conversations about narrowing down choice

How do you want the world to be different because you were in it?

What do you want your legacy to be?

If you knew that you could not fail, which choice/idea would you pursue first?

(Note that we are only suggesting that one choice is made for now, reducing the feeling that the ideas are being abandoned.)

Which idea/project would give you the greatest joy right now? Tell me more about this . . .

When you are ninety and look back on your life, want to you want talk about? What do you want to say you chose to do?

What resources do you need to help you decide?

Conversations that integrate

How might all this fit together?

When you look at this as a whole, what seems to emerge?

As the need to choose/act comes closer, what naturally falls away?

What new whole is ready to form?

What is your body telling you about all of this? (body wisdom)

What do you know now that you will find out in a year's time? (intuition)

How do you think it will all work out? (cognition)

It's here, during this contraction phase, that we encounter a challenge that coaches meet, but one not often discussed in coaching literature – the challenge of the expansive minds of highly creative people, the 'Big-C creatives' we spoke of earlier. When involved in a coaching process, they often have quite distinct challenges including:

- Struggling with creative chaos and overwhelm of ideas.
- Capturing and communicating what is often a torrent of ideas.
- Helping other people understand what may be a highly conceptual and personal idea.
- Difficultly deciding what to choose, focus on and bring into form.
- Acting upon that decision or choice, whilst still managing the continued bombardment of ideas.
- Bringing a different project or goal to coaching every time.
- Not seeming to take the actions or steps they previously agreed to take.
- Pushing against any notion of accountability or focus.
- Sabotaging their efforts in all sorts of ways.

When working with a highly creative person, you may start having lots of worries. Why are they not progressing? They are off on another tangent and not getting anywhere! Is my coaching good enough? Am I doing the right thing? Why isn't the coaching working?

I have argued for years that clients who are highly creative are often tricky to work with and require a deeper understanding from us as coaches. Sometimes a little more structure might help or a different type of coaching activity. At other times a completely relaxed approach or wacky activity is needed. They may also benefit from more of a mentoring style of coaching with elements of teaching regarding the creative process.

Awareness needs to be raised around the challenges of being a highly creative person including the nature of creative chaos, overwhelm and the challenges of focusing. Helping people to understand the environments and circumstances that they work best under and how they can most effectively communicate their needs, are all essential.

You might need to rethink what it means to 'coach' a creative person. This is where I am indebted to Jill Badonsky who, amongst others, helped me to relax my perceptions around coaching, recruit my whole self as a coach and introduce a much broader range of activities into my work.

Learning points

- Coaching helps people move away from expansion, into integration and synthesis.
- Coaching supports the integration of sensory input, ideas, internal awareness, insights gained and a willingness to let go of other possibilities.
- Highly creative people may appear to struggle with this phase.

Chapter 15

The point of creative action

In our model, this is where it all comes together – the maximum point of contraction, a compressed point, leading to action. Moving into action is the only way to bring creative ideas into the physical realm – into reality. It is *creative* ac*tion* or *creation*. Defining action could be complex but really it is about actually doing something, not just thinking about it. So alongside actually putting paint onto paper, writing a paragraph or two, I would also include sharing an idea with your team, which makes it more likely to become reality.

I have left the discussion about planning, goals and steps until now, but clearly they occur through the whole process of expansion and integration as we constantly move between doing and being in our pursuit of creating other or becoming other. Before we talk about this very coach-like stuff, it's worth remembering that creativity works best when a system of helpful practices is happening at the same time. I feel it's our role as coaches, to help each of our clients to discover a system that works for them and then support them to use it regularly.

Goals

Creative goals could be any number of things:

> *'I want to write a book.'*
>
> *'I want to learn to play an instrument.'*
>
> *'I have painted for years and want to hold an exhibition.'*
>
> *'I have a deadline to finish this novel.'*
>
> *'I love making scarves and want to start a creative business.'*

We also have more conceptual goals:

> 'I want to be a more creative thinker.'
>
> 'I keep having all these ideas and don't know what to do with them.'

At work we might have goals such as:

'My team need to come up with more ideas.'

'We need more creative products – our business is failing due to lack of innovation.'

In these examples, there is a massive range of what could constitute a goal. Debates and questions such as what constitutes a goal, an outcome or an aim, can be found in numerous coaching texts elsewhere and general discussion isn't particularly relevant here. In creativity, embracing the shifting nature of goals and the inherent emergence of the creative process is essential. As we saw earlier in the discussion about how creative processes such as painting and the coaching process are similar, there is a need to let go of overly tight outcomes and embrace the emergence of what might be.

Thanks to recent longitudinal coaching research led by David Clutterbuck (2011) we know that an over-adherence to goals in a coaching process is unhelpful. This research reinforces awareness that goals naturally emerge, shift and change through the coaching process. So I prefer to call goal setting 'having a vague idea of what you are working towards'.

There is also some helpful research regarding creativity and goal setting from Shalley (1991), who explored what types of goals and circumstances resulted in the highest levels of creativity. The results apply to both creative goals at home and creativity in a work environment. Shalley found the highest levels of creativity came from a 'do-your-best' creativity goal and difficult productivity goal (basically it's tricky but just give it a go), or a difficult creativity and difficult productivity goal. Conversely, if individuals are given a productivity goal (they have to produce something) or low personal discretion (It's not my choice, I'm not bothered) and a no creativity goal, creativity decreases.

Shalley's findings are in line with what we know about the importance of intrinsic motivation and also highlight the need to encourage our clients to just have a go, reduce high expectations of the outcome and lower pressure, so that people feel able to just do their best with some sort of goal or productivity aim in mind. We also need to ensure they can exercise personal discretion; that they are able to choose and be in control of their own process.

The upshot of this is that we need to discover what type of goals or circumstances work for our clients and also make them aware that in creativity, as in coaching, things shift around quite a lot. If we hold on too tightly we can get really stressed and disappointed but also miss out on lovely things that arise on the way.

Planning and preferences

People often come to coaching wanting a plan. It's comforting to feel that we have a plan, especially if we have wanted to do something different for a while and have been struggling to do it. However, people can be very different in the ways that they plan, set goals and execute tasks. In a longitudinal study, McKee (1991), also cited in Boyatzis and Howard (2013), showed that people have four main preferences when it comes to planning and goal setting. She describes them as:

- Objectives oriented planners: people who respond well to linear, logical goals.
- Domain and direction planners: people who know the direction they want to move in, but move forward without specific targets or deadlines.
- Task planners: people who respond to short-term aims better than thinking about a long-term vision.
- Existential/non planners: people who feel things will somehow work out as they are 'meant to'.

Traditional, liner goal-setting methods, such as SMART (Specific, Measurable, Achievable, Realistic, Timely), will therefore only suit a quarter of people – yes only a quarter – therefore blanket use of SMART goals is unhelpful for the majority of people. Unless we understand this when working with our clients and help them find out what works for them, we risk helping them set goals and to plan in a way that is unlikely to work for them!

If their preference is toward existential/non planner or domain/direction planner, coaching them to make plans and organise in a linear, logical ways may well prove to be ineffectual. Worse, it may alienate your client so that they disengage. For example, it could be that your client turns up for the session with a new creative, exciting idea that has emerged since the last session. If then the session focuses on a linear action plan or the next logical steps, you may well find that none are forthcoming. Your client has moved on.

Helping your client become more aware about how they plan is probably one of the most important things you can do as a coach. Such awareness may develop over time or you could intentionally explore this in the following way:

> *We know that all people plan and work differently; some people have a clear goal and set logical, timely steps to achieve it. Some people kind of know the rough direction they want to go in, and then go with the flow in that direction. Some people don't have a long-term vision and work on what's in front of them. Some people leave life to 'fate' or feel that 'what is meant to be, will be.' As you listen to these four types of planning and goal setting, do any of them resonate with you?*

Yes, this isn't pure coaching and yes we are doing a bit of teaching. We are giving our clients knowledge that may help them during their creative process and wider life in general. Only you can reflect and decide whether this fits with your coaching style and philosophy.

Conversations to explore clients' planning styles

What sort of plan do you need to create?

In the past, when you completed something like this what sort of planning worked for you?

What worked in the past when you needed to set some goals?

What do you know about yourself, that you are willing to admit, when it comes to planning?

> *As your coach, if you came to our next session and haven't stuck to the plan you have made, what would you like me to do?*

Promoting risk taking, action and fast failure

There is a lot of talk in innovation circles about the need to take risks, fail fast, learn fast, adjust and try again. We have also seen how beneficial it is, on a micro level, in helping to build peak performance through deep practice (remember how fast, repeated and adjusted action builds myelin – the stuff that makes neurons work faster). Although I often cite the importance of making mistakes and experimenting as essential to promoting creativity, it might not go down well with someone who wants to produce technically accurate, traditional, pencil drawn portraits. So, our clients need to be clear in their own minds about whether they want to develop a skill, such as technically correct drawing, or draw more creatively, where mistakes are an integral part of the process.

In supporting creativity, promoting fast failure is more than just testing and refining ideas or performance. We are helping our clients build a new muscle important for creativity; the ability to let go of perfectionism and move into action more freely. We will talk about the often crippling effects of perfectionism on creativity later on, but here, a willingness to take risks and fail helps to ensure that any plans are fluid, quick to implement and easily adjusted.

There is value in exploring how the notion of risk taking and failure sits with your clients:

- Do they embrace risk in other arenas? If so in what ways?
- In relation to their creative practice or creative goals, what evidence is there that they can take risks, learn from failure and adapt?
- Are the risks taken very calculated and controlled (low risk)? Or are they very experimental and daring (high risk)?
- What is their perception of the risks they take?
- Do they learn fast from 'failure', bounce back, adjust and carry on?
- What do they feel constitutes success?
- Are they able to reframe and find the learning from a 'failure'?
- Are they happy to play and experiment for a whole day, without having something tangible to show for it?

Small actions

Taking action, however small, is paramount and we all know how difficult this can be. By the time we have finished our journey into creativity and coaching, we will have explored what else gets in the way of taking action and doing something creative. However, addressing the actual act of moving from idea into creative action is probably the single most important thing we can do for our clients.

Having been a therapist and coach for years, I thought I really understood the importance of small steps and small actions, but I really didn't. At first I also tended to underestimate the importance of taking a step even if someone doesn't feel 'completely ready' or they are 'still waiting for the easel to be delivered'. Otherwise, we can end up with a 'one day, some day, maybe' scenario.

Dr Bob Maurer[1] works in healthcare in the US. He makes it clear that if someone is planning to exercise for the first time, going to the gym three times a week is not a small step. It's too much of a habit change: it's too much to add into someone's week; it will impact on family roles and responsibilities (they may also feel compelled to buy Lycra, which should always be carefully thought through). This can all be too much and really set fear in motion and avoidance into action. To Dr Maurer, a small first step in such a case would be to stand up and walk in front of the TV, for one minute during the advert break – an action so small, that it will barely be noticed (Maurer 2004).

So when you are discussing first or subsequent actions with your client, make sure they are really, really small. At the next coaching session, if you find that they have not taken those small actions or have sabotaged them, consider whether they were possibly too big!

Here are some small creative steps:

- If your client wants to start to write a book, they might want to buy a nice pen. That's a small step. Another small step might be to just write two sentences or a short paragraph, but do it really badly and make it as rubbish as you possibly can (it's so much easier to start if your standards are really low).
- If your client wants to hold their first exhibition, a small step might be to Google possible locations for five minutes, make a list of possible pieces to include in the show or come up with some titles for possible pieces of work.
- If your team at work needs to come up with some different ideas for a project, just ask them to spend a few minutes brainstorming alone or five minutes visualising the situation or circumstances involved. Or maybe coming up with five ideas that definitely won't work!
- Sketching for five minutes is a small step, joining a drawing class might just be too big for some.

This is all about getting started or getting going again and, for the stuck, fearful or over perfectionist client, such ideas can work really well. You will often find that your client goes beyond those tiny first steps once they have made a start.

Conversations to reduce pressure and shift into small actions

In what tiny way, could I move this forward right now?

Would doing this just 5% more often make it less stressful?

What am I taking far too seriously about this?

How could I approach this whilst being really gentle and kind to myself?

How can I let go and enjoy the process?

> *Can I find what I seek if nothing changes?*
> *How could I relax and enjoy the process?*
> *In what way is the current situation absolutely perfect?*
> *How could we experiment with lowering standards and expectations?*
> *How can I make this easy/fun?*
> *What worked in the past? or What might work?*

Working 'with' and creating action together

Since training as a creativity coach, I have allowed myself much greater flexibility as a coach. One the most powerful things I started to do is something that Jill Badonsky calls Parallel Universe Time™ (2011). Other coaches have different names for it but, essentially, it means working on something at the same time as your client. For example, your client may have purchased some pencils and a sketch book, but they are not making a start. During the coaching call, you could agree to work in parallel. Your client hangs up and goes off for ten or twenty minutes and actually does something – the tiniest doodle or writes a couple of sentences and so on. At the same time, you also go off and do something, ideally something that you also keep putting off. Working like this is a brilliant way of getting people going and you will often find that once they have started they are reluctant to come back to the call as they are so immersed in what they are doing!

I use this with my creativity coaching clients and I also use it with other types of clients who perhaps have a phone call they need to make or an email that they keep putting off, or something else that is really blocking them. Why not agree to do it then and there? This idea also works well as a group coaching activity, in person or on a group conference call.

Lowering pressure and expectation

The other vastly important piece of learning I gained during my creativity coach training (as opposed to my previous, more traditional coach training) was the problems caused by high pressure and huge expectations that people often have of themselves, the creative process or the outcome. Completing and finishing a piece of work may require a deadline and a bit of a push, but when someone is in the early stages of generating ideas or just trying to get going, pressure generally is not helpful.

When we are coaching creativity there are many ways of easing the pressure. For example, we may encourage very small steps and actions in the way we have just explored. Another way is to tackle the high pressure caused by high expectations and big outcomes from the creative process. Lowering expectations may sound like 'crushing dreams' or 'playing it small' and this approach is in contrast to other approaches that advocate going for the biggest and best! Yet lowering expectations is more about letting go of the outcome enough to make a start and enjoy the process as it unfolds.

Consider this:

- We yearn to write our first book, perhaps our memoirs, and go into it with the expectation that it will be published, read widely and become a best seller.
- We have a strong desire to start painting, but do so expecting a gallery to hang our work and for it to sell.
- We are the main 'creative' in a company that needs a new best-selling line and we are expected to 'invent' something brilliant.

Some people, perhaps only the seasoned 'successful' creatives, respond well to these internal high expectations. For most of us regular people, they can serve to alienate us from our attempts to make a start, prevent us from experimenting, taking risks or failing and, most importantly, relaxing enough to enjoy the creative activity we want to do.

Habits

The importance of habitual action and regular practice in creativity cannot be understated. If you examine the lives of famous creative people, or less known but highly productive creative people, you will undoubtedly see helpful habits and routines in play.

It's easy to see how habits and the regular activity they can produce help people build skills and stay in the process, but they serve an even greater function to my mind:

> *Turning something into a ritual (or habit) eliminates the question 'why am I doing this?'*
>
> Twyla Tharp (2006)

A habit, something we do without thinking about it, such as writing our morning pages or attending our regular pottery class, serves to avoid or at least quieten unhelpful internal doubts or strong external forces.

For some clients, habit forming might have always been a challenge. Questions such as 'when you got into the habit of doing x in the past, how was it?' may well uncover a lifetime lacking in habitual behaviour beyond perhaps sleeping and eating. I say this as I am one such person. I know so well how helpful habits are to creative people, especially highly productive creative people, but it just seems to be beyond me. The only habitual pattern I have discovered is that I do things for three days – that's it. I am reliably informed that it takes twenty-eight days to create a new habit, so it would seem that I am some way off that.

> **Conversations to help form creative habits**
>
> *What unhelpful habits do you have that don't serve you well?*
>
> *There are usually benefits to these unhelpful habits; can you identify any?*
>
> *How might developing some new habits help you right now?*
>
> *What tiny thing could you do each day that would keep you connected to your idea/project/goal?*
>
> *Think about a time when you had to make a new habit or change an old one. What helped you do this?*

Rituals

As well as forming helpful habits, rituals help many people with their creative process. If you are fascinated by this, as I am, you will find lots of inspiration and ideas by looking at other artists, writers, entrepreneurs and creative thinkers. They usually have much to say about their own process and what helps them.

- Many people find that they need to go for a walk or do some form of exercise before creating; or use exercise as a break during creating.
- Rising early and working straight away works for some, whereas others work well through the night.
- Washing or showering is frequently used as part of creative preparation.
- Working creatively at the same time each day works well.
- Many cite food or food preparation rituals.
- Often people may use a particular type of notebook or device.

If you are interested in the rituals, habits and routines of highly creative people, you can find a wealth of stories in *Daily Rituals: How Great Minds Make Time, Find Inspiration and Get to Work* by Currey (2013).

Eric Maisel (2005), one of the first people to use the label 'creativity coach', has much to say about habits and rituals. One ritual that I have found personally helpful is to perform the following before I paint. Maisel calls this the 'Centring Sequence':

1. Come to a complete stop.
2. Empty yourself of expectations.
3. Name your work.
4. Trust your resources.
5. Embrace the present moment.
6. Return with strength.

He recommends doing each phrase to a full breath in and out, so it goes something like this:

(breath in) I am completely (breath out) stopping

(breath in) I expect (breath out) nothing from my painting

(breath in) I am working (breath out) on this painting right now

(breath in) I trust (breath out) my resources, myself, my ideas and materials

(breath in) I embrace (breath out) this moment

(breath in) I return (breath out) with strength

(Maisel 2005, p. 112)

Accomplished painter and one of only a few painters who shifted successfully between abstract and representational painting, Richard Diebenkorn made his internal, thinking 'rituals' clear:

Notes to myself on beginning a painting:

1 *Attempt what is not certain. Certainty may or may not come later (!). It may then be a valuable delusion.*
2 *The pretty, initial position which falls short of completeness is not be valued – except as a stimulus for further moves.*
3 *Do search. But in order to find other than what is searched for.*
4 *Use and respond to the initial fresh qualities but consider them absolutely expendable.*
5 *Don't 'discover' a subject – of any kind*
6 *Somehow, don't be bored – but if you must, use it in action. Use its destructive potential.*
7 *Mistakes can't be erased but they move you from your present position.*
8 *Keep thinking about Polyanna.*
9 *Tolerate chaos.*
10 *Be careful only in a perverse way.*

(cited in Livingston 1997, p. 115)

'Polyanna', if you don't know, is the term given to someone who is continually optimistic and always finds good in everything. Diebenkorn's advice seems very good, especially given the tough path many artists seem to tread.

Learning points

- Integration and a move away from the expansive phase is needed to bring ideas into reality.
- A point of creative action or creation occurs at the maximum point of contraction.

- The types of plans made and goals set should be carefully considered when working with creative people and creative projects.
- People vary in their planning preferences.
- Strong accountability, high pressure and large goals may hinder creativity.
- Small actions and steps may help creativity.
- The habits, ritual and working together may help creativity.

Note

1 It wasn't until I trained with Kaizen Muse Creativity Coaching and embraced the work of Dr Bob Maurer and Jill Badonsky that I started to understand the importance of 'small'. Of course, the word *kaizen* in Japanese equates to 'change for the better' or the notion of continuous improvement.

References

Badonsky, J. (2011) *Kaizen Muse Creativity Coaching Training Manual* (unpublished material).
Boyatzis, R. and Howard, A. (2013) When goal setting helps and hinders sustained, desired change, in David, S., Clutterbuck, D. and Megginson, D. (eds) *Beyond Goals: Effective Strategies for Coaching and Mentoring*. Farnham: Gower Publishing.
Clutterbuck, D. (2011) *A Great Spat over Goals*. Slough: Clutterbuck Associates.
Currey, M. (2013) *Daily Rituals: How Great Minds Make Time, Find Inspiration and Get to Work*. London: Picador.
Livingston, J. (1997) *The Art of Richard Diebenkorn*. Berkley, CA: University of California Press.
Maisel, E. (2005) *Coaching the Artist Within*. Novato, CA: New World Library.
Maurer, R. (2004) *One Small Step Can Change Your Life: The Kaizen Way*. New York: Workman Publishing.
McKee, A. (1991) *Individual Differences in Planning for the Future*. Unpublished PhD Dissertation Case Western Reserve University, Accessed 16/5/16, https://etd.ohiolink.edu/ap/10?0::NO:10:P10_ACCESSION_NUM:case1055356110.
Shalley, C. E. (1991) Effects of productivity goals, creativity goals and personal discretion on individual creativity. *Journal of Applied Psychology*, 76(2), 179–85.
Tharp, T. (2006) *The Creative Habit*. New York: Simon & Schuster Paperbacks.

Chapter 16

Reducing 'blocks' and restrictions

How are blocks created? What restricts flow and reduces forward energy in the creative process?

It is common for people to talk about being 'blocked' in relation to creativity and in coaching we also hear clients talk about blocks and obstacles. So by using the metaphor of a blood vessel, including its structure and function, it's quite easy to relate the blockages and restrictions in a blood vessel, to those that occur in creativity. Remembering that the blood vessel represents the creative process, we can see that flow can be impaired for several reasons:

- It may lack sufficient tone to contract if, for example, it's become stretched and floppy.
- It may be unable to expand, if it's inflexible and rigid.
- It might have a blockage, literally something in the way, like a blood clot or fatty narrowing that restricts or blocks blood flow.

We started to address the first two reasons earlier, but it's the last one that we will look at now. What is it that blocks creativity, gets in the way, restricts flow? How can coaching help?

I actually got very blocked when writing this section. I tried to separate out the causes of creative blocks and write about them separately, but of course they merge together, affect each other and the result is a blocking energy created by multiple factors.

I decided to walk my talk at this point and do some drawing to explore what a blockage in a vessel 'looks like'. Thankfully drawing helped and looking back to Figure 11.4 in Chapter 11 we can see the results of my scribble.

As experienced coaches, we are able to hear the complexity surrounding people's choices, actions and behaviours; why human beings say they want to do something, but often don't. This section is an opportunity to consider some of the factors that when combined, cause a block in the vessel that hinders creative activity (procrastination) or stop it all together (self-sabotage).

Much of the discussion in this section relates to the notion of self-sabotage, which in terms of creativity is a big issue. We will discuss it at length, but in the meantime hold onto the idea that everything we do has an effect elsewhere in our lives – in some way every action sabotages another. The trick is knowing whether we are unconsciously sabotaging our creative efforts, if so, figuring out how to stop.

Like self-sabotage, procrastination is a word frequently used when discussing creative desires. Procrastination, like self-sabotage, is the result of multiple factors combining to produce a blocking or restricting force.

We will explore the complex nature of both self-sabotage and procrastination as we travel through this chapter, but to understand what contributes to them we need to first look at the common reasons that people cite for not doing their creative thing. Exploring, challenging and perhaps dislodging these common factors first, usually unearths the deeper issues at play.

Time

I haven't got the time to take up painting.

I haven't got any space in my week to attend a poetry class.

I haven't got enough hours in the day to do the basics let alone creative stuff.

I have too much work on at the moment.

I'm too busy to finish my book.

My team are busy doing their regular work – they haven't got time to be creative!

We do creative stuff on away days when we have the time!

Lack of time is probably the most frequently cited reason for not getting around to doing something creative, whether it's at home or work. Coaching is great at helping people set nice goals around time management and structuring routines, but when we work with people we often find people sabotaging well-crafted plans. It often becomes clear that *time* could be created or be made available but is *used* in other ways.

One of the benefits of embracing small action, as we saw earlier, is that you don't need to find an hour or whole morning to do something creative. A five-minute sketch, or a paragraph written in minutes while waiting for the kettle to boil, is much more do-able and often results in moments of flow that spread out and find us sketching or writing for much longer. Doing snippets of activity, instead of having to find a whole day or evening, may also help address another problem. These days, time can be often viewed as extremely precious; people seem to want to squeeze every moment of value out of their days. Fear of wasting our time is perhaps one of the most understated modern fears, when choosing activities.

Is it worth doing?

Will it be a waste of time?

What will I have to really show for it?

These questions are often felt, but not often voiced.

Money

I can't afford to attend a class.

I don't have the money to buy a kiln.

I need to reduce my work hours to do this, but we need the money.

There is no money in pursuing my creative practice: art doesn't sell.

I don't have the money to buy x/y/z and can't start without it.

Team away days or time devoted to creativity means people are not working, which costs our business money.

Money and related issues are frequently cited alongside lack of time as the main reasons why people don't do something creative at work or home. Whilst it does play out in a work environment in indirect ways, it's often easier to see how this impacts at home. Unpicking financial issues related to pursuing a creative activity can help people move forward; however, they sometimes struggle to find small or inexpensive solutions or let go of deeply held beliefs about what they need to spend. If we are letting go of being completely non-directive coaches, we could offer suggestions such as:

- Pointers to free online courses that teach you to paint, write and so on.
- Where to find low-cost 'give a try' creativity sessions.
- Examples of artists or other people who create using nothing but found or recycled materials.

Naturally, if clients continue to say they want to paint/write/start a creative business and are still blocked by lack of money, there will often be deeper forces at play and we need to work to uncover what else is going on.

Physical space

There is no space at home for me to . . .

I don't want to do small things: I want to do big things.

I need to hire a studio, but can't justify that.

I want to make a mess and can't do that in the lounge.

I work best if I can leave my stuff out for days.

My neighbours would complain about the noise.

My husband likes the dining table to be kept clear and that's my only place to paint.

My work environment/office doesn't help me be creative.

We are starting to understand the impact of the work environment on creativity at work, and at home it is just as influential. Clearly a very individual issue, it depends on the relationship people have with their living space, who else lives there and what they perceive can or can't be achieved.

For some people, it might feel impossible to 'create' at home – there is just too much to do, too much to keep tidy, too many other people to look after, too many distractions. This is one reason that going to galleries or studios can provide essential inspiration or attending a regular writing class can be so important for some people.

Experimenting with space

I have long resisted getting a studio space outside of my home. In fact, as my children have grown up, I have lost the space I used to have. Eventually I got bored with citing 'lack of space' during discussions with my coach. I actually felt embarrassed that we had tackled everything else that stopped me painting and this was the only reason I had left.

So I decided to carry out a low-cost, low-impact experiment. I found a disused space locally and eventually asked the owner if I could to use it for three months in the run up to the school holidays. No big commitment or contract – easy in, easy out.

The thing with experiments is that they might actually prove very telling and you then have to face what to do with the learning after the experiment ends. I loved it. The space allowed my painting to blossom and my wellbeing soared. Other unexpected things happened to – other plans started to come to fruition. It was really strange, but after the success of the experiment I felt pushed to find a permanent solution, which was still very difficult.

I feel we underestimate the impact of the physical environment on the creative process. If you read about the studios of artists, writers or musicians you start to see how it is just so much more than having some space in which to put an easel or piano. These studios provide a thinking space; a bit like the virtual space created by coaching.

Finding ways for our clients to discover the impact of a change in physical environment on their creativity can be quite a challenge. It can come about naturally if we coach them in different environments and we could design experiments with our clients, so they can experience the impact of having a different space.

Distractions, addictions and obsessions

In our incredibly interconnected world of mobile phones, texts, instant messages, emails and games involving birds, not to mention the massive range of television programmes, abundance of books and magazines, a huge range of weekend activities plus all the other stuff that we have to do during the week, we are constantly bombarded with opportunities to distract ourselves from our creative work.

As T. S. Eliot said in *The Four Quartets* (2001), we are 'distracted from distraction by distraction', but who is to say what constitutes a distraction? Perhaps as Jill Badonsky (2010) kindly suggests, it might be a creative detour that leads us to a different place that is equally valid or even better than where we were headed. And for some creative, whimsical types there are real joys in distractions such as reading a beautiful poem, opening a new book and getting absorbed in it, finding an old record collection and spending the afternoon immersed in music. As we have seen, mindful wandering can actually allow creative new neural connections to take place.

As coaches, we need to work with our clients to raise awareness around distractions, especially if they are, in fact, being used consciously or unconsciously to avoid creative activity and sabotage creative intentions.

Distraction or addiction?

Many people are addicted to something, whether it be exercise, coffee, shopping, gossip and so on. In *The War of Art: Break Through the Blocks and Win Your Inner Creative Battles*, Steven Pressfield (2012) cites addictions including sex, Facebook and doughnuts as ways in which we get a cheap easy fix that keeps us from doing our work. Sadly, this is too often followed by feelings of emptiness. Perhaps we are getting our needs met through our addictions, whatever they may be.

As coaches, we need to help our clients spot unhelpful, addictive behaviours and raise awareness over their function and benefits and drawbacks. Without awareness and acknowledgement of the benefits of unhelpful behaviours, and how they replace unmet needs, are not likely to be tackled!

People

Being in an environment where others don't seem to get you or understand what it means to be highly creative can be very challenging. This could be at work, home, socially or a combination of all three. People can feel they are seen as 'odd balls', 'bucking the trend', 'anti-social', 'disruptive', 'over working' or 'playing around and not pulling their weight', and everything in between.

At work, particularly in a team of people who are very different to them, an especially creative person can at best feel isolated, misunderstood and unsupported. At worst, they might not have the space and time to percolate and develop ideas or products – the very thing they do best.

At home, an aspiring writer, who needs to carve time and space from a busy family life with all of its emotional and social demands, faces similar challenges. It takes good communication, resilience to guilt and courage to say 'I'm not coming to the family picnic today, I need to write' or 'thanks for the invite to the mums' drinky poos but I'm gonna make a cushion tonight'. Clearly, our clients' personal values start playing out strongly in these situations and we will explore those shortly.

Fears

Courage of all sorts is often required when people are developing new ideas, starting a creative pursuit or furthering their creativity in new ways. It could be that the more creative the idea, the more transformative, more off the wall it is, the more courage is probably required. But, of course, it also takes courage to even begin a modest creative pursuit if we have never done it before. Some people talk for years about starting to write or paint but a potent combination of a variety of fears keeps them from even getting off the starting block.

Some of the psychological conditions ideal for creativity we explored earlier included:

- Freedom from the fear of being judged, triggering feelings of 'I'm not good enough'.
- Freedom from the fear of making mistakes.
- Freedom to play.
- Courage to make a start and keep going.

In some ways, we could reduce all the barriers and blocks down to the fears many people share. These include fear of: not being good enough, failure, success, wasting time, being judged, criticism, disappointment, being seen as a fool, being seen – the list is endless.

Deeper challenges can also exist in relation to creativity including fear of: being unable to translate an idea into reality, being judged, disillusionment, rejection, not matching up to earlier standards, being swamped and losing oneself, 'running out of time in life, and, of course, being 'found out' – the good old imposter syndrome.

As we saw earlier, fear has a deep physiological and neurological basis. Our amygdala, the part of the brain which responds to fear, kicks in quite readily when something real or imagined scares us. Even the thought of starting a creative project can produce physical and behavioural responses, including stomach churning and all sorts of avoidance tactics that contribute to self-sabotage and procrastination.

We know that when we use intuitive questioning and deep listening and basic coaching skills, the unconscious fears of our client may come floating to the surface. At the root of many fears we find 'I am not a good enough human being' and 'I will be rejected'.

We could view the purpose of coaching as reducing 'fear' and working to increase self-acceptance and self-worth, all extremely valid, but I would also argue that outside of those things, we need our client to start making small steps in their chosen creative activities. Exposure to the creative activity and process, rather than just talking about it is vital.

We have seen the benefit of small steps in keeping the amygdala asleep. Outside of that, participation is key – we can build on it, reflect on how it went, figure out whether we enjoyed the activity or not, gain a sense of movement and skill acquisition. In activity we use the brain's natural ability to sculpt helpful, myelin rich pathways, so it gets easier and faster next time we participate.

So beyond all our talking about reducing fears and tackling unhelpful cognitive patterns, action is key.

Self-doubt, criticism and comparison

As we have just seen, the words 'I'm not good enough' are a common mantra in creativity. It stops people from starting, hinders progress, colours our perception and our judgement of what we do and what we produce. Self-doubt in creative activities and in creativity in general seems to be a given. Even those people who have reached the heights of creative achievement still have self-doubts. Of course there are benefits to self-doubt – it keeps people questioning and improving – but on the whole it needs to be kept in check.

Self-doubt can massively increase if precious new creative work or ideas are not protected or are critiqued insensitively. As coaches we need to be very aware that creative ideas are delicate and our role is not to provide critique or opinion. We also need to listen for the unhelpful effects of comparison. This can be especially damaging and unhelpful during the early stages of a creative journey or during a difficult time when perhaps personal resilience is low and sensitivity to rejection high. Comparison to others can be helpful if we are resilient enough to use it as a learning tool. However, if we constantly look at what other people are doing, often with skewed perception, it can really knock self-belief, reduce enjoyment in the activity and ultimately might lead us to disengage.

Conversations to help deal with rejection and criticism

Whose opinion matters and if so, why?

How can I strengthen my resolve whilst remaining flexible/learning from experience?

What are you assuming about this that is not helpful?

Think about someone famous who was rejected frequently (there are many), what might have helped them to keep going?

What are the benefits of giving up?

What do you risk by giving up?

What good things might come from this 'rejection'?

How can I remember to say 'So what!' when I receive internal or external criticism?

Overwhelm

Having too many choices, too many ideas or projects in progress, can often contribute to many people's blocked feeling, particularly highly creative people. Generating lots of ideas is part of the 'expansion' that creativity thrives on but can become part of a real block for people if it leads to overwhelm. Perhaps whilst they are working on one project another idea pops into your client's mind. They decide to Google it, start sketching ideas or scribbling thoughts. The idea grows and takes over from the project they were originally working on. Things don't get finished and a sense of frustration and exhaustion ensue.

Jumping between ideas, not developing them from beyond the earliest stages or switching to something else that grabs attention, can eventually lead people into low mood oscillating with high energy and the accompanying proliferation of further ideas. However, identifying the effects of overwhelm in our coaching clients can be tricky if we coach too tightly on one topic or goal without exploring what else is going on in our client's creative mind.

Conversations to explore overwhelm

How easy is it to maintain focus on this project alone?

What other ideas are enticing you at present?

What other projects are you currently working on?

How does your enjoyment of getting new ideas prevent you from focusing?

How can you resist the temptations of overwhelm?

How do you discern what is a helpful side project from an unhelpful distraction?

Beliefs

Strong societal and cultural beliefs exist in relation to creativity. These coupled with personal beliefs about our abilities, what we believe creativity to be and its place in the world, can impact significantly on creativity. Beliefs, whatever they are, can serve as glue that welds together unhelpful factors such as lack of time or money to produce a significant blockage, as shown in Figure 11.4, Chapter 11.

As we know, some personal beliefs often seem quite evident, expressed clearly as 'rules for living'. Other beliefs exist at an unconscious level and cause people to pass judgement on themselves and the world, which although subtle can still have significant impact. We can hear certain beliefs when we listen to our clients. If our listening is sufficiently attuned, beliefs fall out of coaching conversations quite naturally.

Personally, it's not just beliefs that I find fascinating, but how we actively seek evidence to support the beliefs we hold. Our perception becomes truly based on our state of mind. Changing what our perception has been tuned into from childhood to the present day is usually very challenging.

What we believe in relation to creativity relates to beliefs about ourselves, beliefs about our creative work and beliefs about the world.
  Beliefs about ourselves:

- *I'm not creative – I can't think of ideas.*
- *I'm not talented or skilled enough.*
- *I am not creative – I was no good at art at school.*
- *I'm only good at this particular thing.*
- *I'm too old to start changing/doing this.*
- *I'm too stressed/depressed to create.*
- *I'm not clever enough to learn to play an instrument.*
- *I'll be wasting my time/money/effort.*

Beliefs about our creativity:

- *What I have to say/write/do is not important enough.*
- *It's not creative enough.*
- *I'm not trained in _____ so shouldn't try it.*
- *What I create is pointless.*

Beliefs about the world:

- *Life is hard work – therefore creative practices are not real work.*
- *I'll never make a proper living from painting.*
- *Nobody will care about my work.*
- *Being a writer is not a real job.*
- *Real artists go to art school – therefore I am not a real artist.*
- *Most artists/creative people are poor.*
- *There is no market for what I am doing.*

As a coach, what beliefs do you personally hold in relation to creativity? What do you currently do, as a coach, to help your clients become aware of and tackle beliefs that are hindering them?

Over the years, one of the simplest ways I have found to start exploring beliefs is to use sentence completion. Sentence completion is best done quickly, so that people don't start analysing and forming their answers too much.

For example:

People who are creative are . . .

Creativity is . . .

Creativity isn't . . .

I believe that poetry is . . .

I believe that writing a book requires . . .

Successful watercolourists are . . .

People who paint amazing pictures have . . .

Having new ideas requires . . .

I believe I am not creative because . . .

I believe I am creative because...

I believe Van Gogh (or whoever) was an amazing artist because . . .

People aren't creative because . . .

People can become creative by . . .

I am at my creative best when . . .

As coaches we are familiar with helping our clients identify beliefs, be they helpful or unhelpful, to scrutinize them consciously and support them as they assess the basis and evidence for that belief. However, we need to remember that we are often trying to counter years of evidence gathered to support their beliefs and years of 'brain sculpting' according to those beliefs. These beliefs impact so unconsciously, automatically and quickly that we usually don't know the belief is kicking in.

A cognitive behavioural approach can really help. Part of this approach puts beliefs on trial and helps people to find evidence that counteracts the belief – this is central to shifting perception. However, cognition is only one way of dealing with and experiencing beliefs. Whatever we do as coaches, we need to acknowledge how our beliefs are experienced at a physical and somatic, emotional and soul/spiritual level. We also have to take into consideration what neuroscience teaches us; our brain is plastic and can be changed, but it takes repeatedly new input to do so. This is where the behavioural bit is so important but often gets left out as we focus on cognitions. Actions can speak louder and have greater impact than words and can help bypass long held, difficult to shift beliefs and accompanying inner dialogue.

The process of noticing, understanding and re-shaping beliefs can be a long game and may well be a necessary one, but, as I have emphasized before, we also really need to get people moving and taking regular creative action, however small that action might be. We could also encourage our clients to take a 'short-cut' when they feel an unhelpful belief arising that is interfering with their creative goal. When a 'gremlin' or belief says, 'You are not good enough to do this', you could just say, 'so what, I'm going to do it anyway...!' Jill Badonsky suggests you respond in this way, just like a toddler would. If you have never tried this, trust me, it can be very effective!

For example, the gremlin or belief may shout: 'You'll never be a successful writer... you're not good enough!'

You shout back, 'So what, I'm going to do it anyway!'

There is significant measure in just saying '**** it, I'm gonna do it anyway' or 'I don't care what others think' or 'I'd rather do it, have fun and make a mess, than not do it at all'. Otherwise, entering a lengthy debate with ourselves can result in 'paralysis by analysis'. My overall opinion is that there is measure in doing both. We can help clients raise awareness around their beliefs regarding creativity whilst at the same time saying to themselves, 'actually, I am going to do it anyway'.

We also know that there are often helpful aspects to what appears to be an 'unhelpful' belief, and this understanding can be very empowering in terms of creative practice. Working with beliefs is not about annihilating everything that appears negative. Sometimes seemingly unhelpful or negative beliefs can help us ensure that an idea is worth developing and we might question its relevance. As we saw earlier, such discrimination and evaluation is important in determining whether an idea is truly new, original, relevant and worth pursuing.

After eliciting a belief, whether you perceive it to be unhelpful or not, you could look at each belief in turn and ask:

- *How helpful is that belief in relation to your creative goal?*
- *What purpose is this belief serving?*
- *What could you replace that belief with?*

Here are some 'affirmations' to reframe/replace some common, unhelpful beliefs that often arise about the creative process:

- *Creativity exists in all areas of life.*
- *I don't know where this will lead, but I will have fun in the process.*
- *Trying is better than not doing it all.*
- *Creativity is a choice – I can awaken it in me.*
- *There is no right or wrong way to do it.*
- *Creativity is a journey.*
- *Many successful artists/writers were not trained.*
- *I am good enough.*
- *Even though I doubt my abilities, I'm going to do it anyway.*
- *Whose opinion counts anyway?*

Many coaching processes impact on our belief system. When we are coaching creativity we know that lowering pressure and expectations reduces fear and stress; it will also help counter feelings of not being good enough. Approaching a project as playful exploration and letting go of the outcome is very helpful. It promotes the 'openness to experience' that is so important in creativity. We need to release the stranglehold that beliefs exert in relation to creativity, if we are to truly help.

Values

Just as beliefs can serve as the glue that sticks together a multitude of creative challenges to form a block, so does the impact of our value system. Holding conflicting values can cause all sorts of chaos, especially if our values are not congruent with our aspirations or current situation.

Values never exist in isolation; they are always contextual and complex:

- What are my personal values for living?
- What values do I have related to creativity?
- What values do my family/kin have related to creativity?
- What values do my social network/peers have related to creativity?
- What values exist in wider society related to creativity?
- What values exist in the creative domain (e.g. art world, writing profession, my organisation etc.)?

Even if we just look at how personal values for living interact with values related to creativity, we can see how complex things quickly become.
 Consider this:
 Your client expresses a desire to paint big oil paintings. You do some values work and there seem to be some possible conflicts. They express valuing order/organisation/tidiness but they also seem to express a desire to be messy/muddily/experimental, often required for creating large works in paint.
 Consider this:
 Your client really wants to write a book. You both decide to do some work around values and find that they value social connecting/relating/family very highly but also express a need for solitude/peace. They are having trouble finding the space and time to write.
 Can you see what impact this possible values conflict might have? One way to explore possible conflict is to 'blend' values, using circular questions such as:

> *How could you be 'creatively organised'? Or be organised in a creative way?*
>
> *How might playfulness and order sit together?*
>
> *In what way could you have reliable fun and in what way could you have fun reliably?*

Another way is to share knowledge of the creative process in relation to values and the challenges that often arise, for example:

> *We have just been exploring your personal values and seen how important 'control' and 'orderliness' are for you. Research shows us that creativity is often helped by willingness to make mistakes and experiment, so I am curious to know how that sits with you?*

or

> *So achievement and success are very important for you, however, research shows that high pressure and high expectations can be unhelpful in fostering creativity – I'm curious to know what sense you make of that?*

Perfectionism

> *Creativity is allowing yourself to make mistakes. Art is knowing which ones to keep.*
>
> Scott Adams (2015)

Perfectionism is one of the biggest killers of creativity, especially the exploratory and transformation types of creativity that require us to make mistakes, try out ideas, experiment with little expectation. The type of creativity that needs us to be relaxed about making a mess while having no idea how it might work out! This is true whether you want to learn to paint or come up with creative ideas at work. However, different creative goals may require varying degrees of experimentation. It may be, for example, that someone who knows a successful 'recipe' for producing watercolour paintings might not want to let go of the perfectionism that serves her purpose well. However, she still needs to accept that some of the sheets of her nice white sketch pad will get spoiled and that some paintings just won't work out.

Teams needing to enhance creativity and come up with ideas often have to let go of the search for the best idea and focus on exploring and playing, possibly longer than feels comfortable; they may need to accept that the 'perfect' idea may not appear in the time scale that they have allotted. The person who chooses to make a full time career out of a creative practice, be it writing, composing or painting, will understand fully the need to get over the need for everything he produces to work out well. The artist, who really wants to develop ideas or propositions into a body of congruent work, needs to be really comfortable with experimentation, mess and numerous 'failures'.

My eyes were fully opened to this when I gained insight into how art exhibitions are curated, be they major exhibitions or local art events. People only show the things they are really pleased with; their best work. They might show some things in progress, but these are still selected very carefully. No one shows you the absolute rubbish that they have produced en route. You will never see the drafts and re-writings of novels either, only the finished, highly edited and polished, published book (she says chuckling).

Self-sabotage

Fears, self-doubts, beliefs, perfectionism, practical challenges and so on all interact and often result in self-sabotage. Self-sabotage is a real problem for creative goals and, if we are not aware of it, can completely scupper the good intentions and plans that our clients often express.

A large part of the whole coach approach is to help people 'get out of their own way', and the ways we get in our own way and sabotage ourselves are often far reaching and unconscious.

On a personal level, my favourite methods of self-sabotage are:

- Taking on too much work, so I don't have time to paint.
- Poor boundaries, especially with family and friends.
- Getting rid of helpful habits.
- Saying I have no choice, when I really do.
- Poor boundaries . . . again.
- Putting myself and painting last, always.

I could go on and on.

As coaches, it is essential that we help our clients understand how and why they sabotage themselves and there are many ways of exploring self-sabotage. Unpicking the issues previously explored will go a long way, but ultimately there needs to be greater energy for the aspired activity, rather than against it. There need to be more reasons to do something creative than not. We have many ways as coaches to explore decisional balance and I imagine that you are well equipped to do so. For me there are two key questions that I work with in relation to creativity:
The first is:

What are the benefits of not achieving this?

I often ask myself this in relation to painting and am happy to share my answers:

- I don't have to die with a loft full of paintings that no one wants.
- I could spend more time at the gym keeping well
- I could spend more time with my family and friends.
- I don't have to face the fact that I might not be that good at this.
- I would save money and might have a tidier, cleaner home.
- I wouldn't be seen as the 'mad' mum of the playground.

I think you get the picture (excuse the pun). To shift the decisional balance towards painting, it is clear that the 'fors' need to be very potent, very inspiring and compelling.

The second inquiry is:

How comfortable are you with the success that you really desire?

This question is the starting point to a deeper discussion about self-sabotage and comes from Dr Bob Maurer (2004). Using this question, Bob takes his clients back in time to when they were a child. He asks them to imagine they are presenting their desired future self to their parents – the successful businesswoman, professional artist or whatever they want to be. He asks his clients to notice how comfortable they are with how their parents relate to this person. If the parents from the past don't like the person your client desires to become, they are likely to unconsciously sabotage their efforts. At a deep level, we are often still seeking acceptance from our parents.

Self-sabotage is often trying to keep us safe. It is somehow protecting us from rejection and also the hurt that may result from our failures, so, if you repeatedly hear self-sabotage in your conversations with clients, please make sure it gets full attention.

Conversations to explore self-sabotage

What do people mean when they talk about 'sabotaging their own plans'?

What are your favourite ways of sabotaging your plans?

Take some time to explore what success might look like for you. What broader implications might this have?

How comfortable do you feel with the success you desire?

What are the benefits of not achieving your goal?

How do you get in your own way?

If you were at your best, what would you do right now?

What are you assuming about this all that is not helpful?

A final thought about this thing called procrastination

Helping our creative process means we need to help that blood vessel be reasonably free of blocks. It needs to be able to expand, contract and act regularly, which is all about overcoming self-sabotage and procrastination. Like self-sabotage, procrastination is a language short-cut and is used to describe the combined effect of all those fears, beliefs, practical issues and daily stuff. Procrastination results in us not taking action, whether it's regular action or maybe any action at all.

If we unpick the previous issues and find ways to move into action, the power of procrastination should naturally reduce. To me the golden key to overcome procrastination is to take small, really small, fun, low pressure actions; ones that come with few expectations. This, in conjunction with the other 'talking' activities, can move mountains.

Conversations to explore procrastination

When you say you procrastinate, what do you mean?

What are your favourite ways of procrastinating?

What are the good things about procrastinating?

How can you start to notice when you are procrastinating and nip it in the bud?

Are you procrastinating or just having trouble making a decision?

Are you procrastinating or is this part of your process? How will you know when you have procrastinated for long enough?

What would make it easier to engage with your project/passion? What helped in the past?

What thoughts entice your participation? (JB)

Conclusion

In coaching clients with a creative goal in mind, we need to unpick global terms such as procrastination and self-sabotage, as they express the results of many other issues in play. As we do so, we need to work beyond the surface issues initially given, such as lack of time or money, and find what other unhelpful and often deeper things are in the way.

Learning points

- Procrastination and self-sabotage are the results of many other issues.
- Time, money, space and distractions are commonly cited barriers to creative practice, but often mask deeper issues.
- Coaching can work to uncover deeper creative issues including addictions, perfectionism, overwhelm, unhelpful beliefs, conflicting values and a variety of fears.

References

Adams, S. (2015) *The Famous Quote I Never Said*. Online Blog. Accessed 15/10/15, http://blog.dilbert.com/post/122081192901/the-famous-quote-i-never-said.

Badonsky, J. (2010) *The Nine Modern Day Muses (and a Bodyguard)*. San Diego, CA: Renegade Muses Publishing House.
Eliot, T. S. (2001) *The Four Quartets* (reprint). London: Faber Poetry.
Maurer, R. (2004) *One Small Step Can Change Your Life: The Kaizen Way*. New York: Workman Publishing.
Pressfield, S. (2012) *The War of Art*. New York: Black Irish Entertainment LLC.

Part V

An invitation to coach in a different way

I truly believe that if you want to take a more creative approach, working with creativity rather than against it, and you understand the underpinning research, there are unlimited possibilities for your coaching! I hope that with the help of some of the 'evidence' from the accepted sciences you can view your creative practice as evidence based. I am sure that there will be much debate around my assertion of this – do we need each tiny tool and process to be individually researched and evaluated to death or is it sufficient to know that the activity is based on sound principles?

Exploring some of the references and books mentioned earlier will give you a fabulous resource of activities and tools for you to adapt and play with. Do you really need to do another course to get some pencils or crayons and use them with a client?

The activities, tools and case studies in this final part embrace the principles discussed throughout. Namely:

- Evoking and disrupting.
- Playing, laughing and letting go.
- Doing and being.
- Moving and seeing differently.
- Thinking with things.
- Exploring different 'languages' (I don't mean French!).
- Exploring the 'we' of creativity.

Chapter 17

Writing – journaling, poetry and story

As we saw earlier, writing is being used more and more in therapy and research in recent years. In coaching, several forms of writing hold immense value including journaling, writing a life memoir, creative writing, poetry and the process of story making. We also looked earlier at structured writing activities such as a sentence completion exercise when discussing beliefs.

Writing in support of coaching was explored by Doherty (2009) who highlighted its significant value. This included surfacing the 'undiscussables' related to the coaching and issues at hand. Doherty used writing alongside coaching during his PhD, finding that writing accelerated and deepened the coaching process. Doherty offers some great prompts for clients to use after coaching, such as 'The things that I forgot to say to my coach during our last coaching session were . . .'. This glorious prompt opens up the coaching session again, inviting the client to delve deeper and perhaps express what they forgot or didn't feel able to say at the time or things they have only just realised.

When using any form of writing, whether it's within or alongside a coaching session, it's vital to help clients embrace imperfection and put pen to paper; they can always go back and create perfection afterwards if need be. When contemplating 'writers block' I am reminded of the quote from American poet William Stafford:

> *There is no such thing as writer's block for writers whose standards are low enough.*
>
> William Stafford, Poet

It's all about making a start, however small, clunky, clumsy or dreadful the writing may feel.

Journaling

Whether it's a personal journal, reflective journal for learning purposes or 'morning pages' (Cameron 1995) the benefits of journaling can be far reaching. Deepening insight, working through challenges and expressing what cannot be said verbally is not helpful for all sorts of people.

Barbara's story: journaling for wellbeing

'I need to write – it keeps me well', said Barbara who had come to coaching in a state of desperation, rather than desire.

'Tell me your story about writing', I asked.

Barbara: 'I write and I need to write to stay healthy. I know this now but didn't until I was in deep trouble many years ago, but making it a part of my daily life has eluded and frustrated me ever since. Creative writing has helped me through two episodes of ill health in my life. Journaling especially helped in what now seems a truly miraculous way.'

Jen: 'Tell me more about those two times.'

Barbara: 'The first time was in 1981. I had a back injury and the doctor had basically told me to lie flat, take painkillers and wait for it to get better. I was getting more anxious by the day and by that particular afternoon I was at the end of my tether – two months I'd been lying there and I was no better – in fact if anything the pain was getting worse. I was lying on a makeshift bed on the sitting room floor. Around me was a clutter of toys, empty cups and glasses, books and papers and an upright vacuum cleaner. Something snapped and in desperation I inwardly cried for help. Intuitively I had a deep urge to write. An empty envelope and pencil were within reach and words poured on to the page. The verse was philosophical and certainly hadn't come through my conscious thought processes. Then I had an overpowering 'knowing' that I had to stand up, which was very scary because I was going directly against the doctor's advice – and I was alone in the house. Yet that inner prompting was strong and I knew I had to try.

Using the vacuum cleaner to pull myself up, I gritted my teeth as my weight shifted and I lifted myself to an upright position. Carefully, slowly I began to move and was able to take several steps before subsiding back on to the mattress on the floor. Over the following weeks, my back problem slowly got better.'

Jen: 'And what sense do you make of that now?'

Barbara: 'I didn't know what happened at the time, but now believe that that brief expression had been a release and somehow empowering. My nursing career was at an end and yet I knew I would be OK. It marked a turning point in my recovery but also in my career. Afterwards I attended a creative writing course, learned to type and got a job as a secretary in the Health Service. I started to write short stories and my confidence in my writing grew.'

Jen: 'And there was another time when writing helped?'

Barbara: 'The second time took place in 2006. I'd retired from work, my dad had died, we'd moved house twice, I was living in a new area and had been diagnosed and was being treated for breast cancer. It felt like I was in a maze; there was no structure, routine or signposts and it was as if my life

	was on hold. But one day, I was sorting out my bookshelf when a book literally fell on my foot. It was *The Artist's Way* by Julia Cameron and I had bought it some years ago and never opened it. Now I did so, read a few words about journaling and her method of working with 'Morning Pages' and knew that this would help me. So I decided to organise some writing time each morning and followed her instructions to the letter. It took about several weeks but slowly the mists cleared, life regained its rhythm, purpose and a semblance of normality.'
Jen:	'And what's in the way of writing now?'
Barbara:	'I don't know really, but I need to write regularly to support my health. Yet once I'm well, life takes over and in my busyness I don't make time each day. First of all, I can't write to order – once an editor gave me a basic plot and asked me to write a story around it. The shutters came down; I felt I couldn't write around someone else's plot and stopped trying. There's also some sort of inner conflict that keeps me procrastinating and doing anything except write. I will dust, make phone calls, clean – and then find my writing time has gone.'
Jen:	'So various things get in the way. When you look back, what helped get you going, when you were able to write regularly?'
Barbara:	'When I can lose myself in the process and get out of my own way, the words pour out and do make sense. Sometimes the voice doesn't seem to be mine, but these passages turn out to be my best writing – thinking and logic don't come into it much. Making time and having a structure for this in my busy day, though, means that I can write in this unstructured way. I have to trust that that the *magic* will work.'
Jen:	'So what now needs to happen to get this going again?'
	Barbara was silent for a long time and I waited quietly.
Barbara:	'I suppose,' she said slowly, 'if I somehow get into the routine, you know, find a definite half hour during the day when I'm not tired and when I've cleared the urgent stuff of the day, that might help. Hmm . . . the other thing is I tend to get stressed and impatient and blocked if nothing happens straight away. That's where the Julia Cameron's Morning Pages helped me a lot . . . I suppose I could get that out again.'
Jen:	'How feasible is that?'
Barbara:	'W-ell . . . I could start doing the Morning Pages again early in the morning – before I let the other stuff crowd in and take over. If I leave it until later in the day, it rarely happens. That might work I suppose – I can't do both – well I don't think I can . . . I just know that when I start to write again, I will feel so much better.'

Barbara pondered for a moment and then straightened up and I noticed how much her face had changed and she looked hopeful and much more positive.

Poetry

There is a growing interest for using poetry in all sorts of ways, within coaching. In *Poetry as Leadership* (2014), creative leadership coach Sam Chittenden explores this in depth and we will also meet her work using theatre and improvisation in coaching later on. Another coach using poetry at the heart of his work is accountant and coach David Adams. His workshop transformed my relationship with poetry and led me to all sorts of personal insights.

Poetry in business by David Adams

> They thought I was mad when I tried to import an American concept in to the UK business arena: it was like putting up garlic to a vampire or kryptonite to Superman.

When at school poetry was thrust down our throats we almost gagged, until the sixth form and an enlightened school master introduced us to Andrew Marvel, Shakespeare's sonnets, Allen Ginsberg's 'Howl', we began to think differently. I even learned to use my poetry as a means of creating what we might call 'interaction' with girls.

I pursued a career in stockbroking and corporate finance, a world away from poetry, but then again TS Eliot was an investment banker and even in recent times we have heard that Steve Jobs wrote poetry, whilst on acid . . . allegedly.

So, what about using poetry in coaching? Unbelievably, I have found that all sorts of people, whether they feel they are creative or not, have found through doing certain exercises that their minds and even their lives can be changed. This seems to happen whether they profess to like poetry or not. Indeed, at one recent workshop, a very left-brained insurance chief executive said that he always thought poetry was sh*t until that morning. Another called me recently and told me that, whilst I wouldn't remember him, he had attended a session for interim managers that I had delivered a couple of years back, that he had hated every minute of it but that it had changed his life. He had been able to recognise through the exercise we undertook that he was the person who was holding him back, not his family, not his colleagues, not the lack of cash but as, C. S. Lewis (and others) said 'we are what we believe we are.'

A wonderful exercise I enjoy using in coaching is 'I am from'. The original seems to have emanated from 'Where I'm From', a poem by George Ella Lyon (born 1949, Kentucky), which can be found on her website www.georgeellalyon.com. There are even examples of how it can be used for study purposes.

The exercise invites people to use their background. Here is my example, based on the structure of the original poem:

> I am from him of the slitty eyes from Belarus
>
> And he who I knew not from Lithuania

I am from Harpurhey

A poor suburb of Manchester then

As now

But not for long – 5 days perhaps

I am from Eve – yes, Eve Adams and Bert

From Newcastle and textiles

And from a good school

And on the stage

I am from my father who taught me

To read and taught me business

And selling and negotiating

I am from John who taught me about

Girls

And Bryan who taught me drama

And Stanley who taught me about

Accounting

And David who taught me stock-broking

And partners' ways and

I am from the stage and performing

And being the centre of attention

And from my single parent mother,

Whilst my father was fighting

Till I was three.

That's where I'm from

As well as from my clients

As well as from my friends

As well as from my daughters and grand kids

And over 40 years with she

Who also taught me many things

And now, with Dene.

(continued)

(continued)

It's easy to help your clients create their own. (On the other hand please don't be like the guy from Lancaster, Pennsylvania, who said that he was from his ma and pa, his cat and dog and that was it!)

Yet another exercise (possibly best in group coaching) in creativity using poetry is what I call 'Present Reality, Future Reality'. First of all, think of a situation in business or, indeed in domestic life, that you would like to change. It could be your finances, your level of repeat business, your relationship with a direct report or a significant other. It should be something that perhaps you have struggled with for a while or tended to put off.

Present Reality		**Future Reality**

Using the table, jot down a few bullet points in the column headed 'Present Reality' that describes the situation. Then, turn to the third column. Write in that column several bullet points that describe your ideal situation (these need not correspond point by point to the first column).

*Next, write **just one word**, in the central column (that is not one word for each bullet point just one single word that represents what is stopping you getting from present to future reality). And, it's the first word that comes in; the word that comes into your mind before you start judging and analysing. In my experience of using this exercise over the years, there are frequent words such as 'fear', 'time' and 'cash' and there have been words like 'me' and 'inertia'.*

Now write the following on a fresh piece of paper:

I want to write about ....

Add the chosen word onto the dotted line, therefore if the word in the chart was 'fear' then the first line of the poem will be 'I want to write about fear'. You or your client should be reminded that, unlike at school, poems do not need to rhyme or scan they just need to flow with the breathing, but before doing so read them a poem to put them in the mood such as 'Love After Love' by Derek Walcott or 'Faith' by David Whyte, both of which are easily obtained online.

After the reading ask them to write their poem. There may be a few false starts, some attempting a limerick or even a haiku but they then settle down and just write. It is quite amazing what comes out. Here is an example written by MB, CEO of a college of further education – he is a business man not an academic:

I want to write about...... **'*Me*'**

It's not all about me is it? Is It?

I have become something different, but who am I where have I come from?

Where is the boyhood me who ran, laughed, played so mischievously

> *Where is the young man with purposeful stride, determined and with youth on his side*
>
> *The angry young man I left behind that fought to survive, the struggle with self and burning with passion and desire inside*
>
> *Belief and Pride*
>
> *Look at me now still determined, still learning about me, from me and others and I see and feel the change inside*
>
> *All this has shaped me thus far, a far cry from the past me as I look toward the future me*
>
> *Who am I now, what will I become next?*
>
> *Excitement, joy, no more fear, doubt or regret*
>
> *Celebrating with hearty cheer, mischief and fear given way to belief, compassion, living in the here and now*
>
> *Acceptant, contented, proud and me*
>
> *For now!*
>
> If we have time, the delegates then coach each other using their poems, pulling out the subconscious meaning. In some cases, we use the 'Fierce Conversation' techniques of Susan Scott or 'clean language' style coaching. This is extraordinarily powerful. They are also asked to type out their efforts and share when going away from the workshop with life and business partners. Again some lovely stories of greater understanding are generated and, of course, what is said in the room, stays in the room. This is the key to sharing their most intimate thoughts.
>
> This technique has been taken to the boardroom, the living room and the bedroom to great and lasting effect. It enables people to understand their 'partners' better and gives them the deep knowledge to help their mutual development. As we all know development in business and in personal lives is one of the keys to success. This does much more, in my view, it helps people look at themselves and others in a new light and helps them to be more creative, to be more innovative and thus to achieve better results. If, by using these techniques we can change attitudes, our own and others, change cultures, absorb higher values, we will surely reach those higher planes that Maslow talked about.
>
> David Adams, Unlocking Creativity™
> See also Adams, D. *Well-Versed: A Powerful Guides to Business Success* (2015).

Ishikawa: engineering a poem

My work with engineer and coach Peter Mayes has led to some fantastic experimentation combining engineering problem-solving tools and creative approaches. My favourite to date is creating Ishikawa poetry from the starting point of a cause and effect diagram (or *Ishikawa* in Japanese meaning fish), a problem analysis tool often used in engineering.

150 An invitation to coach in a different way

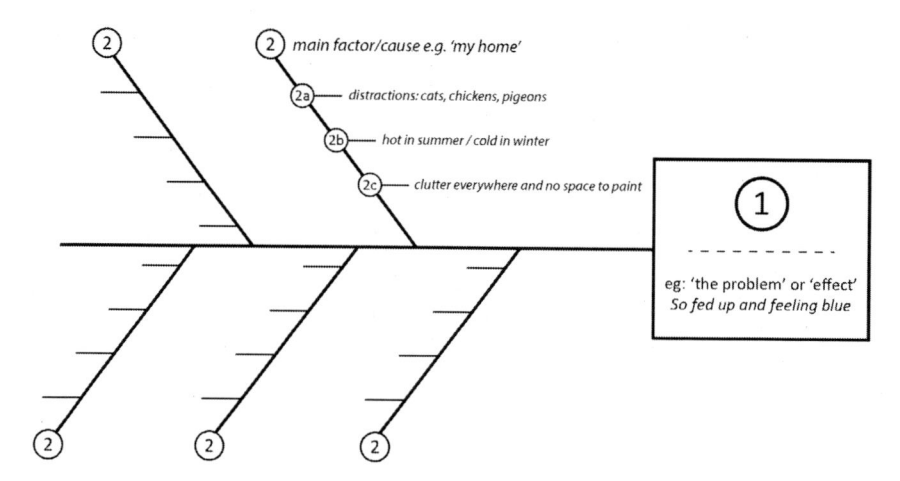

Figure 17.1 Ishikawa: engineering a poem

Using the template in Figure 17.1, insert the problem statement (the effect) in the box on the right (1). This is the 'engineering' stance – being quite logical and analytical about solving a problem, however, the problem can be anything: a personal challenge like lack of confidence or low mood; a lack of income in a business or product that is not selling well; a team that's not performing well and so on.

Next, insert the main factors contributing to the problem. These are the main 'bones' of the fish (2). Try and identify four or five. Next, take each factor one at a time and analyse it, identifying at least three possible causes (2a,b,c) behind each contributing factor. Continue until you have filled in the fish diagram, which results in a sort of mind map.

Next create the poem as follows:

Poem title: .... *(insert the problem statement (1))*

What's that all about?

Perhaps it's... *insert one of the factors (main fish bone (2))*

and then insert the possible causes or reasons behind that factor:

(2a)..

(2b)..

(2c)..

Oh, what do I do?

***Perhaps it's**................................. (insert one of the other main fish bones (2))*

and then insert the possible causes or reasons behind that factor:

(2a)..

(2b)..

(2c)..

Continue in this way, until you have used the main factors to start each verse of the poem, with the causes/reasons creating the lines of the verse. You should end up with around four or five verses in your poem. Here's one a client created during a workshop:

'I am so fed up and feeling blue'

What's that all about?
Perhaps it's the 'place' I am dwelling in?
Distracted by chickens, cats and pigeons
Freezing in the winter, boiling in the summer
No space for clay
Oh what do I do?

Perhaps it's the money?
Trickling streams, insufficient flow
Scrimping and scraping all the time
Never enough for David - he wants new window and a boat!
Oh what do I do?

Perhaps it's me?
Needing solace to create, but so lonely
So many projects, so little return
Managing my ever changing mood
Oh what do I do?

Perhaps it's the work?
Uncertain and flying from famine to feast
Wanting to do it my way, come what may
Unwilling to play the game . . .
Oh what should I do now?

The last line has the words 'Oh what should I do now?' added. In some ways this is an invitation for the client to reflect on their poem and identify some points of action. For this client it became clear to her that she needed to change her working environment; home working was just not for her.

Story

Vogel (2012) notes that 'narrative techniques are evident in coaching even where no explicit narrative methodology is referenced' (p. 1). Stories just tumble out of us naturally – it's one of the main ways we make sense of our world and communicate it to others. Creating 'story' is perhaps the task of coaching but story is also the content of coaching (Vogel 2012).

There are many simple ways to use story in coaching, which embody both the power of storytelling and story writing. All can be done within a coaching session or maybe as coaching 'homework'.

Booker (2005) identifies seven basic plots evident in universal stories which are: overcoming the monster, rags to riches, the quest, voyage and return, comedy, tragedy and rebirth. You will find these in all sorts of novels and films and also 'hear' some of these common storyline's coming through your client's stories. Familiarising yourself with these storylines may give you and your client an opportunity to explore how their story might continue. For example, upon hearing a pattern to your client's story such as a rebirth you could say:

> *I hear that you are going through a period of re-examining who you are and what you do in life. It reminds me of the story of xxxx (mention a rebirth story here, of which there are many including 'The Frog Prince' and 'It's a Wonderful Life'). Do you know this story? In it the character experiences . . .*

This invites the client to recall what can happen in a rebirth story and decide how, or indeed if, it has any relevance to their own story. It can also give them a sense of possible outcomes or perhaps a sense of hope.

The hero's journey[1] is a very well-known storyline. Joseph Campbell described and explored it deeply in *The Hero with a Thousand Faces* (1993). His model is reflected in plots such as *Star Wars* and *The Lord of the Rings* trilogy.

Its familiarity makes it easy to work with in coaching sessions. Familiarise your client briefly with the classic hero's journey story structure, describing the keys elements and stages of this archetypal journey:

- The Hero (your client).
- The preparation, the calling, developing the resources.
- The journey, the struggles/fights, finding the gift/the turning point.
- The return home, the sharing of the gifts and learning.

In your coaching session, or perhaps as homework, ask your client to write their own story, in relation to the current goal or challenge, using the hero's journey as a guide. I think it has merit either way, but only leave this as homework if you feel your client is able to work without support. Otherwise talk through it together, with you prompting, exploring and scribing, so that your client can relax and just talk.

A simpler way is to just provide your clients with some prompts and allow them to fill in the gaps. Mark Beeman from North Western University is doing on-going research into how people fill in the gaps when presented with incomplete stories (Beeman 2015). Our brains seem to hear and understand that if there is gap, the inference is that it should be filled. We can use this to our advantage and provide prompts for our clients to complete, such as:

> **'Once upon a time . . .'** *(Introduce the hero/client and main characters)*
>
> **'One day . . .'** *(A challenge occurs or a choice to change is made. Name this)*
>
> **'And so . . . and then . . .'** *(What happens in the story? What challenges come up, what resources does the hero draw upon, what are the pivotal points?)*
>
> **'In the end . . .'** *(What was the outcome, how did it turn out, what was the main learning?)*

The use of prompts is a simple effective tool in coaching, as we have seen, when exploring beliefs. Knowing your client well and having heard their story to date, together with the challenges, choose an appropriate prompt from which your client can continue writing (or exploring verbally with you, the coach scribing). Here are some suggestions:

- **** (insert client's name) turned the corner. Feeling slightly weary due to the long journey, she now faced a crossroads . . . .
- The end was clearly in sight now and **** felt a surge of energy, which . . .
- She/he had been walking in the forest for some time now and felt quite lost, but suddenly . . .
- The path had been clear until now, but fog had descended quickly and she felt . . .

Again, depending on what would suit your client, you could tailor the prompt to their current challenge, ask pertinent questions or just leave them to write freely and explore what comes up. Much will depend on what you feel your client will respond to best.

Note

1 While I enjoy the hero's journey, I feel it is sometimes over used in coaching. It can lead to a sense of 'this will end well, if I just keep going' or 'unless I overcome this, there won't be a happy ending and I will have failed where everyone succeeds' and doesn't really acknowledge that some things just don't work out! This heroic paradigm has been prevalent in our society for many years and could be seen as the driving force behind entrepreneurship and capitalism. Conversely it perhaps fuels the never ending search for happiness prevalent in society today.

References

Adams, D. (2015) *Well-Versed: A Powerful Guide to Business Success*. St Albans, Herts: Panoma Press.

Beeman, M. (2015) North Western University website. Accessed 15/10/15, http://groups.psych.northwestern.edu/mbeeman/research.htm#Inferences.

Booker, C. (2005) *The Seven Basic Plots: Why We Tell Stories*. London: Bloomsbury.

Cameron, J. (1995) *The Artist's Way*. London: Pan Books.

Campbell, J. (1993) *The Hero with a Thousand Faces*. New York: Fontana

Chittenden, S. (2014) *Poetry as Leadership*. UK: Goodreads.

Doherty, D. (2009) The discovery of 'writing as inquiry' in support of coaching practice, in Megginson, D. and Clutterbuck, D. (2009) *Further Techniques for Coaching and Mentoring*. Oxford: Elsevier.

Vogel, M. (2012) Story matters: an inquiry into the role of narrative in coaching, *International Journal of Evidence Based Coaching and Mentoring*, 10(1), 1.

Chapter 18

Visual processes

Traditional coaching generally relies on our ability to verbalise, think through and describe situations and put our feelings into words. This involves often high levels of concentration and conscious, cognitive processing. This is not the only way. As we know, artists and art therapists use visual language and techniques of all kinds to access internal thoughts, feelings and wisdom and also to communicate this to others.

As coaching evolves we really need to take this on board. There are many easy ways we can use visual techniques that require very little in the way of materials.

Working with metaphor using a visual process

Apparently, Aristotle considered use of metaphor to be a sign of genius. He felt that any individual who had the capacity to perceive similarities between two separate areas of existence and link them together was a person of special gifts. What similarities do two utterly different 'things' share, if any? Perhaps if we understand one thing, it provides learning about the other?

We use metaphor in conversation all the time, but often unconsciously. Listen for metaphor in normal speech and you will hear people say things like 'she's really scrapping the bottom of the barrel with this' or 'I feel like I am in a fog' or 'this is just a seed of an idea'.[1] Creativity and creative thinkers alike, can respond well to working with metaphor, producing profound insights and new ideas. In this section we will look at working with a metaphor in coaching, using visual processes such as drawing and collage.

It's best to help your client find their own metaphors in relation to their creative challenge. A very simple 'what is it like?' when discussing a problem, desire or goal can often elicit a metaphor that you can then work with. If your client can't come up with a metaphor, perhaps offer them some suggestions; however, it's good to find a 'universal metaphor' as they are easier to understand. The sorts of metaphors that people might refer to in terms of their creative process or goals include:

- I am stuck in the mud/walking in treacle.
- I am blocked like a drain pipe/it's like there is a big wall in front of me.
- I am lost/walking in fog/lost in a forest.
- I am overloaded/there are too many pathways/there is too much on my plate.
- It's like an uphill struggle.
- I need to think out of the box.
- I need to get my creative juices flowing.

What other ones can you think of? Listen out for them in conversations and perhaps add to this list.

How you work with the metaphor will depend on the time, space and expectations of the coaching relationship. This chapter gives you just a few creative ways to experiment with.

Drawing my rather full plate

I just have too much on my plate.

This is a frequently expressed metaphor, which can mean many things. In this case, my client had many creative challenges associated with overload and overwhelm of ideas. She also had a young family and busy life in general. She was very stressed and had trouble verbalising the magnitude and complexity of her thoughts. Together we explored this full plate with some of the following questions, while she drew the plate of food on a sheet of paper. Not all these questions were used, but I have elaborated for the purposes of clarity.

What is the plate like? What size is it? What is it made from? Is there just one plate?

What's on the plate? Are there different foods/items? What are they like? Tell me more . . .

What relationship do these items of food have to your creative goals?

How does this plate of food relate to other daily activities?

As you look at this plate in your mind's eye, what is happening? Is the 'food' or 'stuff on the plate' moving around, falling off the plate? Are you touching it, eating it? What is happening?

How are you feeling as you look at the plate?

Is one of the 'foods' tempting you more than others? How does your body feel when you look at it or try to eat it/do something with it?

Are some foods 'richer' than others? Are some foods easier to digest than others?

What choices do you have? Do you have to eat it all? Is a full plate better than an empty one?

Experiment with the plate and contents! Imagine its empty, what happens next? Imagine it stays full, what happens next?

What needs to happen with this plate and the contents?

What would you like to have happen with it?

As you watch this plate, what ideas are occurring to you?

There are endless questions you could ask to explore a significant metaphor such as this. However, if your client draws the plate or represents it in collage, it provides an easy visual prompt to work from and the metaphor starts working itself. By looking together at the client's choice of items, the size and how they are placed, coaching questions naturally 'fall out' and the inquiry develops its own structure.

Drawing my business garden

One particular client had been working with me for a while. She came to coaching with a need to focus on her business. It had become clear very quickly during previous sessions that she is highly creative, generates many ideas and has started several businesses over the years. She often doodles during coaching, so working with drawing was an obvious thing to try:

Jen: 'In one short sentence, what needs to be worked on today?'
Client: 'Short sentence? Ha ha. So the thing that needs to be worked on right now is money . . . I have been working very hard for several years and have created so much but what I earn does not reflect what I am worth and what I am capable of doing. It makes me think of plants in a garden and the plants aren't producing fruit; I am just running around, trying to keep them alive. I have planted too many things. I'm tired.'
Jen: 'Shall we draw that garden and those different plants? How about making a rough sketch to help us think through what is happening in that garden?'

I don't give her time to ponder this much and quickly find some card, felt pens and other materials. 'Make a rough start, while I make us some tea' I casually say. When I return with the tea, the sketch of the plants and garden is developing quickly. I ask some casual questions every now and then and, after about ten minutes, she seems to slow down and pick up her tea; it's time to talk further.

Jen: 'Tell me about this picture?'
Client: 'I am the gardener and I am so tired. At the moment I have moved into a different garden and, although I am really enjoying it here, there is no money at present, just more work, more work that does not seem to yield fruit; I need fruit now, I need some money now.

My husband is frustrated that I have worked so hard, but earned so little (sighs).

These other plants (businesses) that I have grown from seed – there are at least three or four, one of them is quite established and is the only one that provides any income at all; it has some fruit on the tree, but nowhere near as much as it should have, considering the work that I have put in over the last nine years and the potential that it could have.

One of the plants is a business project I started four years ago – it's still a seedling and although there was early fruit (income) the plant has withered away and gone into stasis, like a bulb. This needs to be really left for now and I need to speak with my husband about what I could do with it – he was very excited about it at the start too.

This plant (points to third plant) is half grown and still just coming into form. The thought that pops to mind is that there is no pollination for this growing plant, no way to bear fruit. But it's also still growing it roots (she draws some roots on the plant as we speak).

It occurs to me that I want to grow cactuses really; things that don't need much care or water. At home I don't have any other houseplants apart from cactuses – I don't like looking after things.'

Jen: 'What else occurs to you about this picture?'

Client: 'I am not in it. There is no person drawn in the garden. And also the pollination thing – there are flowers but no apples. I keep hoping the flowers will attract bees; I keep talking to people, networking, meeting people and hoping these flowers will turn into fruit (money). I need to draw some bees (she draws some bees). And the watering ... clearly how I have been trying to water these businesses is not working. And I keep planting more seeds; I need to be honest with myself that these new seedlings (new projects) stop me from watering existing ones and helping them pollinate and fruit.'

Jen: 'Tell me about these bits', I gesture to an area of the picture she has not spoken about yet.

Client: 'These are weeds. I need to be stronger with myself about side projects – there is no tangible, immediate income – I have to let go of the idea and let go of the desire to see it happen and hope that someone else might want to do that (sighs). Just because it's a great idea, doesn't mean I have to be the one to do it.

There is some weeding to be done. Need to let people down. That's hard. but I need to use my energy where its most needed; that's what this is all about. Let me write those three things down.'

She stops talking and writes:

Better use of energy, pollination of flowers, watering system that works better, put other into stasis.

This interactive discussion involving the picture, continued. Every now and then she would add something to the drawing, change something a little bit and write things down that occurred to her. As the discussion drew to a close, I asked:

Jen: 'Are there any obvious decisions or actions that now need to be taken?'
Client: 'It's very clear now. I feel a little sad about the plant but feel much better and clearer about everything else. I'll email you in a couple of weeks to tell you what I am doing.'

Relating to a different other, in this case an evolving drawing, offers a different way to relate to and explore the topic. Its dynamic properties allow us to add to and change as we go along – really crucial in coaching as awareness and insights appear.

Drawing organisational values

A creative session with a board of directors by Kate Taylor Hewett

> There was some confusion over future direction for Sound Communities CIC. A key issue for the three founder directors, Kate, Mike and Mitch, was to be able to explain, clearly and succinctly, what they were trying to do as an organisation. I offered to do a 2.5hour session with the aim being to create a clearly outlined mission and vision in order to help prioritise projects, resources and target applications for grants.

I asked each of the directors to draw the timeline of how they ended up getting involved in Sound Communities, starting as far back as they could see connections in their life. I gave them twenty minutes to do this, with a large piece of wallpaper each, lots of coloured pens and music playing. I had to use a lot of encouragement and be clear that this was not about the artwork, it was about them thinking through and representing their story so it could be shared.

Then, in turn, I asked them to explain their picture to each other and ask each other questions. This took around twenty-five minutes. At this time, I noted down any repeating or important words that came up and put these on post-its. This process led to a deeper self-disclosure than had happened before, even though they had already been working together for over a year, and a clearer sense of each other's motivations. In this case there was significant overlap between what each person thought was important and why they were involved.

We then clustered all the key words and decided which were the most important. I facilitated a discussion around how these key words expressed and might guide the work they do.

I then asked them to draw another image that represented the future they saw for Sound Communities – I gave them ten minutes to do this on a smaller piece of paper.

(continued)

> *(continued)*
>
> *We compared and contrasted the different pictures, explaining what they meant. Although the visions were slightly different, there was significant overlap and space, in the future at least, for each individual to build on what was important for them.*
>
> *We then looked at what these words and images could shape in terms of a vision and mission. In a synchronistic way, rather than coming up with something new, we ended up confirming that their current strapline – 'Connect, Engage, Inspire' – was well suited to their personal and organisational motivations and in subsequent board meetings it has been clear that the directors are much clearer about their current priorities.*

Drawing goals

I use this exercise frequently with groups and individuals and it always elicits rich information, awareness and plans with great ease. Way lay any worries about needing to draw well as it's not necessary for this exercise to work well. Start by asking your client to draw a simple sketch of a desired future outcome such as 'finishing my book', 'a flourishing business' or 'a creative, comfortable home'.

Next, ask your client to draw a second image, on a separate piece of paper, representing how they envisage the current state of their desired outcome – what it looks like at present. Again, it's important to draw attention to the fact that this exercise is not assessing their drawing skills – stick men, symbols and scribbles are welcome.

Once complete discuss the future image first, using light, curious questions such as:

- Tell me about this picture.
- What are the benefits in achieving this ideal outcome?
- What have you done so far to work towards this?
- What gets in the way of this occurring now?

Clearly you will be guided by your own coaching as you discuss this image and the desired, future outcome. Next turn your attentions to the image depicting the current state. You will find that some awareness and ideas have already surfaced during the first discussions, but you could also ask:

- Tell me about this picture.
- What are the main ways it differs from the ideal image?
- What is occurring to you now?
- What needs to happen to move you towards the future image – what steps are needed?

I use this exercise a lot and love its simplicity, pragmatic nature and also its adaptability.

How does your river flow?

Another metaphor frequently heard in everyday conversation, refers to life being like a river. Cited within both coaching (Whitworth et al 2005) and OT, it has been developed into a conceptual model to guide practice (Iwama 2006).

> *The Kawa (Japanese for 'river') model uses a familiar metaphor of nature as an effective medium to translate subjective views of self, life, well-being and the meanings of occupations.*
>
> www.kawamodel.com

The aim of therapy, in this way, is to achieve better flow in the river of the client's life. Although developed for OT, there is a great deal of similarity with the language, concepts and aims of coaching: barriers, obstacles, flow, context, engagement, resources, values and attributes, to name a few.

In its simplest form, the river bed represents the environment both physical and social; the rocks 'Iwa' represent life circumstances, which are difficult to change; the driftwood 'Ryuboku' represent an individual's assets and liabilities; the water 'mizu' is life force, flow, energy, chi; the spaces between the rocks, wood and river bed are 'sukima' – these gaps are the places where flow still exists and are important to acknowledge.

The model can be viewed longitudinally, with the source of the river being the start of an individual's life journey, and the end occurring when the river joins the sea. Twists, turns, falls and the changing landscape of the river are used to narrate a person's life journey to date.

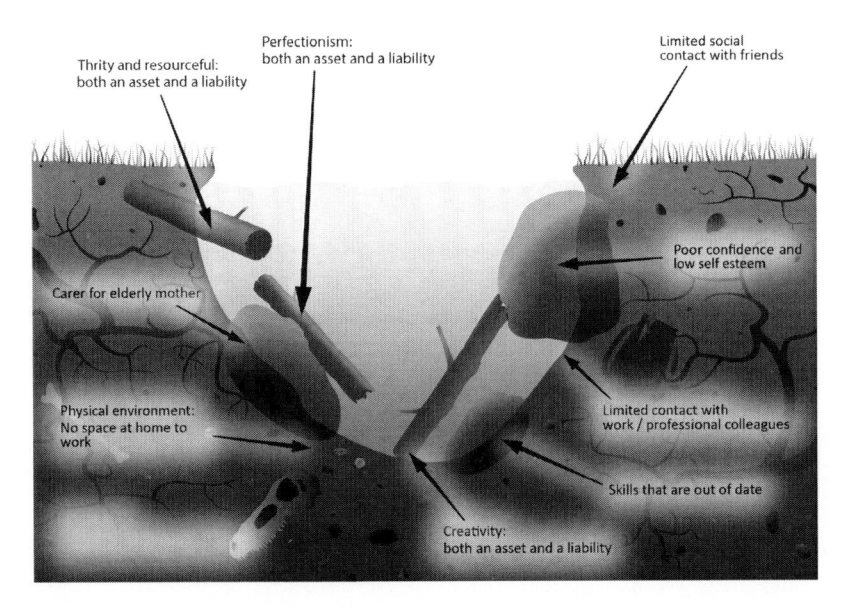

Figure 18.1 Life river cross section

You can also use this model to explore your client's current situation, by looking at a cross section of the river. This can be done with a simple pen and paper sketch or perhaps in collage. This cross section will provide a wealth of coaching insights as clients draw their perception of their rocks (life circumstances, blocks, challenges), their driftwood (strengths, attributes and liabilities), the river bed (the context: the social and physical environment) and the water (life energy or flow).

Figure 18.1 gives an example of a coaching client's river cross section – it has been graphically enhanced to make it clearer to see.

What follows are some questions, which can be used in conjunction with a client's sketch to guide a client's exploration of their life river and find ways of improving flow.

Questions to elicit current situation and desired states

How is your life flowing at present?

If life was like a river, what sort of river would yours be?

What sort of twists and turns might there be in your river?

What would you like your river to be like?

What does being in 'flow' look like?

Questions to elicit obstacles, blocks and life difficulties (Rocks)

How is your river flowing now?

What is blocking your river and impeding flow right now?

What is in the way right now . . . and what else?

If rocks represent difficult life circumstances and personal challenges, what might they be for you?

Questions to elicit resources and strengths? (Driftwood)

What do you consider to be your personal strengths and attributes?

How might some of your personal strengths sometimes be unhelpful?

What resources do you currently have?

How might your perception of the situation be unhelpful?

How do you sabotage yourself sometimes?

How do you block yourself?

Questions to explore the physical and social environment

Who do you have around that is supportive?

Who impacts on this situation in a helpful way and in what ways?

How does your work space/home support you?

How does your work/home environment hinder you?

How do you connect with your wider community?

What opportunities are there to get support or help?

Questions to identify what's going well, what's in flow

What is flowing well in your life at present?

What has worked for you in the past?

What might help now?

Tell me about a recent day or event that went well – what happened?

Tell me about a time when you felt you managed well? What helped?

What is the path of least resistance right now?

Questions to elicit actions or steps forward

What are you realising as we speak?

What occurs to you as one of the most helpful things that would improve the flow?

How can you recruit your natural resources and strengths to help you here?

What would be the easiest and most obvious place to start?

What would be a tiny, tiny first step?

How might this action impact on others?

How can you remind yourself of the helpful things you remembered today?

Using this river model lends itself to illustrating complex concepts and raising awareness of the contextual issues that surround it - sometimes seeing the big picture is easier when we draw it.

One of my biggest pieces of personal learning from the Kawa model has been a better understanding of how my greatest strengths, creativity being one of them, can be either an asset or a liability: as an asset, my creativity helps me to generate unique ideas and see untold possibilities; as a liability, it causes overwhelm of ideas and lack of focus and extreme grumpiness if I am not able to create. Using the metaphor of a strength being a piece of driftwood can help clients see that if the strength is being helpful, the driftwood moves to improve flow in the river, perhaps even levering a rock out of the way. If the strength (driftwood) is being unhelpful, it acts to block the flow. In this way, coaching also helps us to identify and use our attributes more skilfully.

A vision in collage

Making a 'vision' or 'dream' board using collaging is one of the most powerful visioning techniques I have encountered and I rarely let my clients get away without creating a board at some point. Knowing that visioning taps into positive emotional attractors in the brain, enhancing positive behavioural change, adds weight to the use of visioning techniques in coaching (Jack, Boyatzis, Khawaja, Passerelli and Leckie 2013).

If you don't already know how to work with a client to create a vision board, the basics follow, but don't let these instructions contain you. There are many different ways of doing it and some great books to help guide you, including, Joyce Schwarz (2008) *The Vision Board – The Secret to an Extraordinary Life*.

Incidentally, I have worked with clients remotely using this technique, so it's not limited to face to face working, although the following instructions are written from that perspective. Before the session, gather a good quantity of glossy magazines, periodicals, brochures and a few catalogues. Getting a good mix of resource material is essential so ask friends for any different publications – you will need a good box full (I am frequently spotted rummaging through my neighbours recycling box!). You will also need scissors, glue and a large sheet of card preferably A3 or larger.

Help your client generate a question, topic or focus for their vision board such as:

How do I want my creativity to develop?

What do I want my work to look like?

How do I want my business to look?

How can I put creativity at the heart of my work?

Over the coming one, two, five years, what do I want to see happen?

How can I regain passion for my writing?

Or perhaps an outcome statement:

> *Become more creative at work.*
>
> *Finish my book.*
>
> *Improve the cash flow in my creative business.*
>
> *Work with greater ease and happiness my job.*

Help your client spend a few minutes quietly focusing on their question, really letting it sink in. At this point, some people like to completely let go of the question, trusting that they will be guided to choose the images they need, but others like to consciously choose images based on their chosen question.

Direct your client to quickly flick through the magazines, tearing out whole pages with images that they are drawn to. Usually this takes around twenty to thirty minutes, but some people like to spend several days looking for the 'right' images. Encourage them to keep going until they have a large pile of torn, whole pages.

The next stage is narrowing down the choice of images and being a bit more selective. Encourage your clients to use their intuition and reject some images and trim down the ones they want to keep. They might also decide to include some printed words from magazines – that's fine. Before sticking the images onto the large piece of card, it's sometimes helpful to arrange them first!

Once it is complete, ask your client to look at their board and ponder it for a while. Talk them through the following questions including any others that arise:

> *What do you notice about your picture . . . and what else . . . ?*
>
> *What surprises you about the images?*
>
> *What might be missing?*
>
> *What sense do you make of it?*

If your client gets stuck, turn the board upside down or look at it sideways. Do they notice anything different? It's important to resist interpreting the images – it's very tempting, but as with all coaching, the meaning should come from the client, not the coach.

The vision board may well hold meaning and useful insights for many months and years to come, so I encourage people to hold onto them, keep them safe and revisit them at a later date.

Note

1 It's worth noting that highly concrete thinkers and some people with learning difficulties or cognitive problems may not be able to make the necessary conceptual shifts and links to understand or use metaphor in language, so please don't assume.

References

Iwama, M. (2006) *Kawa Model*. Philadelphia, PA: Churchill Livingstone Elsevier.

Jack. A, Boyatzis. R., Khawaja. M., Passerelli A. and Leckie R. (2013) Visioning in the brain: an fMRI study of inspirational coaching and mentoring, *Social Neuroscience*, 8(4), 369–84.

Schwarz, J. (2008) *The Vision Board – The Secret to an Extraordinary Life*. New York: Harper Collins.

Whitworth, L., Kimsey-House, H. and Sandahl, P. (2005) *Co-Active Coaching*. Mumbai: Jaico Publishing.

Chapter 19

Humour and provocation

Humour

In coaching, we use humour in many ways, through our questions, during reflecting back to our clients, to shift pace or mood and perhaps when challenge is needed. We also use it to build relationships and perhaps to play down our opinions or 'self-efface' if the need arises. Shifting 'states' can help take our clients into an expansive, open, disrupted place, full of rich learning. Simple questions like these need to be used with caution, but can be very effective:

How are you taking this all too seriously?

In what way could you laugh at this situation?

How do you find yourself ridiculous?

What might you look back upon, in the future and really laugh at?

Although we don't usually associate being teased or provoked as helpful, it can be powerful when in skilful, well-intentioned hands. Other more provocative questions might include:

What makes you think that you are good enough to do this!

So should we call you Procrastinating Peter?

So are you going to be banging on about doing this until you die or will you actually do something about it?

I'm getting a bit bored now, will you tell me something new now or something I don't know please

The purpose of this approach is often to break a habitual pattern, laugh and release during coaching and make a perceptual and energetic shift. However, using these questions requires the coach to take a risk, let go of certainty and risk not being liked! Clearly a resonant, robust, working relationship is required.

Provocation

The world of provocation in coaching has been experienced in its full glory by Peter Mayes, experienced coach and trainer, who recounts his experiences during training with Provocative Change Works.

> ### Evoking creativity through provocation and disruptive states, by Peter Mayes
>
> *Last summer I attended a program called Provocative Change Works (PCW), designed and facilitated by Nick Kemp. Nick studied with Frank Farrelly and adapted the approach for use by coaches and therapists, but my interest had been sparked initially by Sue Knight and her use of humour in coaching.*
>
> *When I saw these approaches in action, I was intrigued by how light and fluid the coaching seemed to be, but I couldn't work out what was being done and how it was having such a rapid effect. At first glance this type of coaching, these questions and what the coach was doing, seemed completely at odds with all my previous training. The coach interrupted and asked casually about death, money and sex in such a direct way: 'So how long have you got left to live then?' was one such question. Some of the audience took offence and some seemed uncomfortable, but the client seemed completely immersed in the discussion and not offended in any way.*
>
> *I enrolled on the PCW practitioner program and Nick was keen to point out that the gentleness of the nudging to the point of protest was fundamental to the approach. The provocation is about playing Devil's Advocate with the emphasis on the 'playing'. It's like two old friends talking together with good intent, knowing they can tease and push each other.*
>
> *The first part of the training involved gaining an appreciation of the mindset of being provocative with people. Seeing how this worked through videoed sessions of clients was quite a shock and I really couldn't see myself working in that way. At times it seemed like you were insulting, teasing them or ignoring them. Other times you were telling stories that had no relevance to the situation. This seemed to be the complete opposite to how we are trained to coach and work with clients. We are taught to put their needs first, do no harm and so on. Crucial to this way of working is being able to free up your thinking and practice as a coach and not becoming blocked by your previous learning. Much of the training was aimed at us becoming more adaptable, flexible and at ease with the fluid nature of this type of work.*
>
> *As we progressed through the training, people were asked whether they wanted to take part in a PCW coaching session with Nick Kemp and experience at first-hand how it works. The session would be in two parts and recorded so the participant could review the first part before undertaking the second. I'm happy to admit that I tried to hide, but there is no escaping with someone like Nick. He notices everything including my desire to move away and it was at this*

point that I decided to volunteer to be 'the client' and experience what it is like on the receiving end of this approach.

PCW conversations always start with the question 'So what's the problem?' I dutifully described my longstanding fear of driving over bridges, but this first session seemed to be about everything except my issue. We spoke about everything from speeding (driving), to whether I would drive off a bridge, to what would it take for me to drive over a person! The session lasted forty-five minutes but felt like ten minutes and I laughed so much at my own absurdity. At the end of the session Nick asked me for my reactions. I said I was confused; he said 'good' then gave me a recording of the session and asked me to listen to it before coming back next time.

Listening to the recording of the session, I felt like I was listening to another person: I could not see how I had engaged in such completely bizarre discussions. On the next training weekend, a few weeks later, I had the second part of the session. This started with looking at my reactions to the recording and considering how this was affecting me right now. I noticed how my thinking had changed and not just about bridges. I was more at ease generally and wanted to move forward in everything.

I searched for a way to describe this feeling, but the best description I heard was from a fellow student who said 'it's like having the furniture moved around in your head and it just keeps moving'. The formal description of this in PCW is the creation of 'spinning states'. Inducing these states helps to free up the client, gain new perspectives and work with what emerges.

Chapter 20

Evocative environments, evocative objects

Our physical environment the places, spaces and objects around us, undoubtedly affect what we think, remember or feel. Certain places can produce different thoughts and strong feelings such as a mountain top that might evoke a sense of solace, excitement or achievement within us. A dark, dank forest, thick with vegetation and poorly marked paths, can evoke mystery, confusion or maybe an opportunity to be brave. Built environments can also be highly evocative. Think of standing outside a shiny, city tower block, stepping inside the pristine reception and zooming up in the glass lift. Being within a highly evocative environment while we ponder important questions can really shift our thinking and feeling.

Objects can also evoke strong memories or a disruption in thinking and feeling. This might include personal belongings such as a family air loom, a college sweater or other commonly known personal items.

There can be no doubt that coaching clients in evocative places and using evocative items can be an easy way to shift states, add new insights, expand consciousness and stir up the fertile soil, all of which is helpful for creativity.

Evocative environments

You can really use your imagination and creativity here! Just think of the different environments you have available around you – ones that are open freely to the public or ones that you can arrange access to, making sure your client is able to walk up any stairs or manage uneven paths and so on.

My favourite built environments include art galleries, libraries, museums and cathedrals. These can provide rich, psycho-active environments to coach within. We have opportunities to walk and explore twisty, turning, narrow lanes or maybe a route that includes a tunnel or bridge. Perhaps you suddenly 'get lost' on route or there is a road closure. All of these lend themselves to exploring the metaphorical meaning in relation to your client's process and goals:

> *How was our walk today, similar to your current business journey?*
>
> *Standing at this tunnel entrance what comes to mind?*

Standing half way in the tunnel what is occurring to you?

This is a really noisy, busy precinct, a bit like what you describe is happening at work. In such places, what might help?

We have two possible route choices, what might they be in relation to your issue? What do you notice about these choices?

Being inside an art gallery serves many creative purposes, but in this case, *the main aim is not inspiration* (but I defy anyone to not to be inspired and absorb the rich, diverse energy!). The main point is to find places or items in the environment that you could use in the coaching. For example, in a public art gallery, there are many features and tools you could use:

- Many public galleries and museums are arranged such that you walk around in chronological order. This could be used to plan time orientated goals or stages of a project. You could also use it similarly for Time Line Therapy, walking forward and looking back at certain points and learning from the different qualities at each point in time.
- Note the different approaches that artists take to a similar subject, discussing how there are many different ways to achieve a similar goal or work with a similar set of resources.
- You could ask your client to identify a painting or sculpture to which they are attracted and sit with it while contemplating a question or their current goal. You can then coach them through the meaning that this object, perhaps a painting or sculpture, lends in relation to their personal question or goals. Prompts may include: what attracted you to this piece? In what ways does it remind you or relate to your coaching topic? What themes can you relate to in this painting? What do the characters in the painting have to say to you about this? What would you change about this painting/sculpture and why? What does all that tell you?
- Make sure you always bring the learning back to the coaching goal and process, eliciting some insights and possible actions.

The art gallery by Sue Blow

I have been working with a senior academic for some nine months now, but we arranged our first meeting at one of London's major art galleries, for no better reason than that the choice of location suited us both.

Before we met I asked the client to think of some paintings that might represent feelings at the start of the process and those anticipated by the end. This seemed appropriate since the client has connections to art and artists. However, when we

(continued)

> *(continued)*
>
> *met, I was taken not to the painting galleries, but to two very different sculptures. Both were in the same gallery, less than thirty feet apart. The first was small, on a plinth and at eye level. It was constructed from transparent Perspex, with black ink drawn and etched into the inner surfaces. It represents a Cornish tin mine and its power comes as much from the paradox of Perspex illustrating darkness and depth as from the image itself, representing as it does a defunct industry in an industrially challenged part of the country.*
>
> *The second piece is an enormous piece of curved and polished wood, some six feet high and at least that across. Through it is carved a polished tunnel, which is impossible to see through until the viewer is in exactly the right relationship with the curve of the tunnel.*
>
> *The discussion of the choice of piece, relevance to the client's situation, representation of starting point and aspirational outcome has now taken us through four two hour meetings and a lengthy telephone session. It has provided us with focus and inspiration.*
>
> *I have used verbal metaphor as an integral part of my practice for many years, but this was the first time I used physical objects, in close proximity, to such positive effect. I continue to be astonished at the myriad ways in which these two such different and complex pieces are still continuing to give my client support, inspiration and a real means by which to gauge and evaluate progress towards an achievable goal.*

Walking, wandering and wondering

I imagine that many of you naturally go for walks with your clients during coaching sessions, perhaps to just 'get some air' or if you feel stuck or lacking in energy. If you don't, please consider doing so: it really is a fast track route to unblocking, moving energy around and promoting greater clarity. We also know that walking seems to encourage our mind to wander and often ideas appear effortlessly during these times.

You could take your client out for a quick ten-minute walk outside at a pertinent point in the session or you could carry out a whole coaching session based on walking in a rich environment: perhaps a park, forest or alongside a river. Clearly some preparation is needed in terms of having good walking shoes, a drink perhaps and maybe a mat to sit on, so negotiating this into your working contract is important.

An outdoor walk, in a natural landscape, can provide many opportunities for coaching. Taking in prominent natural features such as a forest, or steep hill, muddy pathway or a broad vista, all lend themselves to metaphoric prompts, new perspectives and can free-up our thinking. Here are some possible prompts for enquiries during a walk:

We are about to enter the forest and explore a bit. How is that like your current relationship/business/work issue?

It's hard going through this mud, what might help us find an easier route or is their joy in staying stuck?

From this viewing point, what different perspectives can you see? What different perspectives might there be on your current situation?

Even if you coach on the telephone and don't have the luxury of arranging a coaching session whilst walking, you can still encourage your client to stop half way through a session and go for a walk. Most people have mobile phones and can easily take the phone with them. You don't have to try and talk to your client as they walk, but perhaps agree that they will walk for ten minutes and then stop and call you back. Moving our bodies is essential, especially if we are getting stuck in our thinking.

Outside of the coaching session regular walking, like regular journaling, can really support the overall coaching process. If mindful wandering is the aim, then walking in silence is most helpful. Encourage your client to pay attention to all their senses, sight, sound, taste, touch and smell, as described in the mindfulness section. Encourage them to just notice thoughts that pop in and draw their attention back to their body and the sensory input they notice. The thoughts that arise may well be valuable personal insights or ideas that have been lurking inside, waiting for a time to make themselves known, so encourage your client to take a note pad with them.

I would like to acknowledge the work of Rosalind Turner, walking coach, who has taken me on some fabulous coaching walks over the years.

Evocative objects

In Chapter 9, we started to explore the idea of creative 'doing' as coaching. Here we touched upon the idea that working with a physical object can evoke different thinking and feelings such as those experienced by a sculptor or furniture maker practicing their craft. We also noted the role that through working with 'other', we shape our self (Turkle 2007, Korn 2015). Working with other also promotes subject to object shifting, something that is essential in coaching (Bachkirova 2011). We also know well how personal memorabilia can evoke forgotten or cherished memories.

The evocative objects we could use within a coaching session are as varied as you could possibly imagine. Of course 'the meaning of (such) objects shift with time, place and differences among individuals' (Turkle 2007, p. 307). I know that some coaches have a 'goody bag' containing many familiar, household objects to use in coaching sessions. I have seen coaches use air filters to explore personal boundaries, different sizes and types of spoons to explore managing projects and varied coloured spectacles to explain different perspectives.

Russian dolls by Kathy Denton

I have found my Russian dolls to be invaluable in coaching. They can expose the real dynamics that are occurring within teams, help individuals to address personal conflict situations or help with effective restructuring of a team or organisation. Whilst Russian dolls are traditionally of the Babushka, floral painted lady variety, I have found it worthwhile to source either unisex or some male versions.

The dolls can be used in variety of ways: the different sizes of each doll could represent dominance within a team; the sizes could represent status; the proximity between the dolls can represent how close the team members are mentally and emotionally; the position and sizes can also help explore the dynamics between individuals.

The clients choose a size of doll that best represents the status or dominance or influence of each individual involved. The dolls are then positioned depending on nature or positivity of the relationship. Sometimes the dolls might look at each other, sometimes not. Perhaps the dolls are making full eye contact, perhaps they are glancing sideways or maybe they have their backs to each other.

Case study one: 'J' (SME business owner)

J was concerned that she was feeling increasingly undermined by a member of her team K to the extent that she felt bullied. We used Russian dolls to map out what was happening in interactions between J and K, including the role that two other team members were playing. We then took a 'helicopter view', looking as objectively as possible at the scene below, and talked through what positions the dolls needed to be in for the team to be functioning effectively and for J to feel more comfortable and secure in her leadership of K. We then looked at what actions or behaviours J needed to contribute in order to effect the required change.

Case study two: senior team in a university

The team were planning to restructure the department. We used Russian dolls to map out what was required to deliver on objectives in terms of team structure. Initially we 'ignored' specific individuals and roles that were currently being performed and focused purely on requirements for effective delivery. We then placed specific names on the dolls as appropriate for their ability/attitude to carrying out the role. This led to an awareness that some individuals no longer had a role to play on the team and needed to be supported in finding alternative roles within the organisation. We also saw that others would be more effective in completely different roles within the team. Apart from helping them with the practical issues, using the dolls also highlighted where there were challenging personal dynamics that needed addressing and development opportunities.

References

Bachkirova, T. (2011) *Developmental Coaching: Working with the Self.* Maidenhead: Open University Press.

Korn, P. (2015) *Why We Make Things and Why it Matters: The Education of a Craftsman.* London: Square Peg Vintage Books.

Turkle, S. (2007) *Evocative Objects.* Cambridge, MA: MIT Press.

Chapter 21

Imagining, being and becoming

When exploring the neuroscience of creativity, we discovered that not only does our imagination generate creative ideas, it can also 'simulate' experience. Experiential simulation (Hass-Cohen and Carr 2008) is a powerful, natural human ability and can help us build important creative muscle. It can also serve the coaching process by:

1   Providing a window to the possible states of others – using our imagination to simulate the experience of being another person (Hass-Cohen and Carr 2008).
2   Practicing a desired state using our imagination, helps prime us for 'real life' activity (Robertson 1999) and provides a means to practice the different state we desire (Hass-Cohen and Carr 2008).

The notion of experiential simulation helps us understand why visualisation is a legitimate tool and can assist creative practice. It also explains why many coaching tools aim to simulate and practice resourceful 'states', whether they belong to the client or to someone else.

Windows to other selves

Theories of multiple selves are common within coaching practice and within the tools that coaches often use (Bachkirova 2011). We might call on the strengths and resources of one of our own internal selves or call on help from a muse or archetypal character – in essence, it's the same thing. David Richo (2009), psychotherapist and poet aptly says:

> *The creative process is an activation of many archetypal images and an elaboration of these images into metaphors about ourselves and our world . . . beings like us who are too vast to be depicted in portraits. We are galleries, after all*
> (p. 17)

Depending on your coach training and background, you might call these selves 'resourceful states', 'sub-personalities' or indeed 'archetypes'. Helping our clients become familiar with existing selves as well as developing other helpful states or selves can provide much needed help for creative challenges. These are some selves that clients have identified:

- Little Miss Messy: characterised by her ability to embrace complexity, tangled concepts and general confusion. She is able to weave together complex differences and multiple stances, but it can sometimes seem like an unstructured mess.
- Diana the OTT Diva: she is loud, sometimes a bit too brash. She amplifies interesting things/ideas and like to tell everyone what she has been up to. She is a bit of a drama queen.
- Curious Charles: he ponders and asks interesting questions, but can be quite sceptical, critical and a little nosey. He makes up for this in his ability to see inside and around situations.
- Daydreaming Derek: he is often found starring out of the window, musing over what can seem like irrelevances, but he is so good at dreaming up ideas and different ways of thinking.

(If this approach is resonating with you, I highly recommend the brilliant, witty, creative book by Jill Badonsky *Nine Modern Day Muses and a Body Guard* 2010.)

Personifying particular strengths and challenges and forming them into a character or self can make them more accessible for us to work with. We can then invite the self into the coaching session and ask them for help, with questions such as:

How could Curious Charles help right now?

In what ways is Curious Charles holding you back with this?

How would Bertha the Belligerent (and her natural stubbornness) approach this?

How might Little Miss Messy help you find some creative ideas right now?

How can you get Diana the Diva on board during this performance?

Working with Dire Daisy

Dire Daisy is the creation of a professional friend, Kate, who is in the process of creating glove puppets to support her coaching and counselling practice. She was inspired by Amy Mindell's book *The Dreaming Source of Creativity* (2005). Kate also drew on her extensive study of astrological psychology and personal psychosynthesis and the inherent symbolism of personal archetypal patterns.

Dire Daisy is an emotional sub-personality and was explored to support Kate's personal development during coaching supervision. Reflecting on a recent session, she shared with me how using the glove puppet, Dire Daisy, enabled understanding and had given her some deep insights and also great compassion for this vulnerable inner child.

(continued)

(continued)

> *Dire Daisy lives at the bottom of an empty well amongst rocks, frogs, slime and shadowy shapes. Dark green water weeds hide her as she sinks into the mud at any hint of threat. Watchfulness stalks her and her eyes are wide with tension.*
>
> *She holds on tightly to her memories and what she has learned from her past. Protected by her reflective Eagle cloak, the iridescent blue, green and purple feathers are dimmed by the darkness of the well. Coiled close around her, a huge serpent cherishes, entwines and guards her, black and white diamonds glowing on its unshed fragile skin. Yet Daisy doesn't see the white markings only the black ones that she believes are manacles of the fear that aroused ripple through her. This lonely child is deeply sensitive and reflective and beneath the grime and slime and dark waters, scarlet and orange coals burn brightly: a passive, burning hidden rage.*

Kate's story:

> *I knew there was a strong sad part of me, a sub-personality that held me back in life. Until recently I hadn't found a way of identifying and talking to her, but I felt I needed to. Reading Amy Mindell's book inspired me and, as I love knitting, one evening I found myself knitting a puppet. Over the coming days she grew in my imagination and stitching and gluing, Dire Daisy emerged into the light of day.*
>
> *I showed her to a friend who is also a coach and she advised I have a conversation with Dire Daisy in supervision. There, in a safe space, I asked Dire Daisy why I was blocked when I was trying to advertise a new group. Was she scuppering my efforts – and why? She told me she did not want to do group work; it frightened her, she got angry. Finally, Dire Daisy said she didn't want the word spread about an impending group because strangers could turn up and she felt threatened.*
>
> *At first I was upset and being with my coach was helpful. During subsequent sessions I started to relate to Dire Daisy as just one facet of my wider personality and with coaching new solutions began to emerge. She is powerful and full of strong colours, dark dreams and deep passions. There's a magnetic quality to her that attracts and intrigues people; yet she avoids others when she can and doesn't allow herself to be seen until she feels really safe. I asked Dire Daisy how it felt to be safe and Dire Daisy said that she was comfortable with people she knew and a group that was not too big. I told her I loved and accepted her as part of myself and so would never let anyone hurt her. How would it be, I asked, to allow a trusted friend to come along one day to play? Dire Daisy thought for a long moment and then gave a little nod . . .*
>
> *As a result of making and working with Dire Daisy I have become more conscious of my fear of people; I stop and take notice when I feel anxious and remind myself that I have other inner resources. If I still feel bad, I talk to Dire Daisy and ask what's the matter and we have a conversation. This always seems to help because it takes me one step back from the fear. Recently I identified a much more positive, outgoing, resourceful character (sub-personality). As I explore this new sub-personality, I will create her and use her to support Dire Daisy.*

When working in this way, some people prefer to recruit the qualities of people they admire or respect, perhaps a famous artist or writer, rather than working with their inner selves. You could work with your clients to help them identify three or four people who have really inspired them creatively or who they respect in terms of their approach or creative process. Help them identify what qualities those people hold that they really admire.

When your client feels in need of that quality, be it perseverance, attention to detail, humour, resilience, willingness to experiment, courage, ask them:

How would xxxxx approach this?

or

What can I learn from xxxxx at this time?

You could work in a more sensory-somatic way and ask your clients to imagine stepping into their chosen mentor, and seeing, feeling, sensing and acting like them for a while, to see how they could recruit the desired, helpful state. This can be taken a step further by finding some works by the creativity mentor to read, listen to, watch or look at prior to starting their creative activities.

When I paint, I often start by doing a little ritual to help ground and focus me. I then say to myself 'I wonder who could help me today?' I then find a book or some prose to evoke their 'essence' or I may even start a conversation with that artist as I paint. This works well for all sorts of activities, be they creative or not.

Visualisation – sculpting new pathways

Experiential simulation can also be used to 'practice' a desired creative state and prime us for 'real life' creative activity (Robertson 1999, Hass-Cohen and Carr 2008). Whether your client wants to write a book, start painting, set up a new business, change career completely or just be more creative in their daily life, experiential simulations are hugely beneficial because they:

- Prime our brains ready for the necessary actions to be taken, sculpting new neural pathways.
- Moderate fear by kidding the fear centre of the brain (amygdala) that they have already done the 'thing' several times before, so it's not that scary.
- Identify self-sabotage techniques that arise during mental rehearsal.
- Build a stronger vision, as experience helps us feel and see whether or not we really want it!
- Support stronger behavioural change as visioning has been shown to activate positive emotional attractors (Jack, et al 2013).

Simulating an experience in this way is a form of mental rehearsal that has been used in sports coaching for many years and to great effect. It is also used in the rehabilitation of patients with Parkinson's disease, stroke and brain injury where it is often called Motor Imagery Practice (Dickstein and Deutsch 2007). So in advocating for its use in creative practice, we are building on strong foundations.

Visualisation is one of the simplest ways of providing a simulated experience as part of a coaching session and can easily be done face to face or on the telephone. Using very basic relaxation principles to help your client relax is a good place to start. Then support and guide your client through building a rich, sensory visualisation with them actually involved in the activity they desire. Get your client to describe what they see, hear, feel, smell and so on. What clothes are they wearing? What is their posture and how are they sitting? What expression is on their face? What activities are they doing? Can they feel, see and smell the paint? Can they see the words appearing as they write? Can they really see themselves on stage performing? Are they able to see themselves saying no to their kids and practicing their violin instead?

What happens as they sit with the image? Explore any things that happen. Does someone enter the scenario? Is this a partner or parent? Does your client experience discomfort with the emerging picture or are they relishing it? What happens next?

As the coach, take note of any potential problems or changes that your client identifies. Do they say 'actually, I am not enjoying this as much as I thought?' or 'actually I want to do this for myself, not for others' or 'my husband has appeared and is rather grumpy with me' or 'I feel guilty doing this'. This all provides rich material to explore in coaching.

I often do a visualisation at the end of a coaching session as I find it leaves my clients in a good place from which to take action. Getting your client to practice this visualised simulation in between sessions really strengthens its effectiveness.

There are other ways to simulate experiences. 'Acting as if' could involve volunteering in a role at the theatre or art gallery, dressing up in the relevant attire and making the journey to the desired place, or attending events that are relevant. 'Acting as if' is great, especially in the early stages, as it can really help lower anxiety levels and help a client move into action, but it is stronger if combined with real action.

Being the metaphor

Combining a powerful metaphor with movement and our imagination can produce some fascinating results. Recent research has been carried out by Leung et al (2012) entitled 'Embodied Metaphors and Creative "Acts"'. This explored whether enacting metaphors associated with creativity such as 'think outside of the box' and 'on one hand, then on the other hand' actually enhances creative problem solving. Those coaches working face to face with clients or facilitating group coaching sessions or workshops will find this particularly fascinating, but there is nothing to stop those of you who work primarily with telephone coaching encouraging your clients to move around during a session and take the phone with them.

Leung's research comprised of five studies in which participants were assessed using a variety of standardised measures to measure fluency, flexibility and originality of ideas and divergent/convergent thinking. The studies included actually asking participants to complete the assessments while sitting both inside and outside of an actual box! Another experiment tested the two hands metaphor (on the one hand, then on the other hand) by making gestures first with one hand and then the other, assessing the resultant changes in divergent thinking.

This work provides evidence that embodiment of a metaphor can activate cognitive processes that facilitate the generation of new ideas and connections, in other words creativity. This research goes a long way to support the work of coaches who walk with their clients whilst they coach or use other movement work such as Time Line Therapy.

References

Bachkirova, T. (2011) *Developmental Coaching: Working with the Self*. Maidenhead: Open University Press.

Badonsky, J. (2010) *The Nine Modern Day Muses (and a Bodyguard)*. San Diego, CA: Renegade Muses Publishing House.

Dickstein, R. and Deutsch, J. E. (2007) Motor imagery in physical therapist practice, *Physical Therapy* 87(7), 942–53. Accessed 2/10/15, http://ptjournal.apta.org/content/87/7/942.full.

Hass-Cohen, N. and Carr, R. (Eds) (2008) *Art Therapy and Clinical Neuroscience*. London: Jessica Kingsley Publishers.

Jack, A., Boyatzis, R., Khawaja, M., Passerelli, A. and Leckie, R. (2013) Visioning in the brain: an fMRI study of inspirational coaching and mentoring, *Social Neuroscience*, 8(4), 369–84.

Leung, A. K. et al (2012) Embodied metaphors and creative acts, *Psychological Science*, 23(5), 502.

Mindell, A. (2005) *The Dreaming Source of Creativity*. Portland, OR: Lao Tse Press.

Richo, D. (2009) *Being True to Life*. Boulder, CO: Shambala Publications Inc.

Robertson, I. (1999) *Mind Sculpture: Unleashing your Brains Potential*. London: Bantam Press.

Chapter 22

The 'we' of creativity

Whilst most of this book has focused on the individual who wants to create something or become something different, there is another way of looking at coaching; the natural creativity and coaching that occurs when groups of people come together. When we shift from the 'I' to the 'we' of creativity, incredible things can truly happen.

In the concluding part of our journey, we will examine three very diverse perspectives, which all encompass this shift to the we of creativity. This shift is happening all around us, notes psychologist and creativity researcher Vlad Glăveneau (2010), so as an emerging profession we would be strongly advised to consider what this might mean for our practice.

First, Sam Chittenden explores the use of theatre and improvisation in leadership coaching. Next, in a reflective piece, Dan Doherty discusses how coaching shows up naturally through participating in a choir. Finally, I will discuss how I work with coaching games in a party format, in people's homes, businesses and the wider community.

Improvisation in leadership coaching: knowing what to do when we don't know what to do

Sam Chittenden

A good coaching relationship provides a safe space where a client can explore challenges and choices, and practice 'doing themselves differently'. The more 'real' this practice, the more powerful the insight and the more likely any decisions and changes are to stick.

We use theatre and improvisation techniques explicitly and implicitly in our coaching and other development work at Different Development.[1] These approaches enable coachees to practice doing themselves differently, trying different approaches to entrenched problems, enabling clients to make a shift and find an authentic way to be at their best.

Deliberate or not, all leadership behaviours and communications involve an element of performance. As leaders, we must think not only of what we say, but of how we say it, including the use of gesture, tone and symbol to convey meaning. It is this performative dimension of leading that moves the hearts and minds of followers. But we can get stuck agonising about the right way to do things.

Some of the elements of theatre that can be used to good effect in coaching, include:

- The dynamic of rehearsal within the coaching context.
- The introduction of real and imagined audiences.
- The use of character work to look at the roles we and others play.
- The application of physicality with voice and body work.
- Using acting tools and exercises to develop great connection with an audience (and between coach and client).
- Last but not least, the role of improvisation, spontaneity and play.

Making it up as we go along

Leadership is often improvisational and spontaneous. We have to carve out new paths with whatever resources we have – our current understanding, people and skills and other resources. Like an actor on stage, we may wish that we had a different set, props or supporting cast; but we have to create magic with whatever we have, and from whoever we are. We have to improvise.

In 'Composing a Life', Mary Catherine Bateson (1989) suggests that:

> *Improvisation can be either a last resort or an established way of evoking creativity . . . I believe that our æsthetic sense, whether in works of art or in lives, has over-focused on the stubborn struggle toward a single goal rather than on the fluid, the protean, the improvisatory.*

A leader who can improvise will draw on whatever they have around them, their experiences and resources, being flexible and creative in their approach.

For many people, and in most organisations today, life is complex and unpredictable, and requires flexibility (IBM 2010). A capacity to remain open and flexible, suspending immediate judgements, is a real leadership strength, and a tolerance of mistakes and imperfections is vital. Innovation requires us to question the status quo and to break the rules. Effective leaders work at the edge of their ability and knowledge and are resilient enough to be able to move on and learn from mistakes. They take risks. These themes are explored in more detail in *Rhyme and Reason: The Poetry of Leadership* (Chittenden 2014).

A coaching approach that encourages creativity and flexibility, builds comfort with uncertainty and draws out the full range of skills (and personae) of the client, will equip them to deal not only with the immediate challenges in front of them, but a whole range of issues and challenges that have yet to arise.

Why improv?

Improvisational theatre, also called improv or impro, is a form of theatre where the performance is unscripted and is created in the moment. Modern improv techniques were developed by Viola Spolin in the 1940s–60s and further in the 1970s by Keith Johnstone, author of *Impro: Improvisation and the Theatre* (1979).

The nature of improv develops a greater comfort with the unknown. It can promote risk taking, lower the expectation of perfection and encourage us to take ourselves less seriously. By using provocations to overcome our natural resistance, improv can enable us to 'have a go' at something, stepping outside our comfort zone, experimenting and as a result having a physical experience of doing something different.

This doing, rather than talking about doing, is key. According to Irish Legend's Fionn Mac Cumhail, the sweetest sound in all the world is the music of what happens. Where coaching clients often get stuck is not so much in knowing what to do, but in taking action, just as actors can get blocked; improv can get them moving.

Although it is unscripted and appears unstructured, the discipline of theatre improv is built on a set of tenets. The tenets set out what makes improv work as theatre and also make acting in improv fun and safe.

Presence and focus of attention

Spontaneity is intimately related to presence; if an actor is present, they are able to react in the moment. Self-consciousness, or a focus on what the actor should be doing, is death to their performance (as Declan Donnellan (2002) describes in *The Actor and the Target*).

When people first start doing improv, they are likely to play a variety of 'games' that develop concentration skills and attention to what is going on on stage (rather than on what they themselves are doing). Above all, this develops curiosity and listening skills.

A focus on the goal (the 'target') of the scene, and the ideal of making 'the *other* person look good' invite the actor to forget ego or fear, and concentrate on impact.

Accepting offers and building

In improv, a scenario, storyline or character is known as an 'offer'. In order for a scene to work, other actors need to *accept* rather than *block* the offer. For example, an actor comes on stage and says 'Good morning doctor'. If their partner says 'I'm not the doctor', they block the progress of the scene. Alternatively, if they respond with 'That's a nasty bullet wound' or even 'I'm covering for the doctor. I'm from the temp agency', they have not only accepted but *built on* the initial offer. Success at this requires actors to be 'yay-sayers' rather than 'nay-sayers', at least while on stage. It means repressing our natural urges to reject anything new, especially anything we didn't think of ourselves.

Relationships

Just as a strong connection between the actors in improv enables the kind of team work that results in successful scenes, so do the relationships between characters. Great improv focuses on connections between characters, not just the storyline.

No such thing as a mistake

A fundamental idea in improv is that there is no such thing as a mistake – all mistakes are opportunities. To drum this home, most improv games include an element of celebration, such as cheering when someone drops a ball or misses their turn. Celebrating failure, and the opportunity it can bring, helps us to overcome our fear of failure or of looking foolish. This is generally the biggest block in improv and in life.

Jump then justify

Improvisers must jump into a scene with courage and make something happen. Like leaders, they must step into the void and make something happen, making active choices. Action is key – rather than discussing whether they should or shouldn't go on a treasure hunt, they get out their spades and dig. In this way they cut to the chase.

What you did is what you do

According to Keith Johnstone, improvisers shouldn't try to get better at their craft, they should simply notice what they do and what happens.

Applying improv in coaching

The most important thing to remember in using improv approaches in coaching, is to use them flexibly and spontaneously, as the situation demands, rather than planning an improv session or having a checklist. *Improv exercises in coaching are provocations, working like great questions.* They encourage embodied exploration of the coachee's issues, and help the coachee to notice what it is that they do, and what works.

As with any medium of personal development, modelling is important. If they want to invite a client to play (and, as we will explore later, to make mistakes) they have to be willing to go there themselves. This also means using some presupposition in encouraging clients to give improv a go. It doesn't work to be hesitant or apologetic. Equally, it must be held lightly. One way to overcome natural resistance is to stress the 'let's pretend' or 'what if' nature of the exploration. It is also good to use some radical scenarios – they may not fit, but they will help to overcome natural resistance to other new ideas.

Just as in theatre, there are endless improv scenarios in coaching. Here are a few ways it can be applied.

Presence

We can increase presence within the coaching space by paying attention to what is happening and offering feedback to the coachee on how they impact on us in the moment. Acting exercises such as the Meisner Technique (Jarrett 2015), in which pairs of actors take turns to voice something that they notice about the other, help to build connection and attention to detail. They also focus on simple truths, rather than judgements or rationales.

Accept and build

The principle of accept and build (also known as 'yes, and') is one of the most fundamental in improv, and it translates readily to a coaching conversation. Acceptance (or 'yes') might be about the coachee acknowledging the reality of their situation – rather than wishing it was otherwise. This is a vital step in owning or taking responsibility for the things they can influence, and equally in identifying the things they can't. Inviting them to build (or 'and') from here encourages the coachee to identify real steps and actions.

'Yes, and' also develops an awareness of tensions, without creating immoveable objects:

> *we want to do this . . . yes, but . . . we are short of xx . . . END*
>
> *we want to do this . . . yes, and . . . we are short of xx . . . so . . . .*

This simple shift in language invites a change in mindset (to a creative, resourceful one). Gently bringing a client's attention to their use of the word 'but' can help to highlight their self-limiting beliefs. It can also be used to generate ideas, for example, by brainstorming, and building on ideas and suggestions rather than dismissing them immediately.

What if?

When using improv in one-to-one work, it is the coach's role to offer provocations or scenarios. Sometimes these will be related to the real-life issue, but with a twist, other times not. In the latter case it can be helpful to have a source of 'random' ideas, such as cards with different scenarios or characters, or Story Cubes®. These can also be used to develop confidence in talking about an unknown and unprepared topic.

Many improv techniques involve 'working the actor', when one improviser (sometimes the teacher/director) leads the other with a series of questions or suggestions:

The 'we' of creativity 187

Take something off an imaginary shelf. What is it?

A box.

What's inside it?

A ball.

Bite it. What does it taste of?

Rhythm and pace

Improv is often quick-fire, and involves actors responding rapidly to each other. It can have a ping-pong sense of rhythm and turn taking. Applying this in coaching, and inviting the coachee to respond with what first comes to mind rather than over thinking, can avoid blocking and generate a wider range of possible solutions. It can also get quickly to the truth. In this way of working, the coach's script might be a list of simple questions, or single words – verbs, adjectives, nouns. It can take a few 'turns' to warm up, so needs to be sustained, with commitment. With practice, the coach can take a lead from the coachee's responses and incorporate twists and turns in this simple narrative.

Role and character

One of the richest seams in improv is the creation of different characters or alter egos. Something that the coachee could never imagine themselves doing might become simple if they were, for example, superwoman or a lion. Offering different personae that a coachee can 'try on', for example, when preparing for an interview or a difficult conversation, gives them a wider repertoire to drawn from and can help to build their self-confidence. Whilst having a separate persona can initially free the coachee from habits and self-expectations (giving them 'permission' to behave in a new way), it also helps to stress that its characteristics are not alien but a part (albeit small) of who the coachee is. After all, we are all a little leonine inside.

Celebrating failure

In group coaching, simple improv games (such as name games and throwing/catching) can be used in their purest form to break the ice, build trust and create an atmosphere of learning and support. The tenet of 'mistakes are opportunities' can also be applied more implicitly in group and one-to-one coaching, using questions such as 'what does this make possible that wasn't there before?' and 'what can you learn?'

Cutting to the chase

Great improv gets to the heart of a scene quickly. It is full of action. The actors are committed to their characters and to each other. They are doing things, rather than talking about doing things. The coach can help to cut through obfuscation by asking the equivalent of 'what is this scene about?' or 'what's really going on here?' Equally, they can invite the coachee to action, using pre-suppositional language – 'so what are you going to do?'

Review

In acting training and rehearsal, as opposed to performance, there is time to reflect and to look from an audience or observer's perspective. So, in coaching there is a balance between action and reflection. The coach must manage this rhythm; the ebb and flow between stability and change, vision and reality, action and reflection. Stepping in and out of improv exercises can provide this balance, and create a healthy mix of challenge and support.

Curtain

Using improvisation and theatre techniques is all about doing. In true improv style, it only works if its offer is accepted and built upon. Any reflections on your experiences of using these ideas are warmly welcomed at sam@differentdevelopment.co.uk.

Coaching in the 'key' of life

Dr Daniel Doherty

Throughout my long, professional life I have engaged with the craft of coaching in one form or another. One aspect of my life that has grown in importance over the past five years has been my participation in a variety of choirs where strangers come together to make unaccompanied music under a musical leader. There is no requirement for any musical qualification, no need to sight-read and often we sing songs from many lands without words of notation written down. The benefits of such choirs are increasingly lauded for their capacity to breathe healthy life into the individual and create attunement across a community.

The purpose of this reflective piece is to examine where and how coaching shows up naturalistically within the choir context, including reflecting on coaching-style processes that occur outside of the choir such as over dinner or when walking to a venue together while humming our respective parts.

It is commonly stated within choirs that participation is about 'much more than just singing'. It is about the personal insights that are somehow released in the course of musical creation, and of the affordance that allows us to share private thoughts about other aspects of our lives with others with whom we have created that music. Often we have little idea about each other's work, personal life or domestic circumstances yet somehow singing together allows us to bypass these 'normal' conversational exchanges to explore instead some of the deeper themes that run under the surface of our everyday passage through life.

We find ourselves reflecting on how it is to learn to sing together – especially difficult songs – and how it is to be coached through that process by a choir leader. Much of the time we reflect that this learning curve is enlivening, while at other times it can be excruciating in the extreme. The harder we try the less probable it seems that we will ever put this set of notes together, while others around us seem to soar effortlessly towards harmonic heights.

In that moment of struggle we feel vulnerable and exposed. Yet through these struggles we develop a shared history. Later conversations relating to our lives beyond the context of the choir will offer metaphors and parallel processes from our shared singing experience to draw upon and illumine our conversations.

Coaching themes unlocked through singing together

Much of the singing that I have engaged in recently has alternated between mixed and all male choirs. The themes that this gender contrast has opened up have included reflections on how men and woman respond to being coached differently. We have also looked at the male bonding that occurs while singing together, commenting on how different that seems to the bonding that occurs when men meet at work, in pubs or at sports events. Women who sing with 'we' men in mixed choirs are really curious to know of our experience of maleness and of the effect of sharing low frequency vibes together. They then are prompted to share their experiences of singing with women as compared to a mixed choir. In this way gender and gender difference is open for exploration in a spirit of free inquiry not easily accessible in other social contexts. Men's resistance to feedback and help in general is also a recurring theme, as is male competiveness.

We talk of singing in different languages and of the possibilities and restrictions that the enunciated word brings. When singing in a tongue alien to us, we comment not only on that difficulty, but also on the wonder and beauty of a culture that is magically invoked by the singing of their canon.

We talk of our lives, of our loves, of our past, of our parenting and of our shared humanity with all of its challenges and joys. We talk of addictions, of obsessions, of the ageing process – many of us are older and of our experience of the passage of time in our lives. We even touch upon death. There are times too when the lyrics of a song we have recently sung open up conversation that touches upon intense and keenly felt joys and sorrows in our lives. We sing a refrain over and over to the point where it becomes mantra – 'bury me deep in love/bury me deep in love/take me in/under your skin/bury me deep in love'.

Together, our singing evokes a fugal form of 'call and response'. Here, the narrative (story) passes between the parts of the choir, from bass to alto to soprano then back to tenor, to carry the tune. So too, in a kind of 'parallel harmonic modulation', do the conversations between us all on other topics. We talk of the 'flow' that opens between us as we sing; of when time dissolves and we become entirely absorbed in that moment of creation. By contrast we lament the absence of such flow in the discordant jangle of daily living.

What is it about singing together that opens such generative conversations?

When I ask myself what it is about the coaching experience that allows such different and sometimes raw conversations to be approached and explored, a number of answers emerge. Most obviously we all share the experience of being coached in the here and now by a leader. Hopefully the skilful leader can openly reflect on the coaching process itself, taking it beyond learning the technicalities of the song, to thinking about the way we all create harmonies and resonances in other aspects of our beings – how we learn to sing 'songs in the key of life'.

There seems little question that communal song creates the experience of being in flow – that moment when the goose-bumps appear and spontaneous tears arise from the perfectly formed chord. This creates a common ground, one that enables us to recreate or at least to allow the possibility of that same flow experience to reoccur in individual exchanges.

The choir is, out of necessity, a high-feedback environment and sometimes that feedback is quite rough. This experience of receiving feedback drives us into stark recognition of our 'inner critic'. It helps us learn how to take criticism, as well as to figure out when it is deserved. This opens up conversations about how we deal with 'not being good enough' or of being misunderstood (to be sung to 'Oh Lord, please don't let me be misunderstood') in our wider life. This is powerful juju. There is no hiding place in the choir unless you try and fake it by miming, which some do; this too is ripe for coaching exploration!

Our defences too are shown and there for all to see. We can notice our instinctive reaction to blame the leader or fellow singers for our failure to hit the note, or we can look inside of ourselves and our own resistances. Reflection on all of this, often in intense discussion in breaks between singing, allows us to explore our vulnerability and the patterns we habitually draw upon to deal with that experience.

The act of listening intently as we sing seems to enhance our ability to listen to each other in conversation. In our struggle to gain a harmonic blend, trust grows with those that have directly coached us, but also between those of us who coached and supported each other within our sections. As we meet again and again over time, trust builds and individual conversations deepen, pursuing a theme or an episode in life that unfolds between these singing 'oases'. As we grow to know each other we are sometimes ashamed to think of the poor first impression we had of a person now we know them in all of their authentic fullness. We also wonder what initial impression they had of us. There is also a power in chance encounters with strangers where social status is unknown yet where we can, for example, coach on work issues without even knowing what the other person does for a living.

Learning from singing, applied to the world of coaching – some reverse engineering

Given the power of the parallels between the worlds of singing and coaching, it is hardly surprising that I have experimented with exporting lessons learned from singing approaches into my coaching practice, not least when I have been leading coaching groups. I have experimented with opening coaching groups with a song and with rhythmic exercises appropriated from choir. These have proved successful in attuning the group and also in providing a metaphor for reflecting on the dynamics of attunement and of blending with another's voice. I have shared stories from my singing life and of the innate confidence that breeds in the belief that a 'miracle' will manifest in the moment that we make a piece of work complete. I have reflected on the opportunity in choir and in the conversations around choir to create the environment where synchronicities of perfect timing occur.

In coach training I have reflected on the parallels of performing in front of each other, of dealing with vulnerability but also drawing upon the power of silent support without the need for overt assurance.

There are many psychosomatic parallels to draw upon, recognising that voice rises in different places in the body with different archaic emotions attached to those different somatic sites. This noticing of voice – the coach's voice as well as the client's – helps us better attune to what is going on under the surface in the moment. As well as gaining blend and flow there is also reflection on the power of interruption. There are the parallels to be drawn on the need for a balance between lyricism and restraint in the coaching conversation.

Both coaching and singing help a person to find and express their authentic voice, but there is also an unashamed reach for, or chance discovery of, higher purpose – perhaps a transcendental moment. In singing, we conduct an archaeological dig into the deepest meaning of song, eventually revealing what beauty may lie underneath even the saddest of songs. The same is often true of the themes we pursue in coaching conversations. Then there is the knowing of moments of wholeness where the gestalt is complete and the client knows that all has fallen perfectly into place in their known and as yet undiscovered lyrics of life.

Coaching using party games

Jen Gash

Nothing lights up the brain like play

(Stuart Brown 2008)

Learning and creativity flourish through play. Stuart Brown, play guru, feels that human beings are 'the most youthful, the most flexible, the most plastic (neuroplastic) creatures of all and therefore the most playful and this gives us a leg up on adaptability (as a species)'. Yes, play is that important. Play allows us to see what's possible; an intrinsic part of creativity, but we somehow seem to get fewer and fewer opportunities to play as we get older.

I always believed that if you played a game such as Monopoly with someone you didn't know very well, you would know them extremely well by the end of the game; much more so than through conversation alone. People's drives, skills and sneaky tendencies all pop out as they let go of their mask-like exterior and engage in play. These are some of the main foundations of Discovery Party – a way of working with people using coaching games as part of small parties held in homes and work places.

The idea was born in my early days as a coach out of surprise that so many mums in the playground did not seem to know anything about coaching. I decided to run some 'coaching' evenings with a number of my friends, aided by a bottle or two of wine. It worked a treat and months later people would mention things they had done or things that had shifted as a result of the little 'party' at my house. Over the next couple of years, I built on the idea and developed numerous coaching games and unique tools, which can all be used for these fun, relaxed coaching get-togethers.

Sometimes the parties are a group of friends who know each other really well, sometimes they are groups who don't know each other at all. It doesn't seem to matter. People relax, have a glass of wine, play some games, get chatting and share some deep and not so deep things. Sometimes big 'aha' moments take place during the party, sometimes it is weeks later, but I know that the seeds of possible change are being planted.

People are able to have conversations that never would have taken place otherwise. My favourite moment of recent years was a lady who shared a life dream to become a mahout (an elephant keeper) saying 'of course, no one here can help with that!' However, a voice piped up from the sofa saying 'actually, my brother runs an elephant sanctuary ... I can put you in touch'.

The parties are also great for team events and I have run all sorts of parties, including one for forty-three members of teaching staff at the end of term. Another reason I established the business was to help coaches get known locally, using people's natural networks and friendship groups. I have had all sorts of opportunities spring from running a party.

In Discovery Party we have a raft of games, but one of the easiest to experiment with is a coaching version of pass the parcel. It's always enjoyed by the adults who play and is a great activity to start with. With a small prize in the centre and a sweet treat in each layer, the parcel has around six to eight layers, depending on the size of the group. Inside are a set of coaching questions, one on each layer, graded from fun, gentle enquiry to perhaps slightly more delving questions in the centre. For example, the outer layers could include questions like:

What is your favourite way of cheating or avoiding housework?

If you were a Mr Men or Little Miss character, which one would you be and why?

These get people used to answering and sharing in a low pressure, fun way. Succeeding questions become deeper, such as:

If you had a magic wand, what would you do with it?

Tell us about a time you felt a real sense of fulfilment or achievement?

These are just examples – you can ask all sorts of things and tailor the parcel questions to the needs or purpose of the group, for example, business development related questions, wellbeing questions or creativity questions.

I start by explaining that when the music stops, the personal who opens the parcel gets to read the question out loud and share their answer, before opening the question up to the rest of the group. I do, however, state that there is no pressure to speak and if someone doesn't like the question or can't think of anything, that's fine – no one is made to feel uncomfortable and of course general principles of group-work and confidentiality apply.

We have many other games and usually play around three or four during a two-hour party. As well as being a creative, fun, low pressure introduction to coaching, I also hope that the parties help 'ordinary people' access coaching – coaching is too good to be restricted to the lucky few in corporate jobs.

Note

1 At Different Development Ltd. we work mainly in leadership and executive development, and so the focus of this section is on coaching for leaders, but 'leadership' can be used to mean taking a lead in any realm of our lives, be it work, art, self or community.

References

Bateson, M. C. (1989) *Composing a Life*. New York: Atlantic Monthly Press.
Brown, S. (2008) *Play is More Than Just Fun*. TED talk. Accessed 20/10/15, https://www.ted.com/talks/stuart_brown_says_play_is_more_than_fun_it_s_vital/transcript?language=en.
Chittenden, S. (2014) *Rhyme and Reason: The Poetry of Leadership*. Brighton: Different Development.
Donnellan, D. (2002) *The Actor and The Target*. London: Nick Hern Books.
Glăveanu, V. (2010) Paradigms in the study of creativity: introducing the perspective of cultural psychology, *New Ideas in Psychology*, 28(1), 79–93.
IBM (2010) Capitalizing on Complexity. *Insights from the 2010 IBM Global CEO Study*. Accessed 21/05/16, http://www-935.ibm.com/services/us/ceo/ceostudy2010/index.html.
Jarrett, J. (2015) *The Meisner Technique*. Meisner Technique Studio website. Accessed 3/10/15.
Johnstone, K. (1979) *Impro: Improvisation and the Theatre*. London: Faber and Faber.
Leigh, A. and Maynard, M. (2004) *Dramatic Success*. London: Nicholas Brealey.
Spolin, V. (1999) *Improvisation For The Theater*. Evanston, IL: Northwestern University Press.

Index

ability 39, 55
accept and build principle 186
'acting as if' 180
action *see* creative action
Adams, David 146–9
Adams, Scott 136
adaptability 108
adaptive resonance theory (ART) 46
addiction 128
Adler, Alfred 24, 27
affirmations 134
'a-ha' moments 29, 31, 34, 46, 59, 80, 111, 192
altered states 80
amygdala 45, 46, 130, 179
anxiety 34
archetypes 27, 176
Arieti, S. 46
Aristotle 67, 155
art 5, 9, 15, 17, 55, 63, 77; altered states 80; beliefs about 10–11; developing a vision 78–9; Feroze 57–8; grief and loss 60, 81; Impressionists 61; observational drawing 56; participation mystique 23; perfectionism 136; physical space 127; Picasso on 78; Plato on 13; reality checks 80; resources 79; value of 52; vision board 164–5; *see also* drawing
art galleries 170, 171–2
art therapy 67–8, 84
Assagioli, Roberto 26, 27
Attentional Control Network 38–9
Attentional Flexibility Network 39
autonomy 54–5
Ayres, Jean 44

Badonsky, Jill 46, 71–2, 113, 119, 123n1, 128, 134, 177
Baer, J. 5
Bandler, R. 32
Bateson, Mary Catherine 183
'becoming other' 19, 34, 72, 77, 83, 91, 94
Beeman, Mark 153
Behaviourism 22
'being' 91
beliefs 4–5, 10–12, 17, 69, 103, 132–5, 186
Bently, T. 29
'big five' personality traits 28–9
'big-C' and 'little-c' creativity 51–2
Bilder, Robert 25–6, 37, 45
blocks 90, 93, 95, 96, 124–40, 162
blood vessel metaphor 90–1, 94–5, 96, 97, 99–104, 124, 138
Blow, Sue 171–2
Boden, M. A. 61
body 20, 37, 44, 89–90; *see also* brain
Booker, C. 152
Boyatzis, R. 115
brain 37–47, 51; beliefs 133; experiential simulation 179; fear response 130; flow 83; memory 39–40; networks 38–9; noticing 42–3; sculpting 41–2; sensory processing 44–5; wandering mind 41
Broaden and Build Theory 32
Brown, Stuart 191
Buddhism 14, 43

Cameron, Julia 29, 71, 145
Campbell, Joseph 152
capitalism 16–17
Carson, S. H. 33, 40
Cave, Nick 59, 90
'celebrated self' 21–2, 75
'Centring Sequence' 121–2
chaos 59, 86–7, 101, 113, 122
Chittenden, Sam 146, 182–8

choice 92, 112
choirs 188–91
Chomsky, Noam 51
Christianity 14
Cicero, Marcus Tullius 14, 89
circling ideas 81
Clutterbuck, David 115
coaching: creative 'doing' 76, 83–5; as a creative process 76, 77–82; creativity supported by 76, 86–7; definition of 75–6; enabling contraction 111–13; enabling expansion 105–10; evocative environments 170–3; evocative objects 173–4; experiential simulation 176–81; focus on the individual 19; historical changes 75; humour and provocation 167–9; improvisation 182–8; 'magical synthesis' 46–7; mind, body and soul 20; model for coaching creativity 88–96; party games 191–3; point of creative action 114–23; psychology influence on 21; reducing blocks and restrictions 124–40; singing and 188–91; use of the term 3; vessel metaphor 99–104; visual processes 155–66; writing 143, 146, 152
cognitive behavioural approach 133
collages 164–5
collective unconscious 16, 29, 94
combinatorial creativity 61, 63
communication 5, 56
confidence 83
Confucianism 14
Congdon, K. G. 67, 68
Congram, S. 29
containment 86, 90, 92, 99, 100, 103
context 9
contraction *see* expansion and contraction
convergent thinking 37, 46, 94, 181
Cooper, Pauline 71
copyright 17
counselling 68, 70
courage 129
Coyle, Daniel 42
crafts 5, 15, 17, 55, 63
'creating other' 34, 72, 77, 83, 91, 94
creation 13
creative action 45, 92, 93, 114–23
creative process 59–60, 93, 97–8; client engagement 102; vessel metaphor 99, 104
creative therapy 67–74
creativity: 'becoming other' 19, 72; beliefs about 4–5, 10–12, 132–5; 'big-C' and 'little-c' 51–2; blocks and restrictions 124–40; capitalism 16–17; coaching as a creative process 76, 77–82; concept of 3–8; definition of 5; 'doing' 50, 76, 83–5; evolutionary perspective 38; Feroze 57; Freud 22; Guilford 24; historical context 12–16; Jung 23; Kelly 25; Maslow 26; May 27; memory 39–40; mental illness linked to 33–4; model for coaching 88–96; motivation and 54–5; neuroscience of 37; paradox of 72–3, 87, 92; sensory processing 44–5; supported by coaching 76, 86–7; vessel metaphor 99–104; Wallas 23–4; wandering mind 41; at work 61–3
Creek, J. 9
criticism 130–1, 190
cryptomnesia 23, 40, 94
Csikszentmihalyi, Mihaly 32, 53, 54

Dana Foundation 39
De Bono, Edward 28
'deep practice' 42
dementia 40
Denton, Kathy 174
Diebenkorn, Richard 122
Different Development 182, 193n1
Dire Daisy 177–8
disappointments 80–1
discontinuity 16, 92
discovery 56
Discovery Party 191–3
Disney method 32
distractions 127, 128
divergent thinking 24–5, 28, 34, 37, 46, 94, 181
Doherty, Daniel 143, 182, 188–91
'doing' 50–2, 76, 83–5, 91
drawing 156–61; *see also* art
'The Dreaming' 13

Eastern thinking 14, 19, 44
education 4, 11, 15
Edwards, Betty 71
elaboration 24–5
Eliot, T. S. 128, 146
embodiment 56, 180–1
emotions, positive 32, 34, 47
empathy 5, 26
energy 13, 87; expansion and contraction 91, 92; river model 162; vessel metaphor 99; *see also* flow

engagement 51, 52–3
engineering 88
Enlightenment 13, 15
environment 9, 70, 170–3; *see also* physical space
Erickson, Milton 26, 31
evolutionary perspective 38
expansion and contraction 46–7, 86–7, 89, 91–3, 96; chaos 101; enabling contraction 111–13; enabling expansion 105–10; vessel metaphor 90, 94–5, 97, 99, 100, 103
expectations 119–20
experiential simulation 176–81
experimentation 78
exploratory creativity 61, 63

failure 117, 187; *see also* mistakes
Farrelly, Frank 168
fears 46, 47, 125, 129–30, 179
Feist, G. J. 28
Feroze, Peter Moolan 57–8
'fertile ground' 105–6
'fertile void' 29–31, 40, 94
fish diagram 149–51
flexibility 24–5, 108, 181, 183
flow 37, 53–4, 83, 84, 90–1, 93; choirs 189, 190; engagement 52; expansion and contraction 91, 92; Feroze 57; as natural medicine 51; river model 161, 162, 163, 164
fluency 24–5, 181
fluidity 108
flux 96n1
Fox, Nick 19, 56
Frederickson, B. 32
free will 26
Freud, Sigmund 22, 23, 75
Fuster, J. M. 39, 40, 46, 47, 91, 93

games 191–3
garden metaphor 157–9
gender issues 189
Gestalt psychology 24, 29, 40, 91, 94, 105
Ghiselin, Brewster 59, 60, 91
Gilbert, Elizabeth 31
Glăveneau, Vlad 182
goals 114–15, 123; changing nature of 54; drawing 84, 160; flow 53; planning and goal setting 115–16
God 14

Goswami, A. 16, 92
graduates 62
Grant, A. 76
Greek Mythologies 13
grief 60, 81
Grinder, J. 32
Guilford, J. P. 5, 24, 28, 94

habits 80, 120–1, 187
habituation 69
hallucinations 94, 103, 104n1, 106
Harland, P. 25, 107
Hennessey, B. 54
Heroic paradigm 80
hero's journey 152, 153n1
Hewett, Kate Taylor 159–60
Hinduism 14
Hofstadter, Douglas 51
Howard, A. 115
humanism 15, 26
humour 167, 168

'ideal self' 26
ideas: accept and build principle 186; circling 81; discrimination and evaluation of 134; enabling contraction 111, 112, 113; enabling expansion 105, 106–7, 109; overwhelm 86–7, 101, 113, 131, 164; vessel metaphor 103
images 84, 165, 176, 180; *see also* visual processes
Imagination Network 38–9
imperfection 108
imposter syndrome 85, 129
improvisation 182–8
Industrial Revolution 15
innovation 4, 7, 12, 16; disruption in 63; organisations 61–2, 117
inquiry 78
inspiration 89
integration 47, 87, 93, 95, 101, 122; enabling contraction 111, 112; sensory 44; vessel metaphor 96, 97
intellectual property 17
intrinsic motivation 54–5, 63, 115
Ishikawa poetry 149–51

Jeffery, Maggie 21
Jinn 13
Jobs, Steve 146
Johnstone, Keith 184, 185

journaling 71, 143–5
Jung, Carl Gustav 12, 16, 22–3, 27, 29, 34, 40, 59, 94

kaizen 46, 123n1
Kaizen Muse Creativity Coaching 29, 72, 123n1
Kauffman, B. S. 38
Kaufman, James 5, 33, 52, 54–5
Kaufman, Scott Barry 33
Kawa model 161–4
Keats, John 91
Keifer, Anselm 60
Kelly, George 25
Kemp, Nick 168–9
Klee, Paul 78
Knight, Sue 168
Korn, Peter 55–6
Kyaga, S. 33

language 89–92; *see also* metaphors
lateral thinking 28
leadership 182–3
Leary-Joyce, J. 105–6
left-brain, right-brain concept 38, 47, 92
Leonardo da Vinci 51
Leung, A. K. 180–1
Lewis, C. S. 146
Locke, John 15
Longhurst, L. 31
Lorenz, K. 50
loss 60, 80, 85
lungs 89, 95
Lyon, George Ella 146

Mac Cumhail, Fionn 184
'magical synthesis' 46–7
Maisel, Eric 71, 121–2
Maslow, Abraham 22, 26
mastery 54, 63, 83
mathematical creativity 5
Maurer, Bob 46, 118, 123n1, 138
May, Brian 51
May, Rollo 26, 27, 71
Mayes, Peter 88–9, 149, 168–9
McCrae, J. O. R. 28
McKee, A. 115–16
McNiff, L. 67–8
Meisner Technique 186
memory 37, 39–40, 46, 47, 105
mental illness 33–4, 68, 104n1
metaphors 89–91, 97, 165n1; archetypal images 176; embodiment 180–1; visual processes 155–9, 161–4; *see also* vessel metaphor
Meyer, A 51
Miller, B. L. 40
mind wandering 41, 47, 105, 108, 128
Mindell, Amy 177, 178
mindfulness 41, 42, 43, 47, 67, 108
Mintzberg, H. 63
mirror neurons 46
mistakes 108, 117, 122, 129, 136, 185, 187
Model of Human Occupation (MOHO) 69
money 126
'Morning Pages' 143, 145
motivation 39, 54–5, 63, 115
Motor Imagery Practice 180
multiple selves 176
myelin 42
Myers-Briggs Type Indicator 22, 75

narrative 79, 152
negative capability 91
neuro linguistic programming (NLP) 31–2
neuroplasticity 41–2, 47
neuroscience 26, 37–47, 51, 58, 91; art therapy 67; beliefs 133; coaching model 93–4; enabling expansion 105; *see also* brain
neuroses 23, 34
noticing 42–3

objects: evocative 84, 170, 173–4; object-making 55–6
observation 56
occupational therapy (OT) 68–70, 161
openness to experience 28, 29, 34, 105
optimism 122
organisational values 159–60
originality 24–5, 181
outdoor walks 172–3
overwhelm 31, 86–7, 101, 113, 131, 164

PA model 40, 46, 91, 93
Page, J. 75
painting *see* art
Parallel Universe Time 119
parasympathetic nervous system (PNS) 45
participation mystique 23
party games 191–3
Pennebaker, James 70
people 128–9
perception 43, 46–7, 56, 93, 103, 105, 132
perfectionism 101, 117, 118, 136–7, 161

performance capacity 69–70, 83
Perls, Fritz 24, 31
permeability 99, 103, 104
personality 6, 7, 28–9
persuasion 6, 7
photography 56
physical space 126–8, 161, 163, 170; *see also* environment
physics 16
Picasso, Pablo 78, 90–1
Pillai, Jagan 39
place 6, 7
planning 115–17, 123
plate metaphor 156–7
Plato 13
playfulness 107, 191
poetry 71, 146–51
polymaths 51
positive emotions 32, 34, 47
potential 6, 7
Power, R. A. 33
press 6, 7
Pressfield, Steven 128
pressure 118, 119
process 6, 7
procrastination 94, 101, 124, 125, 130, 138–9
product 6, 7
Progoff, Dr 70
Proust, Marcel 56
provocation 167–8, 184, 185
psyche 19, 20, 21, 23, 26, 68, 69
psychoanalysis 22, 27, 67
psychology 21–32, 94
psychosis 33, 104n1
psychosynthesis 27
psychotherapy 29, 44, 67–8
Puccio, G. 38

quantum mechanics 16

Readman, M. 5–6
reality checks 80, 104
rejection 130–1
religion 14
Renaissance 14–15
resilience 58, 83, 130
resources 79
Reticular Activating System (RAS) 41
reward 54, 63
Richo, David 71, 176
risk taking 105, 117, 184

rituals 80, 121–2
river metaphor 161–4
Robertson, Ian 42
Robinson, Ken 11–12
Rock, David 21, 75
Rogers, Carl 22, 26
role play 187
Romans 13–14
routines 80, 121
Runco, Mark 41
Russian dolls 174

Sawyer, K. 41
Schwarz, Joyce 164
scientific creativity 5
Scott, Susan 149
sculpting 41–2, 47
Segal, R. 28
self-actualisation 22, 26
self-awareness 4, 83, 92, 99–104
self-doubt 130
self-help 26
self-sabotage 45, 124–5, 130, 137–8, 179
sensory system 44–5, 105; *see also* perception
Shalley, C. E. 115
'shared vulnerability' 40
silence 31
singing 188–91
Skinner, B. F. 22
small actions 117–19, 125, 133–4, 139
SMART goals 116
somatic coaching 44
soul 20, 26
space 126–8
Speedy, J. 70
spirit 13, 20
Spolin, Viola 184
Stafford, William 143
Sternberg, R. J. 52
Stober, D. 76
Stone, Ruth 31
stories 79, 152–3
strengths 162, 164, 177
stress 43, 45–6, 47
symbols 12–13, 23
sympathetic nervous system (SNS) 45
synaesthesia 45
systems approach 69, 70

Taoism 14
Tarnas, R. 15

technology 16, 17
Tharp, Twyla 120
theatre 182–3, 184
therapy 29, 44, 67–74
time 119, 125–6
Time Line Therapy 171, 181
Torrance, E. P. 5, 28
transformational creativity 61
trust 190
Turkle, S. 173
Turner, Rosalind 173

values 135–6, 159–60
Van den Berk, T. 23
Vartanian, Oshin 39, 55
vessel metaphor 90–1, 94–5, 96, 97, 99–104, 124, 138; *see also* blood vessel metaphor
vision 78–9, 93–4, 179
vision board 164–5
Viskontas, I. V. 40
visual processes 84, 155–66
visualisation 176, 179–80
Vogel, M. 152
volition 69

Walcott, Derek 148
walks 172–3
Wallas, Graham 23–4
wandering mind 41, 47, 105, 108, 128
wave metaphor 29–30
wellbeing 42, 43, 51, 68, 77, 83
Wertheimer, Max 24
Western, Simon 21–2, 75
Western thinking 14, 15, 19, 80
Whitaker, Vivien 84
Whitmore, John 27
Whyte, David 148
Wicker, B. 46
windows to other selves 176–9
Woolf, Virginia 60
work 61–3
working memory 39, 47, 105
writing 143–54; journaling 71, 143–5; poetry 71, 146–51; stories 79, 152–3; as therapy 70–1
Wundt, Wilhelm 22

Xenophanes 13

Taylor & Francis eBooks

Helping you to choose the right eBooks for your Library

Add Routledge titles to your library's digital collection today. Taylor and Francis ebooks contains over 50,000 titles in the Humanities, Social Sciences, Behavioural Sciences, Built Environment and Law.

Choose from a range of subject packages or create your own!

Benefits for you
- Free MARC records
- COUNTER-compliant usage statistics
- Flexible purchase and pricing options
- All titles DRM-free.

Benefits for your user
- Off-site, anytime access via Athens or referring URL
- Print or copy pages or chapters
- Full content search
- Bookmark, highlight and annotate text
- Access to thousands of pages of quality research at the click of a button.

REQUEST YOUR FREE INSTITUTIONAL TRIAL TODAY

Free Trials Available
We offer free trials to qualifying academic, corporate and government customers.

eCollections – Choose from over 30 subject eCollections, including:

Archaeology	Language Learning
Architecture	Law
Asian Studies	Literature
Business & Management	Media & Communication
Classical Studies	Middle East Studies
Construction	Music
Creative & Media Arts	Philosophy
Criminology & Criminal Justice	Planning
Economics	Politics
Education	Psychology & Mental Health
Energy	Religion
Engineering	Security
English Language & Linguistics	Social Work
Environment & Sustainability	Sociology
Geography	Sport
Health Studies	Theatre & Performance
History	Tourism, Hospitality & Events

For more information, pricing enquiries or to order a free trial, please contact your local sales team:
www.tandfebooks.com/page/sales

Routledge
Taylor & Francis Group

The home of Routledge books

www.tandfebooks.com